TRIAL OF STRENGTH

Also by Joshua Rozenberg

The Search for Justice (1994)
The Case for the Crown (1987)
Your Rights and the Law (with Nicola Watkins) *(1986)*

Trial of Strength

The Battle between Ministers and
Judges over Who Makes the Laws

JOSHUA ROZENBERG

RICHARD COHEN BOOKS · London

British Library Cataloguing in Publication Data:
A catalogue record for this book is available from the British Library

Copyright © 1997 by Joshua Rozenberg

ISBN 1 86066 094 0

First published in Great Britain in 1997 by
Richard Cohen Books
7 Manchester Square
London W1M 5RE

1 3 5 7 9 8 6 4 2

Typeset in Linotron Bembo by
Palimpsest Book Production Limited,
Polmont, Stirlingshire

Printed in Great Britain by
Mackays of Chatham plc, Chatham, Kent

Contents

Contents

Introduction

The trial of strength between the executive and the judiciary reached a state of perfect symmetry on Monday 27 January 1997. In the morning, the Home Secretary tried to persuade the law lords that he, a politician, could behave as a judge. In the afternoon, the law lords tried to persuade the Home Secretary that they, the judges, could behave as politicians. It is a curious effect of our unwritten constitution that politicians and judges may do battle in this way. The premise of this book is that a truce must now be called.

The battle of 27 January took place in the House of Lords. In the morning, five law lords began hearing an appeal by the Home Secretary. Michael Howard, through his counsel, argued that he had the right to decide how long the two boys who murdered James Bulger should serve in custody before being considered for release on licence. This was essentially a judicial decision, but Mr Howard considered it was one that he as a minister should take. The full story – and the way in which judges keep politicians in line – is told in Chapter 3.

After lunch on 27 January, the two teams changed ends. This time, peers were considering Michael Howard's plans to introduce mandatory and minimum sentences for certain types of offender. Some of the law lords who had taken part in the hearing that morning tried to persuade Michael Howard, through his junior minister, to modify his proposals. This was essentially a political move, but the law lords considered it was one that they as judges should take. The full story – and the way in which judges speak their minds to politicians – is told in Chapter 2.

During the afternoon's debate, the Liberal Democrat peer Lord Hutchinson of Lullington QC helpfully summarised the political case against Michael Howard:

The Home Secretary has made many mistakes. As we know, he has acted unlawfully on no less than fourteen occasions. But surely the most unforgivable thing that he has done is to play up for populist political purposes his differences with the judges. That surely is unforgivable in the holder of such a great office. It has done and continues to do grievous harm to the delicate balance in our constitution between the judiciary and the executive . . . The judges have been put in an impossibly difficult position, a position where, inevitably, because of the Home Secretary's attitude, they appear to get involved politically.'[1]

These damning allegations lie at the heart of this book. Michael Howard's frank response can be found in Chapter 1.

Monday 27 January was not the first occasion on which the judges had flexed their political muscles. Exactly a week earlier, two law lords had spoken in the House of Lords against another of Michael Howard's initial proposals. In the Police Bill, he was proposing to allow senior police officers the right to authorise bugging and burglary whenever it would be of substantial value in preventing or detecting an offence for which someone could expect three years in prison. Under Mr Howard's proposals, there would be a measure of judicial oversight but chief police officers would not need prior judicial approval.

Lord Browne-Wilkinson, a leading law lord, pointed out that the government was seeking 'enormously wide powers'. In his view, they should only be exercised with prior judicial authorisation. He referred to the famous eighteenth-century case of *Entick v. Carrington*,[2] which he said established that 'the police, the military or any organ of government have no greater right to enter our property than has any private individual'. He continued: 'That is the bastion of our constitution. It has been adopted by all other common law jurisdictions as the bastion of their freedom. If that freedom is to be taken away, it is my view that the clearest possible need has to be demonstrated for that to be done and the biggest possible safeguards placed to protect our freedom.'[3]

Another law lord, Lord Lloyd of Berwick, said he could not accept that it was 'right for one police officer to authorise another police officer to enter our homes, no matter how senior the first police officer may be'. He had 'a sense of wonderment' that any peer could accept that principle 'because it seems to cut across so seriously one of the basic concepts of freedom'.[4]

After a campaign by Lord Browne-Wilkinson, the Labour party

agreed to support the principle of prior judicial authorisation. Labour's amendment called for every burglary or bugging operation to be approved by a judge of the High Court or above; the Liberal Democrats thought the job should be done by a circuit judge. Both amendments were approved by the Lords: as a result, the government made concessions when the bill returned to the Commons in February 1997. It was agreed that the prior approval of a High Court judge would normally be needed where an operation could affect 'legal, medical or journalistic privilege'.

Political moves to amend the Police Bill had gained the support of serving and retired members of the judiciary. Heading the list of judges who supported both amendments when a vote was called at the end of the debate was the Lord Chief Justice, Lord Bingham. As well as Lord Browne-Wilkinson and Lord Lloyd, two other serving law lords voted against the government: Lord Hope of Craighead and Lord Slynn of Hadley. Five retired judges voted for one or both of the opposition amendments.

In January 1997, Lord Browne-Wilkinson spoke in support of another Labour amendment to the Police Bill. Its aim was to provide additional safeguards before the police could bug solicitors' offices or barristers' chambers and it led to the concession mentioned above. Lord Browne-Wilkinson had been hearing Mr Howard's appeal in the Bulger case at the time the amendment was to be debated: the law lords had to adjourn early so he could speak in the debate.

After Lord Browne-Wilkinson had spoken, a vote was taken on the amendment he had supported. The result was a dead heat.[5] Even so, the government won the day because one of Lord Browne-Wilkinson's fellow judges used his casting vote against the amendment. The judge who did so was acting fully in accordance with convention. He had a casting vote because he was Speaker of the House of Lords. However, he would not have been sorry to see the opposition amendment defeated because he was also a member of the cabinet. He was, of course, the Lord Chancellor, Lord Mackay of Clashfern. It cannot be right for the Lord Chancellor to have so many overlapping roles. Proposals for reform will be found in Chapter 1.

Naturally enough, the newspapers welcomed the law lords' attempts to protect free speech. On this occasion, nobody bothered to accuse serving judges of dabbling in party politics, of stepping in where the Labour party feared to tread. That accusation will constantly be seen in the pages that follow. So too will the claim that the judges are making new law in defiance of parliament. That issue will be examined in Chapter 4.

The principal legal issue that divided the main parties in the run-up to the 1997 General Election was what was to be done with the European Convention on Human Rights. Labour wanted to incorporate it into the legal systems of the United Kingdom; the Conservatives said that would drag judges down into the political arena. Incorporating the convention would be a major constitutional change; nevertheless, it could be done in such a way that the consequences would be minimal. Chapter 5 will explain the effects for us all.

We can learn a lot about the battle between the executive and the judiciary by looking at the two occasions when they came into direct conflict: *Spycatcher* and the Scott Inquiry. The first of these was a victory for the judges: after some hesitation, they rejected the government's attempts to ban the unbannable. Sir Richard Scott's inquiry into the 'arms to Iraq' affair must be seen as a victory for the government: ministers successfully deflected the criticism they received. Both stories are told in Chapter 6.

Although popular mythology still depicts judges as ancient and reactionary, the reality is that many are young and radical. Among the most radical of all are three who while at the bar were briefed exclusively by successive governments, the former 'Treasury devils' Lord Woolf, Lord Justice Simon Brown and Mr Justice Laws. All of them are fine men, generous friends and determined seekers after justice. All of them will be criticised in the pages that follow. The author is confident they will forgive him.

Perhaps there is something about having worked for a government which makes a judge bite the hand that once fed him. Perhaps he knows too well what goes on in Whitehall and Westminster. Perhaps it is simply that governments seek out and brief the brightest and most creative lawyers of their generation, and that these lawyers become the most thoughtful and questioning members of the judiciary. Whatever the reason, the three judges mentioned above – as well as several others – stand accused in this book of being too free with their own views of what the law ought to be. Certainty should not be sacrificed at the altar of justice.

It is difficult to criticise these three judges when their views are shared by most right-thinking members of society. They are fully entitled to develop the law in accordance with well-established principles. Yet if the judges start fashioning laws according to what they – rather than parliament – think they ought to be, any government is bound to respond. First, ministers will criticise the judges for 'unpredictability'. Then they will accuse the judiciary of 'supremacism'. Finally, the government will seek legislation to clip the judges' wings. In the end, the judges – and justice – will be the losers. The warning signs are all too clear in the pages that follow.

We began this introduction with a glimpse at the turf wars, the politicians who wanted to act as judges and the judges who felt they should act as politicians. These overlapping roles should be brought rapidly to an end. Of course, every decision a judge makes is 'political'– in the sense that he is choosing between alternatives. Of course, ministers must act judiciously when taking decisions – otherwise they will be liable to judicial review. Nevertheless, there can be no justification for giving judicial or quasi-judicial powers to politicians such as the Home Secretary, the Lord Chancellor and the law officers. There can be no justification for giving a political role to the law lords and the senior judges.

There must now be a staged withdrawal. If the law lords are to stop criticising government proposals then ministers must stop attacking the judiciary. If the politicians are to give up their judicial responsibilities then the judges must stop playing politics. This may be a counsel of perfection. The alternative is a counsel of despair.

Although this book is not intended as a polemic, I have tentatively offered my own views and conclusions where these seem appropriate. Any opinions to be found in the pages that follow are not to be taken as those of the BBC. Like the judges, I do not seek to dabble in party politics: any criticisms of politicians are aimed at the breed rather than at individuals. They are balanced by equal and opposite criticisms of judges.

In writing the book, I have taken advantage of many people. Several, including Lord Woolf and Michael Howard, kindly agreed to be interviewed. Sheila Thompson of the Lord Chancellor's Department was as helpful as her official duties permitted. A number of authors will see their thoughts reflected in the pages that follow: they receive formal acknowledgement in the notes but this is the place to thank them for the assistance they have unknowingly given me. I have occasionally drawn on my own previous writings where these seemed relevant. Some of the thoughts that follow first saw light in October 1995 in a lecture which the Gwynedd Magistrates' Association kindly invited me to give at Bangor to mark their seventy-fifth anniversary.

David Pannick, Jane Peel, Melanie Phillips and Nicole Smith generously read parts of the first draft: all saved me from embarrassing errors. Other mistakes have no doubt been introduced since the text left their hands, and those who enjoy pointing out errors to authors are encouraged to write to me at BBC News.

Above all my thanks must go to Richard Cohen. It was he who thought of the subject, commissioned this book on a demandingly tight timetable, skilfully edited it and undertook to publish it in a fraction of the time other publishers would require. Pat Chetwyn and Christine Casley turned these ambitions into reality.

My greatest debt of gratitude is to Melanie, Gabriel and Abigail. They realised, even if I did not, how an author must constantly turn his back on those dearest to him to face the unforgiving screen of a word processor. I promised my daughter I would dedicate this book to her gerbils, Mozart and Einstein. If nobody else does, they will consume it with enthusiasm.

Joshua Rozenberg
March 1997

1

Battle Lines

Newspapers have repeatedly said that there is a state of tension between the judges and the Home Secretary. The implication is that this is an undesirable state of affairs. That is a misconception. It is when there is a state of perfect harmony between the judges and the executive that citizens need to worry. A state of tension between the judges and the executive, with each being watchful of encroachment into their province, is the best guarantee the subject can have against the abuse of power.

Lord Steyn, law lord (1996)[1]

Another aspect . . . which must irritate ministers profoundly is the sort of . . . headline JUDGE SLAMS MINISTER or MINISTER WAS PERVERSE, SAYS COURT . . . The very large number of such headlines we have seen in the last few years has led to a recurrent theme in some of the newspapers and journals to the effect that a relationship of personal antagonism exists between judges and ministers, or alternatively that the judges have a political agenda to curb the cumulative effects of a government too long in power, to act, in other words, as another branch of Her Majesty's Loyal Opposition. These notions are fanciful.

Lord Nolan, law lord (1996)[2]

Opening positions

As the General Election of 1 May 1997 finally drew near, the judiciary and the executive were engaged in nothing less than a trial of strength. It was just as much in the judges' interests to talk the conflict down as it was in the government's interests to talk it up. Judges generally tried to maintain their traditional position as impartial arbitrators above the political fray, while some ministers saw political advantage in getting tough with the judges. The media could not escape their share of the blame for fanning the flames of conflict, and indeed some judges might have thought a book like this would only make matters worse. Both sides were right to have been concerned. At risk was justice itself.

1

Taking on the judges

A chance remark by the Home Secretary Michael Howard showed how far relations between the executive and the judiciary had deteriorated by the autumn of 1995. Not for the first time, a High Court judge had decided that the Home Secretary had acted unlawfully.[3] Mr Howard had been challenged by five IRA members who were sentenced to life imprisonment in 1976 for conspiracy to cause explosions. In each case the prisoner's punishment period – the so-called 'tariff' – had been set by the Home Secretary of the day at twenty years. Those tariffs were nearly up. Provided the Parole Board considered that the prisoners were no longer dangerous, they were entitled to be released on licence once their tariffs had been completed.

It was not the practice of the Parole Board to reach a decision on whether it was safe to release an individual prisoner until some six months after it had received the inmate's papers. During this period, it reviewed the case. To make sure the board could reach its decision in good time, the IRA men asked for their cases to be referred six months or so before their tariffs were due to expire. That request was rejected: Mr Howard said it had always been the practice to wait until the end of a prisoner's tariff before referring his case to the board. The men said that meant they would each spend another six months in custody waiting for the board to review their cases.

In court, Mr Justice Dyson decided that the established Home Office practice was unreasonable[4] and therefore unlawful. He said the Home Secretary's policy produced results that were 'manifestly unjust'. It flouted the principles of the common law. It was also contrary to the European Convention on Human Rights, which was relevant in this case because the tariff arrangements had been set up specifically to meet the requirements of the convention. Nevertheless, on the facts of the case the judge decided that the Parole Board had been right not to let the five IRA men jump the queue by hearing their applications immediately they were received: it was the Home Secretary who had been at fault, not the Parole Board.

This was a clear defeat for the Home Office, but one it could live with. In future, cases would have to be referred to the Parole Board some months sooner, but the five IRA men would not be let out any more quickly. It was presumably for this reason that Kenneth Parker QC for the Home Secretary told Mr Justice Dyson that Mr Howard would not be seeking to appeal against his ruling.

However, the next day Michael Howard was making one of his not infrequent appearances on the *Today* programme.[5] John Humphrys asked Mr Howard if he was going to appeal against the judge's decision.

'We're considering that,' replied Mr Howard. 'The practice which the judge found to be unlawful is the same practice that's been followed by every Home Secretary since 1991' (when the law was introduced). Mr Howard added that the judge had accepted that he and his predecessors had acted in accordance with the domestic legislation. However, he said the judge had ruled that the government should also have acted in accordance with the European Convention on Human Rights. Mr Howard pointed out that the European Convention was not part of our law, adding that the government would have to consider whether to appeal on that point.

Asked whether the ruling damaged Britain's claim to the moral high ground, Mr Howard said something quite remarkable:

> Well, I don't accept that, and we'll have to see what the outcome is if indeed we do appeal. The last time this particular judge found against me, which was on a case which would have led to the release of a large number of illegal immigrants, the Court of Appeal unanimously decided that he was wrong. So we'll have to see what happens if we do appeal. These things are quite difficult to predict . . .

Here was a personal attack on a serving judge. The judge himself, no doubt choking over his cornflakes as he listened on the radio, was hardly in a position to telephone the *Today* programme; he appears to have decided that any subsequent comment would merely inflame a sensitive situation. As a result, Michael Howard was not challenged at the time. Was the Home Secretary simply trying to suggest that Mr Justice Dyson was wrong on this occasion? In that case, why had he not immediately sought leave to appeal? Was he suggesting that this particular judge – one of the most clear-minded of those who handle judicial review applications – was unduly prone to error? If so, he had no justification for doing so. Many listeners thought he was trying to belittle the judiciary as a whole in the eyes of the public.

Understandably, Mr Justice Dyson has chosen not to speak about the experience of being attacked in public by a minister. However, another, more senior, judge was more willing to comment on the Home Secretary's interview.[6] 'I think that was dreadful,' he said. 'It was outrageous – a complete breach of the conventions. The Home Secretary is entitled to say he was disappointed, he's entitled to disagree with the decision, entitled to seek leave to appeal and entitled to appeal. If the Court of Appeal had said the judge was wrong then he would have been entitled to say the judge was wrong. But for the Home Secretary to say, "Well, what do you expect, this judge was soft about something three months ago and the Court of Appeal said he was wrong" – that's not legitimate.'

The senior judge thought it was a very dangerous thing for politicians to start making personal comments about the judiciary. 'Judges aren't making personal comments about politicians,' he said, 'they're simply applying what they believe to be the law. It may be that they're wrong, but that's their job. What is more, the judge cannot respond. How would the Home Secretary have reacted if the judge had issued a statement in response pointing out how often the Home Secretary had been overruled?'

The judge said he had thought at the time that the Lord Chancellor should have been 'sticking up for the judiciary, and saying to Mr Howard, it's parliament that's supreme, not the Home Secretary.' He added that as a party politician the Home Secretary had no authority to make the law.

Questioned about this case a year later, Lord Mackay was suitably judicious. 'It's quite natural for someone who has had his decision overturned to feel a certain difficulty with it,' he said. 'It may be perfectly proper for him to explain in terms that are appropriate precisely why he feels that way.' Then came the warning: 'I think ministers in particular require to consider what it is appropriate for them to say in particular circumstances. They have to respect the position of the judge and his responsibility, but there is scope for difference of views as to precisely what is appropriate in particular cases.'[7]

In parliament, there are conventions about the extent to which a judge's decision may be questioned. Reflections against the judges are generally out of order. In 1973 the Speaker of the House of Commons told MPs they could argue that a judge had made a mistake or was wrong; however, he ruled that reflections on a judge's character or motives could not be made except on a motion before the House.[8] Mr Howard can hardly have been arguing that Mr Justice Dyson was wrong on this occasion because the government was not seeking to

4

challenge his decision: it follows that his comments might not have been permitted in the Commons. If ministers are unable to attack judges in parliament, one wonders why they feel able to do so on the BBC.

Another senior judge was willing to speak on the record about the risks involved in unwarranted criticism of the judges. Without referring to any minister in particular, Lady Justice Butler-Sloss said that if politicians made concerted attacks on the judiciary without any serious basis for doing so there was a danger they would be 'knocking at one of the pillars of society'. Lady Justice Butler-Sloss said they might be undermining in the minds of the public 'part of the establishment which is a crucial part of making society work in this country'.[9]

Judging by her family links, Dame Elizabeth Butler-Sloss was hardly a lefty judge. Her late brother Michael Havers had been a Conservative MP: Mrs Thatcher had given him both the longest recent period in office as Attorney General (eight years) and the shortest appointment as Lord Chancellor (four months).[10] Yet here she was, apparently telling Conservative ministers that they were damaging the social structure of Britain. It was a strange state of affairs.

Interviewed by the author in 1997, Michael Howard firmly denied that he had been making a personal attack on a member of the judiciary. His *Today* interview had not been a reflection on Mr Justice Dyson's character or motives. The senior judge who described the Home Secretary's remarks as 'outrageous' had misrepresented what Mr Howard had said. Indeed, Michael Howard was not prepared to accept that his interview had upset the judges at all. 'I don't think there was any basis on which any sensible judge should or could have been upset by it,' he said. Mr Howard added that he was in contact with a number of judges, and none of them had ever made any point of this kind.

Why had he said he was considering an appeal when his counsel had deliberately not applied for leave? Home Office officials said Kenneth Parker QC had not been acting on instructions from the government when he said the Home Secretary would not be seeking to challenge the court's adverse decision. In any case, said the Home Office, Mr Parker had changed his position once he learned that the five IRA men were considering an appeal against the judge's refusal to let them jump the queue; in those circumstances, Mr Parker had told the court, the Home Secretary would consider appealing against the point on which he had lost. Home Office lawyers pointed out that they had twenty-eight days in which to apply for leave to appeal, whatever had been said in court.[11]

Asked to explain his comments about Mr Justice Dyson, Mr Howard said they had to be seen in the context of an interview in which he had said it was 'becoming increasingly difficult to predict what is likely to happen in this area of the law'. In pointing out that the judge had been overruled on a previous occasion, he was simply giving an illustration of the unpredictability of judicial review. 'I was using the fact that that judge had been reversed on a previous occasion as an example of unpredictability,' he said.[12]

Some listeners may not have understood the Home Secretary's remarks in this way. The author is happy to have given Mr Howard a chance to explain publicly what he meant.

A month after making his remarks about Mr Justice Dyson, Michael Howard received another setback from the courts. This time, the case was brought by the founder of the Unification Church, Sun Myung Moon, whose numerous followers are popularly known as the Moonies. Mr Moon wanted to travel to Britain from his home in South Korea for purposes he described as 'entirely private and religious'. Mr Howard decided he should be refused entry to Britain on the ground that his presence 'would not be conducive to the public good'.

In court, Mr Moon's counsel argued that he should have been told about Mr Howard's concerns and been given a chance to respond to them before the Home Secretary had reached a decision on whether to exclude him from Britain. Mr Justice Sedley agreed, and granted Mr Moon's application for judicial review of the Home Secretary's decision. The judge noted that Mr Moon had been given permission to enter Britain three years earlier; he concluded that Mr Howard had not met the required standards of procedural fairness.[13] Despite his victory, Mr Moon cancelled his visit.

Speaking a day later in the House of Commons, a Conservative MP described the judgment as an 'extraordinary' decision: he said it was yet another example of the 'contempt with which some members of the judiciary seem to treat the views of this house and of the general public'.[14] That was not a gauntlet the Home Secretary was prepared to pick up. Back on the *Today* programme the next morning, he returned to his theme: 'I think it is becoming increasingly more difficult to predict how the courts are going to react in what is clearly an expanding area of the law,' he said.

On the face of it, that was fair comment. Judicial review is indeed an expanding area of the law; the more it expands, the more difficult it is for ministers to know when they will fall foul of it. Yet many listeners will have drawn a different inference from Mr Howard's remarks – that he was accusing the judges of making up the law to suit themselves. The Home Secretary firmly denied that he was suggesting any such thing.[15] However, as part of its report on the case *The Times* quoted unnamed Whitehall officials as saying that ministers were 'gunning' for the judges after a series of humiliations in the courts.[16]

During the year that followed, Michael Howard was working on plans to cut back the judges' sentencing discretion. The genesis of these proposals – and the judges' response – will be described more fully in Chapter 2. Nevertheless, their effect was clear even before Mr Howard published his Crime Bill in October 1996. It was to drag the judges into a political arena where they were no match for the gladiators of Whitehall and Westminster.

Opinions vary on whether this was the Home Secretary's deliberate intention or merely a consequence of his attempt to smoke out the Labour opposition. Mr Howard said neither was true: he had put forward his proposals because he believed they were right. At all events, his critics believed he was at best indifferent to and at worst enthusiastic about damaging the reputation of the judges. He had put them in an impossible position: one where they had either to sit back and watch legislation brought forward which they thought was not in the public interest or respond and be drawn into politics against their wishes.

The Master of the Rolls broadly agreed with that analysis. Lord Woolf, second in judicial seniority only to the Lord Chief Justice, said he very much hoped that the Home Secretary was not acting deliberately, just to get into a confrontational position. 'I don't believe that's what he's doing,' said Lord Woolf, 'but I do think that will be the consequence of what is happening. The judiciary have been trying hard enough to make that clear to the Home Secretary, so it is regrettable that he has felt it necessary to go about things in the way he has.'

The dangers of confrontation were huge. In Lord Woolf's view, what was at stake was the objectivity and the impartiality of the judiciary:

> I think it is extremely important that the independence of the judiciary should be maintained. It is equally important that the objectivity and impartiality of the judiciary should be maintained. On the whole, I think the public today do believe that the judiciary are objective and impartial. But if we get sucked in to what are perceived by the public to be political issues – which they don't want judges to be involved in – then that would damage the credibility of the judges in the eyes of the public.[17]

This was a telling indictment, and goes to the heart of the key issue in this book. It came from a judge who was profoundly liberal in outlook, generous in spirit, hugely energetic and determined to seize every opportunity to improve the legal system. Understandably disappointed when he was passed over for appointment as Master of the Rolls in 1992,[18] he was both delighted to get the key civil–justice job in 1996 and sad that the vacancy had been created by the illness of his good friend Peter Taylor. Not content with drawing up a blueprint for a new streamlined civil–justice system, he set about reforming the Court of Appeal, bringing in outstanding young lawyers for a few months at a time to assist the judges in reviewing applications for leave to appeal[19] while insisting his fellow appeal judges worked longer hours in 1997 to clear the backlog.

Was Michael Howard worried that his sentencing proposals would damage public respect for the judiciary? 'If the judges want to debate these issues, they're entitled to do so,' he said. 'We ought to be able to have a sensible debate without anyone falling into disrepute as a result of that debate.'[20]

This may have been true in theory, but it was hardly realistic: Michael Howard's recent proposals had certainly drawn the judges more closely into the sentencing debate. Did Mr Howard accept that the judges' descent into the political arena had damaged their standing in society? Mr Howard thought hard before answering:

> I don't know. I think it is quite important that in general judges should not descend into the political arena. That is the principal reason why I am opposed to incorporation into our law of the European Convention on Human Rights. I think that the decisions taken on the interpretation and application of the convention come very close to the political arena. I think it would be much more difficult for our judges to keep out of

the political arena if the convention were incorporated. So my general view is that I would like to see judges as far from the political arena as possible; but I recognise that in a public debate – of the kind that is entirely legitimate – over my sentencing proposals, judges may have something to say and they should say it.[21]

This was an honest and revealing answer. Michael Howard recognised that, in general, judges should not descend into the public arena; indeed, he thought they should keep as far away from it as possible. He was right. Unfortunately, as he also recognised, he had left the judges with little option.

Taking on the government

It's the little things that remind you how much the judges are walking on eggshells. In November 1996, the Court of Appeal overturned yet another decision taken by Michael Howard: once more, the judges decided he had acted unfairly. On this occasion, it was about Mr Howard's refusal to grant British citizenship to the owners of Harrods, Mohamed Al Fayed and his brother Ali. In challenging the Home Secretary's decision, the brothers said Mr Howard should have given his reasons for rejecting their claim. That argument was dismissed by the appeal judges: parliament had said specifically that no reasons needed to be provided. However, Lord Woolf – who was presiding over the court – said that under the normal principles of fairness the brothers should have been given a chance to answer any areas of concern in the Home Secretary's mind before Mr Howard had reached his decision.[22] Because they had not been given that chance, the Home Secretary's decision could not stand.[23] This was an important change in the law.

No doubt Lord Woolf could have expected newspaper headlines of the sort mentioned by Lord Nolan in the quotation at the start of this chapter: the court had, after all, decided that the Home Secretary's procedures were not fair. Yet the Master of the Rolls thought that sort of criticism would in itself have been unfair to Mr Howard: the Home Secretary was not to know that the Court of Appeal – in overturning a High Court ruling by a majority of two to one – would find his procedures had been unfair. Lord Woolf therefore took the trouble to say at the end of his judgment that the court's decision did 'not involve any criticism of the Secretary of State or his department'. To emphasise the point, he even went so far as to issue a press release. This said that the court's decision reflected 'no discredit on those responsible for the decisions under review'. It continued: 'No criticism can be made of those who advised that the procedure followed was appropriate, nor of those who followed such advice.'

Although judges had issued summaries of their judgments before[24] this was the first judicial press release to emphasise a point that was not fundamental to the decision (or, as the lawyers say, which was *obiter*). On one reading the press release went slightly further than the judgment in exonerating the Home Secretary and his advisers: this was surely unprecedented. It was a sign of the times that Lord Woolf felt obliged to speak up for the Home Secretary in this way. Mr Howard had acted unfairly and therefore unlawfully and he had been ordered to pay the Al Fayed brothers' legal costs. In the normal course of events, this was surely a decision worthy of criticism. Why then had Lord Woolf let him off the hook?

Two possible answers spring to mind. The first is that the judges were making new law, and Mr Howard could hardly have been blamed for not anticipating it. The second is that Lord Woolf was desperate not to inflame an already tense stand-off between the executive and the judiciary.

Several of his fellow judges thought Lord Woolf was wrong in law: they believed he should have found in favour of Mr Howard.[25] The Master of the Rolls was, of course, the first to acknowledge that judicial review cases (like the Al Fayed brothers' application) are concerned with the way a decision is taken, not the merits of the decision itself. However, some colleagues suspected that Lord Woolf may have been too keen to remedy the apparent injustice done to the brothers: they believed he had adopted arguments put by the brothers' counsel in order to get round a statute which plainly said the Home Secretary need not give any reasons for refusing to grant British citizenship.

One of the two judges who were sitting with Lord Woolf had made his disagreement public: in a dissenting judgment, Lord Justice Kennedy said:

> The plain intention of parliament was to relieve the Secretary of State of the burden of giving reasons . . . If the Secretary of State must nevertheless canvass with the applicant a matter or matters which in his view weigh against the grant of citizenship that, in every case where there is ultimately a refusal, means the reason or reasons for refusal will

have to be disclosed. If, as may often be the case, the Secretary of State has only been troubled about one matter, then the unsuccessful applicant will be in no doubt as to the reason for refusal and the Secretary of State will in reality have been required to assign a reason for the refusal, which is precisely what [the legislation] says should not occur.

Interviewed the next day, Lord Woolf firmly denied that he was trying to circumvent a provision that he might not have liked. As he had stated in court, there was an overriding duty on anyone exercising a discretion to do so fairly. That duty had not been excluded by parliament. Even so, Lord Woolf seemed to accept that the Home Secretary could not have been expected to know that he had a duty to give applicants the chance to respond to his concerns. As he indicated while giving judgment, the law had not been clear. 'Until this court decided otherwise,' said the Master of the Rolls, 'it was perfectly reasonable to take a different view of the procedural requirements on an application for naturalisation.'

Asked whether his comments showed that relations between the judiciary and the executive were particularly sensitive, Lord Woolf said that did not necessarily follow: it was more that judges were expecting the media to misconstrue their decision as 'slapping down' the Home Secretary. He said both the executive and the judiciary should take corrective action to avoid the damaging impression of unnecessary confrontation.[26]

Lord Woolf was accused of trying to have his cake and eat it. He was obviously trying to be fair to both Mohamed Al Fayed and Michael Howard. He was also trying to obey the commands of parliament while observing the principles of administrative law. Above all, he was trying to achieve justice without raising the political temperature.

These attempts to square the circle were not fully appreciated. In a leading article, the *Daily Telegraph* accused Lord Woolf of political activism: the paper argued that the judges were there to interpret law, not make it.[27] On the same day, an article in *The Times* suggested that Michael Howard had come out of the case well: 'On the Tory benches and indeed in sections of the Tory press,' the *Times* author suggested, 'it is no disadvantage to be seen as the enemy of liberal judges, the man who said no to Mohamed Al Fayed.' The article argued that in a week which had seen Mr Howard reversed in the courts three times in as many days[28] the bruises he had sustained were, in the eyes of those he was keen to impress, 'badges of honour'.[29]

Not all commentators believed that the judges had been taking on the government. Some even seemed to think that the judiciary was in league with the Conservatives. Will Hutton, editor of the *Observer*, apparently believed that the judges who were appointed by Lord Mackay had 'come from the same milieu as his party colleagues'.[30] Writing in November 1994, he said in his best-selling book *The State We're In* that the judiciary – which, strangely, he described as 'the third branch of government' – had not thrown up many obstacles to the Conservatives. Apparently with approval, he quoted the former Conservative MP Lord Gilmour describing the judges as 'lambs under the throne'.[31] Then Mr Hutton said:

> The long-standing tradition of Britain's judiciary being more executive-minded than the executive, in Lord Atkin's famous dictum, came into its own in the 1980s with the law providing almost no refuge from the ambitions of the Conservative party to enlarge the centralising power of the state. The judges went along with the government's efforts to ban *Spycatcher*; and local authorities found that they had no redress for the various initiatives that curtailed their autonomy, entrenched by custom and practice but not by law.[32]

No less a person than the Lord Chief Justice has described this as 'an amazing passage'. Lord Bingham thought that John Major and his colleagues, together with the government's lawyers, 'would find this description of the judges' role hard to match up with the world they live in'.[33] Indeed, nobody could seriously suggest that leading judges like Lord Taylor, Lord Bingham, Lord Nolan, Lord Woolf and Sir Richard Scott were followers of the Conservative party by the mid-1990s. Lord Atkin's accusation that his fellow judges were 'more executive minded than the executive' was made during the dark days of the Second World War;[34] their approach was repudiated shortly afterwards;[35] and later they were authoritatively described as 'expediently and, at that time perhaps excusably, wrong'.[36] The government actually lost its attempt to prevent publication of *Spycatcher* (although the courts narrowly upheld a temporary ban while the action was being heard).[37] Finally, it is difficult to see how the judges could (or indeed should) have blocked local-government reforms passed by parliament.

Not even the Lord Chancellor could expect any favours from the judges. In March 1997, the High Court found that Lord Mackay had acted unlawfully in repealing the exemption from High Court fees for people on income support. Lord Justice Rose and Mr Justice Laws even refused Lord Mackay leave to appeal. Soon afterwards, he gave in gracefully, reinstating the exemption for all courts.

Judicial appointments

Despite the assumptions of journalists like Will Hutton, the senior judges are a modern and liberal-minded group of people. That does not mean they are soft on crime; nor does it mean that they are unresponsive to the public's concerns. It simply means they seek to act in the broad public interest rather than in the interests of short-term populism.

Perhaps it is therefore all the more remarkable that by 1997 virtually the entire serving judiciary had been appointed to the bench on the advice of Conservative ministers. In practice, the power over judicial appointments shared by the Prime Minister and his cabinet colleague the Lord Chancellor is almost unrestricted.

Sometimes the system works to the advantage of the Lord Chancellor. A good example of this involved the appointment of the two most senior members of the English judiciary in May 1996. Lord Taylor of Gosforth had been forced to retire early as Lord Chief Justice after doctors found that he was suffering from an inoperable tumour. As Lord Chief Justice, he mainly presided over the Criminal Division of the Court of Appeal: it was from there that his successor was expected to come. Lord Mackay, who had found himself the third Lord Chancellor to sit on the woolsack[38] during 1987 (after Mrs Thatcher had told Lords Hailsham and Havers that their services were no longer required), now found that he would be working with three Lords Chief Justice (Lord Lane, Lord Taylor and whoever was now to succeed him). It was a unique turn of events.

The most senior judges are appointed by the Queen on the advice of the Prime Minister. Before sending a name to the Palace the Prime Minister seeks advice from the Lord Chancellor. It has always been understood that the Lord Chancellor consults senior judges before making an appointment. Indeed, it was said at the time of Lord Taylor's enforced retirement that Lord Mackay would be consulting widely on the choice of his successor.

For that reason, Lord Justice Russell, who was then the most senior judge in the Court of Appeal Criminal Division, decided to take judicial soundings. Himself included, there were twenty-three judges sitting in the Court of Appeal who were sufficiently experienced in criminal work to preside over criminal appeals. Five of these judges were not approached: the three who were considered potential candidates (Lord Justice Rose, Lord Justice Kennedy and Lord Justice Auld[39]) as well as two who happened to be unwell at the time (Lord Justice McCowan and Lord Justice Leggatt).

That left eighteen appeal judges. Fourteen of them said their preferred candidate for Lord Chief Justice was Lord Justice Rose.[40] Three judges voted for Lord Woolf. One did not express a preference. Nobody supported Sir Thomas Bingham.

Lord Justice Russell passed this information on to the Lord Chancellor. Lord Mackay replied that the judges' views were important and that the Prime Minister would have them in mind when advising the Queen on an appointment. The judges were content in the knowledge that their views would be passed to Downing Street.

To their surprise, the judge most widely tipped for appointment in the days that followed turned out to be Sir Thomas Bingham. As a result, Lord Taylor decided to pay another visit to Downing Street;[41] he had already seen the Prime Minister in February of that year. Lord Taylor wanted to know why John Major had apparently ignored the judges' advice. The Prime Minister responded by saying he had not been told that Lord Justice Rose was the judges' choice for the job. By then, apparently, it had already been offered to Sir Thomas Bingham.[42]

Many of the judges were very angry at this. Believing that John Major had been kept in the dark about their views, they felt that the Lord Chancellor had ridden roughshod over them. However, they said nothing about the incident at the time.

There is no suggestion that Lord Mackay behaved unconstitutionally. He was fully entitled to recommend the candidate he thought most suitable. Nevertheless, the episode shows how much power the Lord Chancellor has. If he chooses not to consult those who know the candidates best, or chooses to recommend an appointment that they do not support, there is little they can do about it. It is not just the public who are left in the dark about important legal appointments. The judges, too, are treated like the proverbial mushrooms.

It was no surprise to find that Lord Justice Rose was the candidate Lord Taylor favoured to succeed him. Like Peter Taylor, Christopher Rose was a northern grammar-school boy who went on to Oxbridge.

Lord Justice Rose had supported Lord Taylor's attacks on the Home Secretary's sentencing proposals, and Lord Taylor in turn had gone out of his way to endorse Lord Justice Rose's remarks.[43] In recent years the Lord Chief Justice has devoted much of his time to criminal appeals, and apart from Lord Justice Kennedy there were not many other judges of the right age with strong experience of criminal work.

By contrast, Tom Bingham had not even been considered a runner. As Master of the Rolls since 1992, he heard the most important civil appeals, a position that broadly reflected his practice at the commercial bar. The judges of the Court of Appeal Criminal Division had nothing against him personally and indeed they greatly admired his intellect: it was simply that they felt the Lord Chief Justice needed a strong background in criminal work.

Nevertheless, Lord Mackay thought that Lord Bingham was the best man for the job. It was not just that he had been the first judge to support the Lord Chancellor's attempts to break the barristers' monopoly on advocacy in the higher courts, nor that he had supported the government's view of public interest immunity law in contrast to that taken by Sir Richard Scott.[44] Lord Bingham was clearly in sympathy with Lord Mackay's fundamental approach to the legal system – that the system required reform and it had to live within its means. He supported moves to close some of the expensive judges' lodgings: under that proposal, judges would make a provincial city their permanent base instead of travelling round the country on circuit.

As for the doubts about his lack of criminal experience, these were of little consequence to the Lord Chancellor. Lord Bingham had handled criminal trials as a judge of the Queen's Bench Division and he had heard criminal appeals as a Lord Justice of Appeal. Moreover, he agreed to serve on the basis that he would not spend all his judicial time on criminal appeals. These are not usually the most demanding fare, especially for a man of his intellect. Instead, he announced that he would be doing some judicial review work as well. This was not, he insisted, because he was concerned at the direction in which judicial review was going: it was simply because of the importance of the subject. He also said that he would be hearing some civil appeals.[45]

Critics called Lord Bingham's appointment 'political'.[46] In a sense, they were right: the most senior judicial appointments are made on the advice of the Prime Minister. He or she always takes advice from the Lord Chancellor, but sometimes that advice is not accepted.

It was Lord Mackay's practice to put more than one name on the list of judicial candidates he sent over to Downing Street; he would then indicate the strengths and weaknesses of each one, making his own preferences fully apparent. The present author disclosed[47] that Lord Mackay was unable to say his first choice for senior political appointments had always been accepted by the Prime Ministers he served. At the author's suggestion, Lord Mackay was questioned on this point by the House of Commons Select Committee on Home Affairs.[48] The Lord Chancellor's answer supported the author's inference that a Prime Minister – either John Major or, perhaps more likely, Margaret Thatcher – had not always accepted Lord Mackay's preferred choice:

> **Sir Ivan Lawrence QC MP**: I think you answered – just to confirm – to Peter Butler that all your recommendations had been accepted?
>
> **Lord Mackay of Clashfern**: *I was careful not to say that* [italics added]. What I did say was that I make these recommendations in confidence to the Prime Minister, I have never been disappointed by any recommendation that the Prime Minister has made to Her Majesty during my time – neither surprised nor disappointed – and that I could fully support each one of them.[49]

The committee quoted – apparently with approval – the present author's assertion that the Prime Minister's involvement in the appointment of the most senior judges was 'nothing short of naked political control'.[50] Members confessed to 'some qualms about the role of the Prime Minister in appointment to the senior judiciary'. In particular, the committee did not see how he or she might be better informed than the Lord Chancellor might be in making recommendations to the Queen. The committee, despite its loyal Conservative chairman and its in-built government majority, then said: 'we therefore question whether the Prime Minister should play any part in appointing judges.'[51] This was precisely the present author's concern.

It was a concern that was ignored by the government. The committee's report, which broadly supported the existing arrangements, was warmly welcomed by the Lord Chancellor. No changes were made to the appointments system.

It is fair to say that Lord Mackay promoted independent-minded judges regardless of their political views. Yet the present system relies on the Lord Chancellor putting aside political considerations when making his recommendations. This may be difficult enough, but the Prime Minister is also required to forget he is a party politician. This is surely too much to expect.

Labour's view

Labour's Lord Chancellor-in-waiting, Lord Irvine of Lairg QC, said that politics should never enter into the appointment of any judge. Speaking in October 1996, he stressed that 'the role and independence of the judiciary will be vigorously upheld by the next Labour government'. He then put forward ways of strengthening the lay element in the panels that interview candidates for appointments below the level of the High Court. Lord Irvine suggested the system could be extended to the more senior appointments, while making it clear that the ultimate decision was for the Lord Chancellor to make. He revealed that Labour favoured an Advisory Committee on Judicial Appointments, including 'representatives of the judges and the professions as well as a strong, high quality lay element'.

What worried the judges was a sub-heading in the printed text of this speech which referred to a 'Judicial Appointments *and Training* Commission' (italics added). The judges believed that to remain independent they needed to keep complete control of their own training: it looked as if Labour wanted to take that away from them.

It was perhaps ironic that the man who aimed to succeed Lord Mackay of Clashfern as the senior judge of England and Wales was another Scot. Both men came from humble backgrounds, both did brilliantly at Scottish universities and at Cambridge, both had brief academic careers before success at the bar. Nevertheless, Lord Irvine of Lairg – 'Derry' to his friends – was as different from Lord Mackay as it was possible to be: 'Derry's not really a practising Scot,' as someone once said.[52]

Lord Mackay had never established a legal practice in England. Nor had he ever sat as an English judge. By contrast, Lord Irvine had made his career at the English bar, and sat as a part-time judge in the English courts. Lord Mackay was not even a member of the Conservative party when Mrs Thatcher invited him into the government in 1979 as Lord Advocate.[53] Lord Irvine's life had been closely bound up with the future of the Labour party ever since he met and befriended the man who was to lead it, John Smith, when they were both law students at Glasgow university.

Derry[54] Irvine had been a potential Lord Chancellor ever since 1987, when the Labour leader, Neil Kinnock, nominated him for a peerage. Mr Kinnock's failure to win the 1992 election only improved Lord Irvine's chances of getting on to the woolsack: as we have seen, John Smith, who succeeded Neil Kinnock, was a close friend. John Smith's untimely death made Lord Irvine's appointment even more of a certainty: not only had he accepted Mr Smith's successor, Tony Blair, as a pupil in his chambers in 1976, he had also taken on the woman Mr Blair was to marry, Cherie Booth QC. Lord Irvine retained the role of pupil-master long after his most famous pupil had given up his practice at the bar, acting as Tony Blair's mentor and intellectual confidant.

Despite his long apprenticeship for the role of Lord Chancellor, Lord Irvine of Lairg was not well known outside the Labour party before the General Election of 1997. As the election drew closer, Lord Irvine made a few more formal speeches and gave one or two interviews; despite this, he was still something of an enigma.

As we shall see, Lord Irvine had no time for upstart judges. He criticised what he saw as judicial supremacism[55] and warned the judges not to engage in political controversy.[56] His critics used these comments to suggest that Lord Irvine was being reactionary, more conservative indeed than Lord Mackay. They also suggested he was trying to soften up the judges for a Labour government, warning them not to interfere with the decisions he hoped soon to be making.

That sort of comment made Lord Irvine furious. In his view, outspoken judges risked giving the false impression that when hearing applications for judicial review 'they may have a political agenda in which their decisions are arrived at because of a hostility to a particular act of parliament'. As for the suggestion that he was softening up the bench for a Labour government, 'nothing could be further from the truth'.[57]

In reality Lord Irvine was trying, while still a member of the parliamentary opposition, to decide how he would occupy the great office of state that might soon come his way. Lord Mackay had lost the confidence of the judiciary: that meant the judges could not be relied on to behave in exactly the way that a Lord Chancellor would wish. If Lord Irvine were to receive the Great Seal of England,[58] he would have to find a way of asserting his authority while gaining the judges' respect. It was not an easy task for someone with less judicial experience than the most junior full-time judge. For all that, Derry Irvine was known for his commanding intellect and his huge capacity for work. If he were to achieve his ambition, it looked as if he would need to use both these talents to the full.

Judicial independence

For the time being, at least, the judges do enjoy a large measure of independence. No judge – not even the Lord Chief Justice – can tell another judge what to think or do.[59] Our judges are widely acknowledged to be incorruptible: there is no suggestion that any of them would take a bribe. Lord Nolan, the law lord brought in by John Major to improve standards in public life, observed that 'in some countries less happy than ours, it may need great courage for a judge to decide a case against the government. In this marvellous country, all that happens if you decide a case against the government is that you get rather a good press, and very possibly promoted.'

As an example of this happy constitutional practice, Lord Nolan mentioned Brian Smedley. He was the judge who presided over the Matrix Churchill 'arms to Iraq' trial in 1992: the case collapsed with the acquittal of all three defendants after Judge Smedley ordered ministers to disclose documents for which they had claimed immunity.[60] At that time, Brian Smedley was a circuit judge. Promotions from the circuit bench to the High Court bench are relatively rare, but Judge Smedley became Mr Justice Smedley in 1995. Lord Nolan understood it had given great satisfaction to the Lord Chancellor and his officials that this appointment, which in other countries might have been regarded as astonishing, caused no surprise whatever in the profession, and went virtually unnoticed by the media.[61]

Some modest proposals

In England and Wales, the three great organs of state overlap in many ways:[62]

The Lord Chancellor is a leading member of the executive, the legislature and the judiciary.
The law lords are members of the legislature and the judiciary.
The law officers are members of the executive who exercise quasi-judicial powers.

These overlapping roles have been tolerated because most of the time they work. The system relies on individuals of the highest moral and intellectual calibre deliberately suppressing some of their natural instincts. Lord Mackay almost admitted as much when he said: 'The judgment, discretion and *good faith*[63] of those operating our constitutional arrangements is of the greatest importance . . . As long as we have people in public life with the necessary qualities – and I believe that we are very fortunate in that respect – I think our arrangements work at least as well as, perhaps better than, many others.'[64]

We expect a great deal from our senior judges and ministers, but we cannot rely on an unlimited supply of almost superhuman beings. The time has now come to remove some of their responsibilities.

The Lord Chancellor

The Lord Chancellor is a member of the legislature (where he is 'Speaker' of the House of Lords), a member of the executive (the highest-paid cabinet minister) and a member of the judiciary (presiding – when he chooses to sit – over the appellate committee of the House of Lords[65] and the Judicial Committee of the Privy Council).[66] Towards the end of 1996, a serving law lord argued that the Lord Chancellor should be deposed as head of the judiciary. Lord Steyn, South African-born and a commercial lawyer by training, sympathised with those who thought it was inappropriate for someone like himself – a member of both the judiciary and the legislature – to be calling for a greater separation of powers in the United Kingdom.[67] That did not deflect him from his plea.

As a proposal, it was far from new. The present author suggested in 1994 that it was time for the Lord Chancellor to hang up one of his three wigs.[68] Indeed, as long ago as 1856 there were calls for a Minister of Justice to take on some of the Lord Chancellor's responsibilities.[69] However, in the summer of 1996 Lord Mackay reaffirmed his support for the Lord Chancellor's tripartite role. In Lord Mackay's view, there were 'great strengths in the existing arrangements'. As he explained: 'I have often felt that when I am among judges I am a lone politician and when I am among politicians I am a lone judge. Yet I believe that, far from undermining either the executive or the judiciary, this combination of roles requires the Lord Chancellor to be particularly sensible of the perspectives of each one.'[70]

Lord Steyn was not impressed. He thought the Lord Chancellor should cease to be head of the English judiciary. In his view, the current position was no longer sustainable on either constitutional or pragmatic grounds. Little of value would be lost by the reform, he believed: the Lord Chancellor would still retain all his other functions and it would make little difference to the law lords or the Privy Council if he no longer sat with them. Indeed, Lord Steyn said much would be gained by the change:

> It seems to me that there are positive disadvantages in the Lord Chancellor being both a cabinet minister and head of the judiciary. A Lord Chancellor gives the appearance to the public of speaking as the head of the judiciary with the neutrality and impartiality so involved. The truth is different. Under governments of all complexions, the Lord Chancellor is always a spokesman for the government in the furtherance of its party political agenda. Even in matters affecting the administration of justice he is, as Lord Hailsham explained, always subject to collective cabinet responsibility.

Lord Steyn recalled that the effect of financial constraints on the administration of justice had recently been a controversial issue. As a cabinet minister, he said, the Lord Chancellor was influenced by the Treasury perspective. 'The view of the judges is rather different,' said Lord Steyn drily. 'They do not wholeheartedly share the modern adoration of the deity of economy. On the whole, they put justice first.'

In Lord Steyn's view, the head of the judiciary in England and Wales should be the Lord Chief Justice. To some extent, he already is. The Lord Chief Justice is the most senior *full-time* judge in England and Wales, and reporters can hardly be accused of giving a misleading impression if they omit the phrase 'full-time' from his job description. Certainly, the judges themselves feel much closer to the Lord Chief Justice of the day, someone they will have known and perhaps worked with for years, than they do to the Lord Chancellor. They may have treated the former Lord Chancellor, Lord Hailsham, as their 'shop steward', the man who represented their interests in Whitehall and Westminster. That was not how they viewed Lord Mackay of Clashfern. His reputation after nearly ten years on the woolsack was as the Lord Chancellor who managed to offend many of his fellow judges.

That criticism was articulated by yet another law lord, this time a retired one. In 1994, Lord Ackner said it was 'a very remarkable, deeply distressing and much to be regretted fact that since 1989 the government have managed to antagonise virtually every component part of the administration of justice. Through . . . the Lord Chancellor and his department, they have alienated the bar, the solicitors and the professional judges.'[71]

Recalling these remarks in November 1996, Lord Ackner traced the origin of this alienation back to Lord Mackay's famous Green Papers on the future of the legal profession, published at the start of 1989. These, said Lord Ackner, were produced at the behest of a sub-committee of the cabinet's economic committee, chaired by the then Chancellor of the Exchequer, Nigel Lawson. Lord Ackner argued that many of the Lord Chancellor's proposed reforms were Treasury-led. If they were designed to save money, Lord Ackner implied, their aim could not also be to serve justice.

It is perfectly legitimate for a government minister to keep within a departmental budget: indeed, one would be concerned if he did not. Whether that is an appropriate course of action for someone who is also head of the judiciary is another matter. There is every reason for suggesting that the Lord Chancellor should give up that role. Two demanding full-time jobs ought to be enough for anybody.

Not surprisingly, successive holders of the office have been reluctant to give up their judicial status. Viewed from the government's perspective, the confusion of roles may be highly convenient. In November 1996, Lord Mackay visited the European Court of Human Rights in Strasbourg. His visit was advertised by officials as an attempt to persuade the court to change its procedures: the government wanted a new system for vetting proposed judges; it asked for advance notice of the court's main areas of concern so it could be better prepared for the final hearing; and it was seeking a wider application of the so-called 'margin of appreciation' – which allows governments more leeway when complying with the convention.

A few hours before Lord Mackay arrived in Strasbourg, the human rights court delivered a judgment in favour of the United Kingdom. It was about a short erotic video called *Visions of Ecstasy* which the British Board of Film Classification had refused to license for distribution: the censors thought the film, about the sixteenth-century Spanish mystic nun, St Teresa of Ávila, might fall foul of the English law of blasphemy. Their decision was challenged by the film's director, Nigel Wingrove. However, the European Court said the ban fell within the margin of appreciation allowed to the authorities in Britain. Conveniently for the court, this was just the sort of approach Lord Mackay had been intending to urge on the human rights judges; Strasbourg officials insisted it was a pure coincidence that the court happened to give that particular judgment on that particular day.

Lord Mackay was well received by judges and officials in Strasbourg. He may have left London as a party politician doing the government's bidding, but by the time his plane arrived in France he had been transformed into a distinguished judge. The people he saw at the court were accordingly polite and circumspect in their public comments after meeting him; for his part, he was as charming and tactful as ever. The government was well satisfied with his visit.[72]

Reaction at home was not so favourable. The Law Society's *Gazette* interviewed Nigel Wingrove's solicitor, Mark Stephens. He said it was 'unprecedented that the Lord Chancellor of any country should go to the court in this manner'. No other country has a Lord Chancellor, of course, but the point was clear enough: as another solicitor said in the same report, it was 'particularly shocking that Lord Mackay, a judge and head of the legal system, should be playing politics in this way'.[73]

It may be shocking to find a judge playing politics, but surely that is a legitimate role for the longest-serving member of the cabinet? The Lord Chancellor may not look like a party politician, he does not have a seat in the House of Commons and he does not attend party conferences. Nevertheless, he is still a political figure who leaves office on a change of government. What *is* shocking is that our constitution still requires one person to wear so many wigs.

During his period in office, which lasted from 1987 to 1997, Lord Mackay stoutly defended his three roles as legislator, minister and judge. Even as he approached his seventieth birthday, he was still bearing those three heavy burdens with a twinkle in his eye. His staff were unexpectedly fond of him: women, in particular, could see through his dour exterior to the warm and generous man beneath.

This was not his public image. He was seen as a strict Sabbatarian (which he was) and a teetotaller (which he was not). Although his wife dutifully appeared at his side on state occasions he kept his family well out of the public eye: in office he was an intensely private man, quite unlike the modern politician.

Indeed, as a politician he was not a total success. His attempt to change the divorce law looked set to founder in the summer of 1996, although in the end the Family Law Act was passed by parliament. It was a warning that no piece of legislation, however innocuous it might appear, was immune from the uncertainties of party politics. It was also a lesson that contentious legislation generally needs to be piloted through parliament by a minister with a seat in the House of Commons; perhaps not surprisingly, Lord Mackay did not share that view.

As we have seen, critics said there ought to be three Lord Mackays in the government. Strangely enough, by 1996 there were. Apart from Lord Mackay of Clashfern himself, there was the Lord Advocate, Lord Mackay of Drumadoon QC, and the Minister of State at the Department of Social Security, Lord Mackay of Ardbrecknish. This multiplicity of Mackays sometimes caused confusion. In August 1996, the Lord Chancellor was invited to address the Commonwealth Law Conference in Vancouver. Understandably enough, Scotland's senior law officer was booked on the same flight. The airline on which they were both to travel noticed that among the first-class passengers there were two people called Lord Mackay. Assuming this could only be an error, they removed one from the list. The Lord Chancellor checked in first. The Lord Advocate was not amused to be told there was no room for him on the plane.[74]

There should be no room in the British constitution for a three-headed Lord Chancellor. Members of the House of Commons insist on choosing their own Speaker: in the past, they have rejected names put forward by the government of the day. It is remarkable that members of the House of Lords are prepared to accept a cabinet minister in a similar role. However, if they wish to keep the Lord Chancellor on the woolsack then they are entitled to do so. What is no longer appropriate is for the Lord Chancellor to remain a judge as well as a cabinet minister. He should give up his judicial office and move to the House of Commons.

The law lords

The law lords are full-time judges who join the legislature as members of the House of Lords.[75] They may continue to take part in debates after they have retired as law lords. As we shall see in Chapter 2, they do not hesitate to speak and vote against government proposals involving the administration of justice. This has its dangers.

One way of reducing those dangers would be to abolish the law lords. From time to time critics[76] have suggested that instead the Court of Appeal should become the highest court in England and Wales.

This would plainly have some advantages. It would make justice quicker: cases would be resolved without having to wait for a hearing by the law lords. It would save money, not just for the country but also for the unsuccessful litigant who would be spared the costs of what could be the third hearing in court.

On the other hand, supporters of the law lords point out that they sometimes overturn decisions of the Court of Appeal: these supporters say it is important that there should be an ultimate court to put right the mistakes of the lower courts. The law lords' critics accept that their decisions are final, at least as far as the courts of the United Kingdom are concerned; that does not mean they are right. Moreover, it hardly adds to the lustre of the legal system when the judges disagree so profoundly. In the *Fire Brigades Union* case discussed in Chapter 3, the union won with the support of just three judges in the House of Lords and two in the Court of Appeal; the remaining five judges involved in the case all found against the union.

Another reason for keeping the law lords is to preserve something of the unity of the United Kingdom. If the House of Lords ceased to sit judicially, there would be three final courts of appeal – in London, Edinburgh and Belfast. Even so, the present unity may be illusory rather than real. Not many appeals reach the law lords.[77] There are no criminal appeals from Scotland. In civil cases, the Scottish courts do not consider themselves bound by decisions of the law lords on appeals from other parts of the United Kingdom.

These days, as we have seen, an important consequence of making our most senior judges members of the House of Lords is that they are able to take part in parliamentary debates. From their perspective, it gives them a chance to influence (and, indeed, sometimes propose) legislation. Abolishing the law lords would leave only the Lord Chief Justice, the Master of the Rolls and their predecessors as legal peers: they would be the only judges with the right to take part in parliamentary debates.[78]

The former Conservative Home Office minister John Patten saw no justification for the law lords' parliamentary role: he thought the answer was simply to take away the law lords' right to vote (and, presumably, speak) in the House of Lords. 'Our judges used to be a shadowy lot, rarely emerging for anything approaching political comment,' he said. 'In the mid-1990s, increasingly they have created their own judicial soapboxes and regularly pop up on the *Today* programme, so there seems no reason why they should automatically be represented in that chamber at all. Their position in the Lords has become blatantly unjustifiable – and deeply unjust.'[79]

Mr Patten exaggerated the frequency with which serving judges appear on the radio. Moreover, it is hardly fair to say the law lords should lose their constitutional position *because* they are interviewed by the BBC. Nevertheless, he was fundamentally right: it is hard to justify the right of senior serving judges to take part in a political assembly, even if they sit on the cross benches.[80]

Lord Mackay tried his best, though. He believed the fact that ministers and judges were also legislators had 'tremendous advantages in practice'. In his view, 'the presence of the most senior members of the judiciary in parliament enables the legislative process to draw on a tremendous and unique concentration of legal expertise. The benefits of this,' he said, 'are to be seen not just in relation to technical law, but in relation to the whole range of legislation that is put before parliament.'[81]

There are, notwithstanding, pitfalls for the law lords. In 1996, it was Lord Hoffmann's misfortune to fall into one of them.

The story began in October 1994 when the Conservative MP, Neil Hamilton, issued a writ for libel against the *Guardian* after the newspaper had accused him of accepting cash for asking parliamentary questions. His legal action was stopped by the High Court in July 1995 because at that time article 9 of the Bill of Rights 1689[82] prevented the courts from investigating anything done by an MP in the course of his parliamentary duties. The court held that it would not be fair to allow Mr Hamilton to continue with his action because the newspaper could not defend itself: to have argued that its allegations were true would have required an investigation of Mr Hamilton's parliamentary duties, which would have been a breach of his privilege as an MP.

This decision came as a disappointment for the Conservatives: it would have suited the government very well if one of its supporters had persuaded a jury that the allegations made against him were not true. Yet if Mr Hamilton's libel action was to go ahead, article 9 would have to be repealed.

Fortunately for Mr Hamilton, and indeed for the government, Lord Hoffmann – a serving law lord – was willing to take steps in parliament aimed at letting MPs waive the protection given by article 9. Lord Hoffmann's amendment to what was to become the Defamation Act 1996 was passed by a majority of 100 peers during the Third Reading debate.[83] As a result, Mr Hamilton resumed his legal action – only to abandon it in September 1996, the day before the High Court hearing was expected to begin. There was said to have been a 'conflict of interest' between Mr Hamilton and his fellow plaintiff, Ian Greer, who was then an influential lobbyist. The next day, the *Guardian* famously called Mr Hamilton 'a liar and a cheat'.[84]

If the libel case had gone ahead it would have been highly political, with leading members of the government called to give evidence against the *Guardian*. Why then had Lord Hoffmann backed moves to let it go ahead? According to media reports, he had put down his amendment as the result of a conversation with the Lord Chancellor. The amendment had been drafted by government lawyers and, although the government had declared itself officially neutral, it seemed there had been an unofficial whip to persuade Conservative MPs to vote for the changes. When Lord Hoffmann saw that his amendment was becoming politicised, he decided to abstain.[85]

It seemed clear that Lord Hoffmann had been sucked unwittingly into politics by a fellow law lord who just happened to be a member of the cabinet. The Lord Chancellor, in turn, was obviously doing the government's bidding.[86] What then did Lord Hoffmann have to say at the end of the day?

'I am not sure that I would have got involved in *l'affaire Hamilton* if I had realised how politically divided the vote on the Third Reading was going to be,' he admitted. 'That said, I think the amendment was right and not improper for a law lord to propose. It was a matter of general constitutional principle.' Lord Hoffmann explained that he had intended that Neil Hamilton 'should be able to sue if he wished to do so and that, if he had a good case, he should win and that, if he had a bad one, he should lose'. Lord Hoffmann said it seemed that Mr Hamilton had concluded at the last moment that his case was a bad one, but that had nothing to do with the principle of the amendment.[87]

As Lord Hoffmann said, he would not have got involved had he known how political the issue was going to be. Judges can be forgiven for political naïveté: little is done to prepare them for their promotion to a court that happens to be part of parliament. Yet the moral is plain: law lords should keep well away from politics – and politicians.

The law officers
The government's chief legal adviser is the Attorney General, not the Lord Chancellor. The Attorney General has a deputy called the Solicitor General. Confusingly, both are normally barristers.[88] Together, they are known as the law officers.

The Attorney General is a member of the government. He and his deputy have normally been MPs. Although the Attorney General is not usually a member of the cabinet he sits on cabinet committees and sees cabinet papers.

He also has certain quasi-judicial powers. He 'superintends' the work of the main prosecuting agencies[89] and decides personally whether to bring a prosecution in the most difficult cases. He can stop any prosecution at any time by entering what is called a *nolle prosequi*. He must decide whether to bring contempt of court proceedings against journalists and others. He also decides whether a sentence passed in the Crown Court is 'unduly lenient' and therefore worthy of review by the Court of Appeal.

There is a conflict of interest between the Attorney General's political role and his quasi-judicial role. Speaking towards the end of 1996, Lord Steyn reviewed the supposed safeguards against abuse:

> First, in his quasi-judicial function the Attorney General is not subject to collective responsibility and he does not take orders from the government. But he may seek the views of other ministers and they may volunteer their views. Secondly, it is said that the Attorney General is not influenced by party political considerations. On the other hand, he may take into account public policy considerations. These conventions are weak. Their efficacy depends on Chinese walls in the mind of the Attorney General.[90]

Lord Steyn recalled that in 1990[91] Lord Woolf had called for the creation of a Director of Civil Proceedings to take over the Attorney General's function of bringing civil proceedings in the public interest. Lord Steyn went further: he said the Attorney General, as currently constituted, should lose the power to bring criminal proceedings as well. Either the Attorney General should become an independent lawyer outside the government or he should remain in government and hand over to an independent lawyer his power to bring criminal and civil proceedings. In either case, the independent lawyer would remain accountable to parliament through a select committee.

This proposal, coming from an independent-minded law lord with an international perspective, deserves the fullest consideration. It would bring the United Kingdom into line with many other countries. However, if it is implemented – as indeed it should be – it will probably be for practical considerations as much as constitutional ones. There are not as many eminent practising lawyers in the House of Commons as there once were, and it is becoming harder for governments to find suitable MPs for appointment as law officers. This is no doubt because practice at the bar and membership of the House are seen increasingly as full-time jobs. Those who are successful at the bar no longer feel under any obligation to suffer a loss of income by entering politics; those who seek success in politics (like, for example, Tony Blair) must abandon their careers at the bar.

The former Labour Home Secretary, Lord Jenkins of Hillhead, summed up the problem very well in a House of Lords debate on the Scott Report in February 1996. After dismissing the Conservative Attorney General, Sir Nicholas Lyell, as 'a modest man with much to be modest about', the Liberal Democrat peer said that 'the race of great lawyer-politicians which has fortified our politics for two and a half centuries has become effectively extinct'. Lord Jenkins continued:

> From Erskine at the beginning to Shawcross or perhaps Monckton at the end, it underpinned our politics. Now it is dead; killed, I think, by the petty and excessive demands of modern constituencies. Brougham would not have been much good at coffee mornings. I would not set Sir Edward Carson to move from advice bureaux to bridge parties. One ought to recognise that the present holder is the last station on the line. Future governments, I fear – in itself I regret it, because the old system worked well – ought to look for law officers outside politics. It is only in that way that they will get silks worthy of the tradition.[92]

The *Daily Telegraph* caught up with the story in January 1997. 'Tony Blair has been warned that he does not have legal talent among his MPs to fill the key law officers' posts in a Labour government,' the paper reported.[93] It pointed out that the only candidate for the post of Attorney General in a Labour government was John Morris QC, a member of parliament since 1959 and the only survivor of the last Labour cabinet expected to serve under Tony Blair. The *Telegraph* suggested that the Solicitor General would have to come from the House of Lords. Lord Williams of Mostyn QC was seen as the most likely candidate.

As the newspaper pointed out, the Solicitor General for Scotland is not a member of either the Lords or the Commons. The post used to be held by a Scottish MP until the Conservatives ran out of suitable candidates: among the last MPs to hold it, in the early 1980s, were Nicholas Fairbairn and Peter Fraser (later Lord Fraser of Carmyllie). Not for the first time, England may follow Scotland's lead.

John Morris was one of just three Recorders – part-time judges – left in the House of Commons by the spring of 1997. There was one from each party,[94] but this happy division of political colours did little to justify an undesirable anomaly. A defendant who receives what he considers to be an unduly harsh sentence may object if he realises that he has appeared before an avowed supporter of Michael Howard's plans for tougher sentences; the victim of an assault may complain if he thinks his assailant has been treated too lightly by a Labour or Liberal Democrat MP. That is not to say that any particular holders of these offices would pass inappropriate sentences: it is simply that those in court may think they would.

By tradition, in certain types of case the law officers – the Attorney General and his deputy the Solicitor General – appear personally in court on behalf of the government. These appearances are not particularly frequent: for example, between June 1987 and December 1989 each law officer appeared in court on average once every six months.[95] In the early years of this century it was the custom that the Attorney General personally prosecuted alleged poisoners and those accused of killing police officers. Yet in 1910 when Dr Crippen was charged with the murder of his wife, the Director of Public Prosecutions, Sir Charles Mathews, persuaded the Attorney General, Sir William Robson, not to interfere with his choice of counsel ('the case does not seem to me to be a very difficult one and, in my opinion,' wrote the Director of Public Prosecutions soothingly to the Attorney General, 'it would be safe in the hands of Muir and Travers Humphreys . . .').[96] It looked from the correspondence as if the Director of Prosecutions feared the Attorney General would not have handled the case as effectively as specialist counsel would; perhaps Crippen might have been acquitted had the Attorney General appeared in person.

Certainly the law officers' recent attempts at advocacy have not been an unmitigated success. The Attorney General and Solicitor General no longer personally prosecute in run-of-the mill murder cases: they are more often to be seen representing the government in public law cases or at one of the two European courts.[97] Because the oral tradition is not as well established in Strasbourg and Luxembourg as it is in the United Kingdom, advocates there have a much easier time: instead of engaging in an intellectual exercise with the judges they can generally get away with reading a speech and answering questions.

However, in June 1996 Sir Nicholas Lyell failed in his efforts to persuade the European Court of Justice that the worldwide ban on exports of British beef might be contrary to European law. With the support of a bevy of officials, the Attorney General put up a creditable performance, but the European judges seemed unmoved by the fact that a member of the government had taken the trouble to address them and they proceeded to dismiss his application to have the ban lifted or modified.

Even less impressive was the performance in July 1996 of the Solicitor General Sir Derek Spencer. He appeared on behalf of the Attorney General in contempt-of-court proceedings against the publishers of five tabloid newspapers, claiming they had created a substantial risk of seriously prejudicing the prosecution of a man called Geoff Knights. As the High Court was to explain later:

> the lives of Mr Knights and his erstwhile girlfriend Miss [Gillian] Taylforth had long been of interest to the general public. This was in part the result of her having a major role in a popular television programme[98] with a consequential public interest in her love life; in part because of their activities together [in a lay-by] on the A1 where a police officer had made an arrest alleging activities of a sexual nature between them there (which arrest had been followed by a libel action concerned with the same activities); and in part because of Mr Knights' own colourful past.'[99]

It looked like a clear-cut case of contempt: Mr Knights' trial had been stopped because of what the judge called 'unfair, outrageous and oppressive' reporting; he said it was also 'unlawful, misleading, scandalous and malicious'.[100] Nevertheless, when the proceedings opened Sir Derek Spencer seemed unprepared for the questions he was asked by the judges: the hearing had to be adjourned early for his benefit. Not only did Sir Derek proceed to lose the case (the judges did not consider that any of the newspaper reports created a substantial risk that the course of justice would be seriously impeded or prejudiced), his lawyers then failed to lodge an application for leave to appeal to the House of Lords within the required fourteen days.[101]

This left the government paying the newspapers' hefty legal costs. It also left the media in a much stronger position than they had been before the case began, which was presumably not what the Attorney General had in mind when he started proceedings.

The consequences were soon apparent. In January 1997, the London *Evening Standard* inadvertently published prejudicial information about three men who were currently on trial accused of breaking out of Whitemoor prison in Cambridgeshire during 1994. It was the second time this had happened – other newspapers had been involved on an earlier occasion – and the judge, Mr Justice Maurice Kay, decided that the trial should go no further. Counsel for the Attorney General told the judge that in the light of the Geoff Knights case the Attorney General would have to take account of the previous publicity in deciding whether to bring contempt proceedings: there could be a problem in isolating the prejudice caused by the *Evening Standard* article.

After some thought, the Attorney General decided to go ahead. In March 1997, Sir Nicholas Lyell announced that he would be seeking leave of the High Court to bring proceedings for contempt of court against the *Evening Standard*, its reporter and the paper's editor, Max Hastings. Although the General Election was less than two months away, Sir Nicholas had ignored all political considerations in reaching his decision: a lesser man might have found some reason for delaying legal action against an influential newspaper editor whose support his party might value in the forthcoming election.

As Solicitor General, Sir Derek Spencer also failed to persuade an Old Bailey jury that Szymon Serafinowicz, an eighty-six-year old who in his youth had commanded a police unit in Nazi-occupied Byelorussia, was fit to stand trial on mass murder charges under the War Crimes Act.[102] Given the evidence that the defendant was suffering from Alzheimer's Disease, this was understandable: Sir Derek had put up a creditable performance in court. Why, though, had he chosen to take over the prosecution brief? It appears that the Solicitor General thought that in a case of this importance a law officer should lead for the Crown, particularly as the Conservative cabinet had pushed the War Crimes Act through an initially sceptical parliament. However, these were spurious reasons. It is unlikely that the jury realised they were being addressed by a government law officer, even if they understood what a law officer was: Sir Derek was referred to as 'Mr Solicitor' throughout.[103] It was also wrong to give the impression that the government as a whole had some interest in getting a conviction, perhaps because it wanted to justify its support for the War Crimes Act: prosecution decisions should be as far removed from governments as possible.

In 1992 Sir Nicholas Lyell had appeared in an important case before a larger-than-normal panel of seven law lords. At that time, the judges were given little help in interpreting obscure acts of parliament: they were not allowed to look up parliamentary debates in *Hansard* in order to work out what parliament thought it was doing when it passed the legislation. The law lords were considering whether to lift that rule and had asked the Attorney General for his views. Sir Nicholas said they should not consult *Hansard*: he argued that the exclusionary rule had a 'sound constitutional, practical and legal basis which had stood the test of time'. Lifting it might even have been contrary to the Bill of Rights 1689.

No fewer than six law lords disagreed with the Attorney General on this point. Only one of them was persuaded, and he turned out to be the Lord Chancellor. Lord Mackay was worried about how much it would cost if lawyers had to consult *Hansard* whenever there was a case involving statutory construction.

It cannot have been right for a member of the government to sit judicially in a case with crucial implications for the resources of his own department.[104] It was even less acceptable for one of his government colleagues to appear before him as an advocate. Both Lord Mackay and Sir Nicholas Lyell behaved on this occasion with the utmost propriety; nevertheless, justice was not seen to be done.

Even if no other changes are made, the time has surely come for the law officers to give up their attempts at advocacy. As with so many other things in life, the job is done better by those who do it for a living. It is often said that a man who is his own lawyer has a fool for a client. A government whose members represent it in court is equally foolhardy.[105]

Giving up advocacy is only the first stage: the overlap between the Attorney General's quasi-judicial and political functions must be brought rapidly to an end. The *Spycatcher* case, discussed in Chapter 6, demonstrated the potential conflicts of interest: on some occasions the Attorney General was acting on behalf of the government while at other times during the same litigation he was acting as an independent guardian of the public interest. The Scott Inquiry, discussed in the same chapter, exposed even greater conflicts of interest, with members of a government that had been less than frank with parliament having to rely on legal advice from a member of that government – one, moreover, whose 'absence of personal involvement' in 'important constitutional and legal issues' rendered him 'personally at fault'.[106]

In this chapter we have maintained that politicians should no longer encroach on the judiciary's territory. It seems only fair to argue in Chapter 2 that judges should keep out of politics.

2

The Sentence of the Judge

I believe that, on suitable occasions, judges should be prepared to speak on matters affecting the law and the courts, to answer criticism and to explain policies. I also hope that if judges do speak out on topics which concern the public they may overcome the widely held belief . . . that judges are out of touch or even, as has been said, 'live on another planet'.

Lord Taylor, Lord Chief Justice (1994)[1]

Our constitution is delicately balanced, with a constant tension between parliament and the executive on the one hand and the judiciary on the other. In this tension lies our historic and unique concept of liberty and its protection. A politicised judiciary will upset that balance and erode our protection.

Melanie Phillips, columnist (1996)[2]

A politicised judiciary?

If we are moving towards a more politicised judiciary, the politicians are largely to blame. Even the most senior politicians indulge in a spot of judge-bashing from time to time. For example, in October 1995 the Conservative chairman, Dr Brian Mawhinney, told his party conference that people should let judges know when they were dissatisfied with them: 'Magistrates and judges are good people, but they do not act in a vacuum. They are your representatives, so praise them when you agree with them and let them know if you are dissatisfied. The expression of the public's view on sentencing does have an effect, so keep on having your say'.[3]

Needless to say, this appalled the judges. As shadow Lord Chancellor, Lord Irvine of Lairg QC accused Dr Mawhinney of 'whipping up write-ins to bring pressure on judges to give tougher sentences'. Asked about Dr Mawhinney's remarks in the House of Lords, the Lord Chancellor managed to put some distance between himself and his government colleague. 'I consider that, in the passage referred to, my right honourable friend was not seeking to express a policy of Her

35

Majesty's government,' he said firmly. Lord Mackay pointed out that the party chairman had said also that the judge who passed sentence in a particular case would have heard all the evidence; people should take that into account before they thought of writing in. Lord Mackay was sure Dr Mawhinney would not have been in favour of people writing abusive letters to judges.[4]

This was a patent example of a government minister making political capital out of the judiciary: Dr Mawhinney seemed intent on dragging judges down to the level of politicians. Yet his comments were simply reflecting the opinion of his audience (members of the Conservative party) and of the newspapers that influenced them (such as the *Daily Mail*); at a time when 'law and order' was a key political issue, the judges were considered soft on crime.

Had the judges done anything to deserve this opprobrium? As far as they were concerned, they had been trying faithfully to fulfil the aims of the Criminal Justice Act 1991. This legislation, however imperfectly, attempted to enact the moderate policies associated with Douglas Hurd,[5] the Home Secretary who had persuaded sceptics that the moral duty of avoiding a custodial sentence whenever possible coincided with the political imperative of clearing overcrowded prisons. Since Douglas Hurd's day that policy had shifted into reverse: the judiciary was less convinced than the Home Office of the need for a U-turn. If the judges were sounding like more like Her Majesty's opposition during the mid-1990s, it was only because the Labour party was not opposing very much: in the aftermath of the 1992 election Labour was exhausted and disillusioned while in the run-up to the 1997 election the party was determined not to appear weak on law and order.

The judges themselves must also bear some responsibility for the exposed position in which they found themselves. They seemed unsure about how far they should go down the road of public debate. There were times when the former Lord Chief Justice, Lord Taylor of Gosforth, thought it right to use the mass media. In 1992 he said: 'The judiciary does not need to put itself into purdah by refusing ever to speak out of court about its work and about legal issues. Silence is attributed to arrogance, complacency or inability to answer criticisms.'[6]

He repeated these remarks on subsequent occasions:

No doubt at one time it was acceptable for the judges to restrict their pronouncements to giving judgment or passing sentence. But the shift in public attitudes under the growing influence of the media calls for a different approach from the judges.

It is simply no longer sensible to remain silent when so much attention, much of it highly critical, is focused on the courts and the judicial process. In the absence of any reply it would be assumed against the judges either that they were so arrogant and complacent as to believe they could ignore criticism or that they had no good answer to it.[7]

However, there were limits: Lord Taylor also said that 'openness must be tempered by moderation and discretion.'[8]

The question of how far the judges should speak out on policy issues is one of the most difficult posed in this book. If they say nothing, governments will walk all over them, implementing changes which may be contrary to the interests of justice. If the judges say too much, they will generally come off second best in a battle with skilled, elected politicians. Our judges should not keep their own counsel. They must also be wary of politicians who draw them into the public arena in order to ensnare and humiliate them.

Judges and politicians

There are four key areas where the judges must exercise caution and discretion. The first of these is all the more dangerous because it takes place out of sight.

The secret meeting

Senior judges sometimes have private meetings with politicians. These carry risks. In the late autumn of 1990, two judges went to see the Home Secretary, David Waddington.[9] One was Lord Justice Glidewell; the other was a circuit judge. They were calling on behalf of the Judicial Studies Board, the body that trains the judiciary. Unusually, they had been shown an advance draft of a Criminal Justice Bill which was shortly to come before parliament. One particular clause was worrying them. It told the courts they could not send an offender to prison unless he had committed an offence which was so serious that prison was the only appropriate sentence. On the face of it, this seemed perfectly reasonable. Yet offenders commonly commit a number of relatively minor offences as part of the same criminal enterprise or over a period of time. The clause meant they would escape prison, however many offences they were convicted of, so long as none of their crimes was particularly serious.

In conversation with the two judges, Mr Waddington agreed to make a concession (which struck them as pre-arranged). It applied to offenders facing more than one charge. If the offender had not committed an offence which was so serious that only a prison sentence was justified, the courts would be able to select two 'associated' half-serious offences and add them together. If these two offences taken together were serious enough, the offender could still be sent to prison.

This attempt to toughen up the law turned a reasonably lucid provision into one that was much harder to interpret. It might be possible for the judges to agree on what sort of offences were so serious that prison was the only justifiable sentence. It would be more difficult to say what pairs of offences would justify imprisonment. There was also a much more fundamental objection, which the judges explained to Mr Waddington. As Lord Justice Glidewell had already said publicly: 'Time and again, judges get somebody in front of them of, say, 20 – with fourteen previous convictions, having been burgling steadily since the age of 15, none of them perhaps enormous crimes. Is the public really going to accept that even on the third or fourth offence the burglar should be left out in the community?'[10] That was what section 1(2) of the Criminal Justice Act 1991 obliged the judges to do.

When the legislation took effect in the autumn of 1992 it proved, in part at least, a disaster.[11] Faced with universal criticism, ministers blamed the opposition parties and the judiciary for not alerting them to the pitfalls ahead. In 1993, Kenneth Clarke, then serving briefly as Home Secretary, claimed publicly[12] that the Lord Chief Justice of the day, Lord Lane, had been consulted in advance about the more controversial proposals in the legislation. Mr Clarke made it clear that, so far as he was aware, Lord Lane was satisfied with the outcome of his discussions with the government. In fact this was not the case, as the Home Office minister, David Maclean, had to admit later. It turned out that Mr Clarke was recalling what he had been told about a discussion in 1989 between Lord Lane and the then Home Secretary Douglas Hurd. Mr Maclean accepted that this discussion could not have been interpreted as approval for a bill that was not published until much later. Mr Clarke told Lord Lane's successor that he had not intended to mislead anyone about the attitude of the judiciary to the 1991 legislation.[13] Nevertheless, he made no attempt to correct the impression he had given.

Before long the government had to amend section 1 of the 1991 Act, and a further section which stopped the courts taking account of an offender's record.[14] Ministers had been fortified in their task by a speech in which Lord Taylor had suggested these two provisions ran 'counter to all the principles of good sentencing policy . . . and in fact defy common sense'.[15] Although the Home Office minister, John Patten, had said the 1991 act would 'affect the way in which the courts operate and the way in which offenders are dealt with for many years into the future', part of the legislation was repealed after less than twelve months.[16]

With the benefit of hindsight, we can see it would have been better if the judges had made their concerns about the 1991 legislation known much earlier. As we have seen, the 1991 act was not brought into force until more than a year after it had been passed.[17] During that period, Lord Lane was well aware of the likely problems. He thought that he could do no more than wait for a suitable case to reach the Court of Appeal and then give guidance on how the law should be understood. In the light of his experience with politicians, it is easy to see why he was reluctant to attack the government's proposals in public. Perhaps he failed to realise how unworkable the bill was becoming after it had been amended in parliament; perhaps he felt it was inappropriate for him to intervene. It would have been better had he done so.

The first formal meeting between a Lord Chief Justice and a Home Secretary seems to have been in 1980, when Lord Lane met William Whitelaw. The former Home Office minister Lord Windlesham tells us that 'in conditions of great secrecy, a dinner party was held on neutral ground in a private room at a West End club'.[18] The two men brought their deputies, Lord Justice Watkins and Leon Brittan, as well as senior officials. The meeting was a success, but the emerging relationship between the executive and the judiciary was shattered a year later when a newspaper[19] story, directly attributed to the Home Secretary, wrongly accused the judges of thwarting government reforms aimed at bringing down the prison population.

Lord Lane was furious, his suspicions of politicians reinforced. It was not until Douglas Hurd took over at the Home Office that Lord Lane found a politician he respected. From 1986 onwards, the Lord

Chief Justice and his deputy held regular meetings with Mr Hurd in his room at the Home Office.

When Michael Howard became Home Secretary in 1993 he established a good working relationship with Lord Lane's successor, Lord Taylor: the two met regularly and corresponded frequently. They had similar backgrounds: both were outsiders from Jewish immigrant families who had relied on intellect rather than wealth or background to reach the commanding heights of the establishment. As a barrister, Michael Howard had even appeared before Lord Taylor. However, by the autumn of 1995 a certain *froideur* had set in. Until then, it had been assumed that the two men saw eye to eye.[20] Not so. 'You don't know the half of it,' said one source. It turned out that Lord Taylor often had to head off the wilder notions that the Home Secretary sought to implement. Unfortunately, nobody was prepared to be drawn on what these notions might have been.

Lord Taylor's successor, Lord Bingham of Cornhill, also knew Michael Howard extremely well, having 'led' him in a lengthy case: the two men worked together when Tom Bingham was a QC and Michael Howard was not. As Lord Chief Justice, Lord Bingham of Cornhill was not opposed to having talks with ministers, provided there was something to discuss. Lord Bingham went to see the Home Secretary in the autumn of 1996 to express the judges' concern about Mr Howard's sentencing proposals: the Home Secretary appeared unmoved.

Michael Howard said subsequently that the two men met 'quite often'. The degree of consultation between the Home Office and the judges over the implementation of policy or decisions involving the criminal justice system was greater than ever before. 'In terms of practical co-operation,' he said, 'a great deal goes on which never reaches the public domain, and that is something which I greatly value.' He did not want it to be obscured by the 'high-profile differences' on some of the government's proposals.[21]

There are also meetings at higher levels of government. When Lord Goddard was Lord Chief Justice (between 1946 and 1958) he had dinner annually with the Prime Minister of the day. Lord Taylor reinstated the convention, meeting (though not dining with) John Major at least once a year. This arrangement was never publicly acknowledged. There can be little doubt that Lord Taylor spoke of his concerns about Michael Howard's sentencing plans when he met the Prime Minister early in 1996. As we saw in Chapter 1, it was at a subsequent meeting that Lord Taylor complained about the choice of his successor.

Should Lord Taylor have made clear to senior ministers his opposition to the government's sentencing proposals? Some members of the government believed he was descending into party politics. Government sources told the *Independent* at the time that 'Judges cannot expect to operate without interference from politicians if they interfere in political decisions themselves. Politics is a hot kitchen.' The paper's kitchen source said that 'If the judges are stupid enough to put themselves in the firing line by opposing an absolutely central package, it will be they who are damaged, not the government.'[22]

Lord Taylor disagreed. Sentencing policy, he said, 'is a matter upon which the judges who administer it are entitled, and I believe obliged, to comment before a major change is made in the law'.[23] We shall see later in the chapter what happened when his private comments reached the public arena.

The public rarely gets to hear about meetings between ministers and judges. It may of course be in the public interest for the judges to speak in confidence. Ministers may be more willing to accept advice if they can change their minds without attracting too much public attention. Yet once judges have been consulted it is all too easy for ministers to depict them as acquiescing in a policy which they may not support. Nobody is suggesting that senior judges should no longer meet ministers. However, their meetings should be private rather than secret. We should be told when the meetings are taking place, even if their contents remain confidential. That way, there will be less scope for misunderstanding – or worse.

The multi-skilled judge

Another danger arises when the judge blurs the roles of legislator and tribunal. A judge should never have to rule on legislation to which he has given his personal backing. Unfortunately Lord Taylor fell into this trap too.

On the day the Birmingham Six were cleared after serving sixteen years in prison the government announced that a Royal Commission would be appointed to examine the effectiveness of the criminal justice system. The Commission was asked to consider whether a court should be allowed to draw inferences from a defendant's silence in the face of police questions. By a majority of nine votes to two the Royal Commission recommended that the law should remain unchanged.[24]

This did not suit the Home Office, or indeed the Home Secretary. Michael Howard rejected the majority view of the Royal Commission and in December 1993 introduced legislation. There was strong criticism at the time, but Mr Howard was greatly encouraged by the support of the Lord Chief Justice. In Lord Taylor's view it was 'sensible' that a jury should be able to take account of the defendant's refusal to account for himself. One detail worried the Lord Chief Justice,[25] and Mr Howard obligingly revised his proposals to fall in with Lord Taylor's wishes. Lord Taylor's influence was demonstrated by the government's decision to reject a separate proposal[26] of which he disapproved, even though the Royal Commission had supported it.[27]

The necessary legislation was passed by parliament and came into force in April 1995. It provides that at the end of the prosecution case the court must make sure that the defendant knows he can give evidence and knows the effect of failing to do so; the magistrates or jury can then draw such inferences as appear proper from the defendant's failure to give evidence or answer questions.[28]

The effect of this legislation was considered by the Court of Appeal in October 1995. Since it was the first time the provision had come before the court the appeal was heard by the Lord Chief Justice sitting with two High Court judges. Nobody involved in the case seemed to have taken exception to the fact that Lord Taylor had expressed his support for the amended section while the provision was going through parliament. Given his views at the time it was hardly surprising that Lord Taylor should have resisted what he saw as an attempt by the appellants' counsel, Michael Mansfield QC, to 'drive a coach and horses through the statutory provisions'. Mr Mansfield had argued that a court should draw adverse inferences from a defendant's silence only in an exceptional case, where there was no reasonable possibility of an innocent explanation. Giving judgment in the Court of Appeal, Lord Taylor rejected this attempt to marginalise the effect of the new law. He said in effect that the statute meant exactly what it said: the plain words of the statute did not justify confining its operation to exceptional cases.[29]

This story leaves one feeling uncomfortable. It cannot have been right for the Lord Chief Justice to sit on the appeal when his support for the legislation was well known. There is no doubt that Lord Taylor handled the matter with perfect propriety; nevertheless, he should have stood aside in favour of another judge. The appellants might be forgiven for thinking justice had not been seen to be done.

The injudicious jibe

As we shall see in Chapter 3, judicial review can be used by the courts to overturn ministerial decisions. The judges insist they are not concerned with the merits of a decision: merely the way in which it has been taken. Provided the minister has behaved fairly and reasonably, the courts must not overturn his or her decision merely because they would have taken a different view themselves.

While respecting this approach, some judges have been tempted to say what they would have done if they had been sitting behind the minister's desk. A good example of this was a case brought against the Ministry of Defence by four homosexuals who had been dismissed from the armed forces.[30] The ministry's policy was to dismiss 'anyone . . . sexually attracted to a member of their own sex – irrespective of whether they engage in homosexual conduct'. Three men and a woman, all homosexuals with exemplary service records, were dismissed as a result of this policy and applied for judicial review.

Their applications were dismissed by two judges sitting in the High Court. Mr Justice Curtis said that in his view the applications failed 'on their merits as well as in law'. Lord Justice Simon Brown said he had 'great sympathy' for the four applicants: he refused their applications 'with hesitation and regret'.

Lord Justice Simon Brown began a robust and memorable judgment with the observation that 'Lawrence of Arabia would not be welcome in today's armed forces'. He added: 'I have to say that the balance of the argument . . . appears to me to lie clearly with the applicants. The tide of history is against the ministry. Prejudices are breaking down; old barriers are being removed. It seems to me improbable, whatever this court may say, that the existing policy can survive for much longer.'

The Defence Secretary took the view that allowing homosexuals to serve would damage the effectiveness of the armed forces. In Lord Justice Simon Brown's 'own opinion' that was 'a wrong view, a view that rests too firmly on the supposition of prejudice in others and which insufficiently recognises the damage to human rights inflicted'. He urged the government to reconsider its policy afresh and consider what had happened when other countries had lifted their own bans. However, because there was nothing unreasonable in the way the

43

decision had been taken,[31] he felt unable to grant an application for judicial review.

The judge knew his judgment would arouse strong feelings:

> There will, I know, be those who think this judgment pusillanimous. There will be others who think that in the course of it I have stepped beyond the bounds of permissible judicial comment. Naturally I disagree with them both. I believe that the ministry are properly entitled to succeed on the challenge, but I believe equally that the applicants are entitled to know my personal views on the merits . . .

Many people would agree with Lord Justice Simon Brown's views: his sense of justice shines through these remarks. Yet he should never have made them. In 1950, the Attorney General, Sir Hartley Shawcross, said that if 'judges permitted themselves to ventilate from the bench the views they might hold on the policy of the legislature, it would be quite impossible to maintain the rule that the conduct of judges is not open to criticism or question'.[32] In 1996, the Lord Chief Justice Lord Bingham agreed: 'it is indeed obvious,' he said, 'that if judges were to ventilate personal criticisms of government policy unnecessary for the decision of the case before them, it would only be a matter of time (and not a very long time) before those who were the subject of criticism replied in kind. It is undesirable, and plainly damaging to the independence of the judges, if they become protagonists in a debate in which they have no constitutional right to participate.'[33]

Lord Bingham's words took a little while to sink in. Two days later Mr Justice Laws upheld Michael Howard's refusal to allow a Nepalese youth, Jayaram Khadka, exceptional leave to remain in the country. The young man had been brought to Britain as a fourteen-year-old by Richard Morley, a businessman, to honour a promise to the boy's father who had saved his life on a mountaineering expedition.

Mr Howard was accused of wrongly confirming the deportation decision in March 1996, despite an Immigration Appeal Tribunal's 'strong recommendation' that the young man should be allowed to stay on compassionate grounds. However, Mr Justice Laws said:

> I am unable to conclude that the Secretary of State's decision in this case was beyond the range of responses open to a reasonable decision-maker. Many may regard the result he arrived at as harsh. It may be said that

there are some aspects of the case which make it unique, or all but unique. But the policy (despite my criticism of the way it has been expressed) is a coherent one, and its application is on reflection perfectly understandable.

The judge properly concluded that Mr Howard's decision was 'taken as the people's democratic representative'. If he were to overturn it, he would usurp that role, which he said it was no business of his to do. He insisted that his personal view of the merits of the case had 'no relevance whatsoever.'[34]

Mr Justice Laws was right to say that his personal view of what the Home Secretary had done was irrelevant. Whether he was right to suggest Mr Howard's policy was 'harsh' is another matter. Although the judge was careful to ascribe this view to 'many people', some might have suspected that Mr Justice Laws was one of them.

Here was another judge whose profound sense of moral duty was apparently threatening to colour his judgments. Sir John Laws and Sir Simon Brown are rightly regarded as two of the finest members of the judiciary. Nevertheless, if judges even hint at their personal views, however much we as observers may share them, they make it harder for us to accept that they leave their own opinions outside the door of the court when they hear applications for judicial review.

That said, these were two examples where the judges' obvious personal sympathies did not stop them from ruling in favour of the ministers. The cases clearly demonstrate that the judges fully obeyed the rules of judicial review – despite their better judgment.

The parliamentary campaign
It is a remarkable fact that senior judges are able to mount parliamentary campaigns against government bills. We shall see shortly what happened when the judges tried to block Michael Howard's sentencing proposals. Although it was not the first occasion on which the judges had spoken out against ministers, the campaigning judge is a relatively novel phenomenon.

The former Lord Chief Justice Lord Lane was the first judge to mount a public campaign: unfortunately he picked the wrong subject. As we have seen, Lord Lane kept silent in the face of some misconceived sentencing proposals although he had previously delivered a ferocious onslaught on the government's plans for reform of the legal profession.

Speaking in 1989, during a House of Lords debate which was to

45

continue for nearly thirteen hours, Lord Lane argued that letting the government decide who should have the right to speak in the courts would lead to 'control by the executive of the principal means available to the ordinary citizen of controlling that same executive'. He continued: 'No doubt the fears which I have expressed will be pooh-poohed in some quarters: of course they will. But loss of freedom seldom happens overnight . . . Oppression does not stand on the doorstep with a toothbrush moustache and a swastika armband. It creeps up insidiously; it creeps up step by step; and all of a sudden the unfortunate citizen realises that it has gone.'[35]

In the light of this criticism, the Lord Chancellor modified his proposals and allowed the senior judges a veto over any plans to extend the right of advocates to be heard in court. Whether the same result could have been achieved without the use of such colourful language is another matter.

There is no doubt that the judges face a dilemma. Sometimes they should fight with all their might against short-term measures introduced by cynical ministers. On other occasions they would do well to remember that they are unelected functionaries who must obey the will of parliament. Broadly speaking, they should speak only when justice is at risk. It was understandable that Lord Lane declined to launch a public campaign against what was to become the Criminal Justice Act 1991. With hindsight, this seems to have been a mistake.

On the whole, it is better for the judges to speak out and risk being wrong than for them to stay silent and not show that they are right. They must decide which course to take. Nobody ever said it would be easy, but making nice judgments is what judges are meant to be good at.

Speaking their minds

There was a time, not so long ago, when the judges were seen and not heard. That golden era ended abruptly in 1987.

More than thirty years earlier, the BBC had tried to lure judges out of the shadows; the attempt was to backfire in spectacular fashion. In 1955, the BBC wanted to invite a number of judges to take part in a series of lectures on the Third Programme about great judges of the past. The Lord Chancellor, Viscount Kilmuir, was consulted, and he in turn consulted the three Heads of Division.[36] In a letter to the BBC's Director General, Lieutenant-General Sir Ian Jacob,[37] he said that as a general rule it was 'undesirable for members of the judiciary to broadcast on the wireless or to appear on television'. This was because of 'the importance of keeping the judiciary in this country insulated from the controversies of the day'. In a striking passage, Lord Kilmuir added that 'So long as a judge keeps silent his reputation for wisdom and impartiality remains unassailable: but every utterance which he makes in public, except in the course of the actual performance of his judicial duties, must necessarily bring him within the focus of criticism.'[38]

Although this letter had no statutory authority, its strictures were immortalised as the 'Kilmuir rules'. The BBC's request, far from persuading judges to speak, meant that for three decades no judge would broadcast without express permission from the Lord Chancellor. As recently as 1986, the year in which he became a Lord Justice of Appeal, the present Master of the Rolls Lord Woolf gave a public lecture about judicial review.[39] He agreed to allow his remarks to be recorded by the BBC,[40] but because of the Kilmuir rules he felt unable to give the BBC an interview on the same subject.

Ticking off the judges

While the Kilmuir rules were still in force, senior judges could expect a ticking off for stepping out of line – even if they were speaking from the bench. An example of this, taken from 1985, shows why the Lord Chancellor should never again claim the right to tell judges what they may or may not say.

At the end of 1984, just a day before parliament was to rise for the Christmas recess, the government published an Administration of Justice Bill. Hidden away towards the end, unmentioned in the government's press release, was a clause dealing with applications for judicial review. The law says that anyone who wants to challenge an administrative decision by way of judicial review must first ask the High Court for permission to start proceedings. If an applicant is refused leave by the High Court he can try again in the Court of Appeal. Clause 43 of the government's bill would have taken away that right to 'renew' an application for leave before the Court of Appeal. So if the High Court were to refuse leave an action would have been over before it had started.

In support of its proposals, the government argued that leave to apply for judicial review was almost always granted if there were a case worth answering and that renewed applications to the Court of Appeal therefore wasted a large amount of judicial time. However, in January 1985 a taxpayer who had been refused permission by the High Court to challenge the decision of an Inland Revenue Special Commissioner tried again in the Court of Appeal and was granted leave by Lord Justice Ackner and Lord Justice Purchas. The two judges said in court that they were 'troubled' to find that the Administration of Justice Bill would take away the right to bring a case like the one before them. Although the case was unusual, the judges said it demonstrated very strongly the merits of the existing rule in an area where so much of the legislation was directed towards preventing alleged abuses of power.[41]

The then Lord Chancellor, Lord Hailsham, was far from pleased with this demonstration of judicial independence. It seemed to him 'a clear breach of the constitutional rules and conventions about the separation of powers'. Lord Hailsham 'sought and obtained apologies' from the two judges.[42] He told parliament that while it was perfectly legitimate for the judiciary to criticise the law as it stood, it was 'utterly improper for a Court of Appeal judge or any other judge speaking on the bench to criticise matters passing through parliament'.[43] They had ample means 'to make their views known in the proper quarter. This could be done quite easily by approaching the Lord Chancellor privately, or in public on the floor of the House of Lords through the mouth of one or more of the law lords.'[44]

There is no reason why a judge who made a comment in the Court of Appeal should have been publicly humiliated by a Lord Chancellor who believes that same judge might say what he liked if he were a member of the House of Lords (as Lord Justice Ackner subsequently became). And there was no logical reason why a judge should have been allowed to *criticise* the existing law – which Lord Hailsham permitted – if the same judge were not allowed to *support* the present law, which was what the two appeal judges had done. Still, the judges had the last laugh. Despite offering a number of concessions the government was defeated on a vote in the House of Lords and the clause disappeared for good.

The suspicion must be that Lord Hailsham was annoyed by

criticism of a policy he supported: on this occasion he seemed to have been acting as a party politician rather than a senior judge. The incident demonstrates yet again that the Lord Chancellor should divest himself of one of these responsibilities. If anyone is to give judges a ticking-off, it should be the Lord Chief Justice.

Kilmuir rules OK?

In 1987 the new Lord Chancellor, Lord Mackay of Clashfern, abolished the Kilmuir rules as one of his first acts in office. No legislation was required: he simply declared at a news conference that from then on it would be up to the judges to make up their own minds. Lord Mackay thought that a system requiring the judges to seek his consent before taking part in public discussion was 'rather artificial and difficult to reconcile with the concept of judicial independence'.[45] As he explained at the time, 'if a person has been appointed a judge and that trust has been placed in him, I think he should be able to decide what to do if he is approached by the media'.[46]

Although this was a sensible, perhaps even an inevitable, move, it produced the unfortunate consequences we have already seen – that some judges spoke out when silence would have been preferable. In an attempt to avoid the risk of injudicious comments Lord Mackay decided in 1989 to tell 'all judges and full-time judicial officers in England and Wales' how he thought they should handle approaches from the media. He used the device of a formal letter to the Lord Chief Justice, Lord Lane: he had in fact discussed its contents with Lord Lane before he sent it. This letter, which was not published at the time, still represents current policy and is therefore worth quoting in some detail:

> The nature of their office makes it necessary for judges to be very cautious about their exposure to the media, and they must avoid public statements either on general issues or particular cases which might cast doubt on their complete impartiality. Above all, they should avoid any involvement, either direct or indirect, in issues which are or might become politically controversial.
>
> However, experience has demonstrated that there are cases in which the media, in a spirit of enquiry, wish to explore matters affecting the legal system so as to secure a wider public understanding of the working

of the law. The value of such programmes may be enhanced by the participation of the judges and there may well be a case for those judges who wish to do so to take part in them.

In the current climate the number of such programmes may increase, with a consequent increase in the number of judges who are asked to participate in them. The guidance set out in the enclosed annex[47] may be helpful for judges who are minded to accept invitations from the media.

I would also like to emphasise that I am always available to give advice in any case where an individual judge would find it useful as, I know, are [the Lord Chief Justice] and the other Heads of Divisions, and the Presiding Judges. As a general principle, if a judge, having considered all the relevant circumstances, including such matters as the reputation of the source of the invitation as well as the subject matter of the interview, has any serious doubts about the wisdom of participating, he or she should decline the invitation. But the final decision about whether any judge should appear on television or radio or give an interview in a newspaper is one for him or her alone.

At the risk of stating the obvious, I should add that I do not think this policy can extend to pronouncements by judges about individual cases. When a judge has decided a case or imposed a particular sentence, in my opinion it is not appropriate for him, or any of his brother judges, to discuss it publicly out of court, whether or not the matter has finally been disposed of on appeal.[48]

The annex enclosed with the letter suggested some questions the judge might like to ask before agreeing to be interviewed. What kind of article or programme was intended? If it was to be a radio or television interview, would it be 'one-to-one or a three-way discussion'? If it was to be recorded and edited, would extracts be intercut and used as part of a documentary? 'What guarantee could be given to the judge that the integrity of the views he expresses would be preserved?' And so on.

An even more restrictive letter was sent to all judges in 1991 by Sheila Thompson, the Lord Chancellor's Head of Information.[49] With it was a paper, 'approved by the Presiding Judges and the Judges' Council', which attempted to dictate to the judiciary when they could talk to the press (or even, in some cases, the Lord Chancellor's press office). This paper included the following remarkable paragraph:

> Circuit Judges and District Judges should always, save in an emergency, consult one of the presiding judges[50] before speaking to the

50

Press Office [emphasis added] and should never speak directly to the press without consulting a presiding judge. High Court judges and judges of the Court of Appeal should likewise consult the Heads of Division.

By what authority could the Lord Chancellor's press office tell the judiciary the circumstances in which they were allowed to speak to the media? By what authority could even the Lord Chancellor lay down such instructions? Asked about the matter in the spring of 1994,[51] the press office confirmed that what appeared to be strict instructions were merely 'advisory'; they were not binding, nor could they be. Officials confirmed that every judge was independent, not only of the Lord Chancellor but also of other judges. They maintained that the document was being rewritten. In January 1997, the Lord Chancellor's Department said the document would be replaced 'within the next few months'; it was still 'not quite ready for distribution'.[52]

This reaction did not seem to betray much sense of urgency: it seemed the Lord Chancellor was prepared to allow misleading advice to remain in circulation for some six years. This suggests Lord Mackay was not unhappy to leave judges with the impression that he and his staff had much greater power to control their dealings with the media than they enjoyed in reality. After lifting one questionable restriction – the Kilmuir rules – he had imposed another one – the Sheila Thompson letter.

There was no suggestion that Lord Mackay wanted to change the letter he himself had sent the judges in 1989. Two points stand out from it: his insistence that judges should avoid any involvement in issues which are or might become politically controversial, and his view that a judge should seek advice from someone like the Lord Chief Justice if he or she had any doubts about a media invitation. What happens when the Lord Chief Justice himself decides to get involved in matters which are, without doubt, politically controversial?

Lord Taylor's legacy

Lord Taylor of Gosforth served as Lord Chief Justice of England for just four years, his career sadly cut short by ill-health. He will be remembered for many accomplishments in the course of a long and successful career. In June 1996 when he retired he was best known as the judge who decided to take on the Home Secretary.

This particular trial of strength became public in October 1995 when Michael Howard made a stirring speech to his party's annual conference. Mr Howard took sentencing as his subject.

First, he dealt with the issue of early release from prison. As the law then stood, most prisoners were released after serving half their sentences. Those sentenced to more than twelve months were supervised and supported by a probation officer for a period after their release.[53] These provisions had been brought in under a Conservative government as recently as 1992.[54] However, Mr Howard didn't like them. 'It's time to get honesty back into sentencing,' he said. 'No more automatic early release. No more release regardless of behaviour. And no more half-time sentences for full-time crimes.'[55]

The inference from these remarks was that criminals would serve more time in prison. An 'annex' to his speech, published by Conservative Central Office, made no attempt to suggest otherwise. The only clarification it offered was that prisoners serving one year or longer would be 'eligible for a small period of earned early release'.

Four months later, Mr Howard was giving a very different impression. He told a meeting of the Criminal Justice Consultative Council[56] that he was aiming to make a change in the impact a sentence had on the offender in the dock. 'That does not necessarily mean a longer sentence,' he admitted. He reminded his audience, which included some twenty-five serving judges, of a Practice Direction which had been issued by the Lord Chief Justice when the last set of sentencing changes came into effect. The courts were asked to 'have regard to the actual period likely to be served, and as far as practicable to the risk of offenders serving substantially longer under the new regime than would have been normal under the old'. Just to make the point completely clear, Mr Howard said: 'My new proposals will certainly raise the same issues, and some similar guidance will be needed.'

So there never was any intention to make prisoners serve longer in prison. Instead of being sentenced to two years and released after one, the prisoner would only be sentenced to one year in the first place. But a Home Secretary who told his party conference he wanted judges to pass shorter sentences would not have had quite such a warm reception.

The second proposal in his party conference speech was the introduction of life sentences for 'serious violent and sexual offenders'. The phrase – not immediately accessible – refers to those convicted of a serious offence of violence and those convicted of a serious sexual offence. In Mr Howard's view, there was a 'strong case for saying that anyone convicted for the second time of a serious violent or sexual offence should receive an automatic sentence of life imprisonment. They would only be released when they no longer posed a risk to the public. And if they continued to pose a risk, life really would mean life.'

It was not until some months later that the public learned how the life sentence would operate. The judge would set a 'tariff' – a punishment period – and when that period had expired the Parole Board would decide whether the prisoner was safe to be released. This was in line with the arrangements for so-called 'discretionary lifers' – prisoners serving life for offences other than murder.

The Home Secretary had one more proposal for the party faithful in October 1995. 'If prison, and the threat of prison, are to work effectively,' he said, 'there's a strong case for greater certainty in sentencing – for stiff minimum sentences for burglars and dealers in hard drugs who offend again and again and again.'

Those last words were carefully chosen. The annex explained that 'offenders over eighteen who had already been convicted of three such offences would face such a sentence'. The word 'face' was chosen with even more care. Mr Howard did not actually say these offenders would *receive* such a sentence. He left the door open to allow exceptions. Nobody spotted this at the time – which, presumably, was what the government wanted.

Mr Howard had politely informed Lord Taylor of his proposals three days earlier. Lord Taylor immediately made his disapproval clear. Mr Howard said he was not prepared to back down. He accepted that there would be a difference of opinion, but he hoped Lord Taylor would keep his views to himself. From Mr Howard's point of view, this proved unwise. Lord Taylor decided he would make his views as public as possible.

During his speech Mr Howard said that he wanted to hear what the judges thought about his proposals. He didn't have long to wait: Lord Taylor's response was as devastating as it was swift. Within two hours the Lord Chief Justice had knocked Michael Howard off his own story.

In a statement issued from his office, Lord Taylor conceded that long sentences were sometimes necessary to protect the public. Nevertheless, he did not believe that the threat of longer and longer periods of imprisonment across the board would deter habitual criminals. 'What deters them is the likelihood of being caught, which at the moment is small.' Lord Taylor insisted that judges must be free to fit the particular punishment to the particular crime: 'Minimum sentences are inconsistent with doing justice according to the circumstances of each case. Instead of limiting discretion by introducing unnecessary constraints on sentencing, the police should be provided with the resources they need to bring criminals before the courts in the first place.'[57]

Michael Howard's initial response seemed to miss the point. 'The judges are perfectly entitled to their views,' he said, 'but it's parliament that decides these matters.' That was true of course, but what worried Lord Taylor was that Mr Howard was announcing his intentions without first consulting or even informing parliament.

Other judges shared those concerns. One stressed that it was parliament that was supreme – not the government of the day – and ministers could not make law by comment, observation or soundbite.[58] The judges were perfectly willing to implement legislation passed by parliament, however misguided they considered it to be. What they resented was a minister trying to tell them what to do.

Michael Howard firmly rejected this criticism. 'This is the way in which democracy works,' he said. A political conference was 'a major democratic occasion' and he saw 'nothing inappropriate in announcing proposals for reform of the criminal justice system at a party conference'. His announcement had been followed by a detailed White Paper and then a bill.[59]

It came as no surprise to find that the judiciary resented any attempt to restrict its sentencing discretion. Judges and magistrates generally think they are better than politicians in deciding what the right sentence should be for the defendant in front of them. In the words of Lord Donaldson, who was Master of the Rolls from 1982 to 1992, 'One of the essential skills of the good sentencing judge is to be able to spot the exceptional case in which a habitual offender can be reformed by being given a chance.'[60] In the first interview Lord Lane ever gave for broadcast – long after he had retired as Lord Chief Justice in 1992 – he urged the government to scrap the sentence of life imprisonment for murder because it was mandatory – it left the judges no discretion.[61]

Michael Howard's enthusiasm for restricting the courts was not shared by all his cabinet colleagues. The Lord Chancellor, Lord Mackay, said that although minimum sentences already existed for some minor offences, such as motoring, there were 'quite substantial difficulties in the law of minimum sentences in some other cases'. That was because there were often exceptional cases. Lord Mackay said he would 'expect that Michael Howard would wish to put forward ways of dealing with that'.[62]

Did this mean the Lord Chancellor had put pressure on the Home Secretary? When pressed on this point, Lord Mackay was characteristically Delphic:

> The precise discussions that go on in parliament, so far as I am concerned, are confidential and I am not therefore willing to disclose the nature of my communications with the Home Secretary. I have a great number of these at different times and in respect of different subject matter; and the views which ultimately come out are the views of the government as a whole – subject of course to modification in the light of discussion in parliament. So you may make what speculation you wish about how these particular views are arrived at, but you may take it that I am not without the possibility of expressing a position in relation to matters of that kind within government.[63]

In Lord Mackay's terms this was virtually an admission that he had leaned on the Home Secretary. He subsequently said almost as much in a newspaper interview.[64] Sure enough, by the time he addressed the Criminal Justice Consultative Council[65] Mr Howard was saying he had always intended to provide for exceptions 'for the genuinely hard cases where the minimum [sentence] would inflict injustice'. His comments came in response to an incautious intervention from the council's chairman, Lord Justice Rose.[66] The judge had told a reporter that a mandatory life sentence for a second offence of rape would lead to more murders. 'Rapists will think they may as well kill their victims,' he said, 'there's no point in leaving them alive if the sentence is the same.' A mandatory punishment would also discourage rapists from pleading guilty, because there would be no incentive to admit an offence for which the sentence was inevitably life imprisonment.[67]

Mr Howard was due to speak to the council just a few days later. He added a withering rebuke to his planned speech. The Home

Secretary told Lord Justice Rose he found the judge's argument 'difficult to follow'. Mr Howard suggested that any rapist who calculated his likely penalty would know the tariff would reflect the seriousness of the offence. In addition, life imprisonment was already an optional penalty for rape:

> If the threat of a life sentence is, perversely, an invitation to murder, then parliament should not have made life sentences available for a range of serious offences such as going equipped with a firearm or the more serious drugs offences. Indeed, taken to its logical conclusion this line of argument suggests that there should not be a life sentence available, even on a discretionary basis, for murder.

All this did nothing to convince Lord Taylor. The Lord Chief Justice therefore took the opportunity of a public lecture in March 1996[68] to repeat and reinforce his criticisms of the Home Secretary's proposals.

Lord Taylor insisted that his objections were not based on constitutional grounds. Although the former Master of the Rolls, Lord Donaldson, had maintained, perhaps extravagantly, that the Home Secretary's proposal to transfer responsibility for the time which a criminal spent in prison from judges to politicians involved 'a constitutional change of epic proportions',[69] Lord Taylor said that parliament would be perfectly within its rights to pass a law introducing minimum or mandatory sentences and the judges would 'conscientiously apply that statute as they do every other'. Nor were Lord Taylor's misgivings based on the likely increase in the prison population: that, he said, was not a matter for him.

Instead, his objections were all founded on sentencing policy. He had four points to make. First, 'the fundamental objection to minimum sentences [for burglars] is that they will cause injustice. They will fetter the judge's discretion to take account of all the circumstances of the burglary and the burglar.'

Second, minimum sentences would prevent the courts from giving discounts for a plea of guilty. Recent legislation[70] had endorsed that principle. Discounts encouraged criminals to admit their guilt and so enhance their prospects of rehabilitation. An early plea of guilty also saved time and money in court.

For his third criticism, Lord Taylor adopted the arguments of Lord Justice Rose. 'In stark terms,' said the Lord Chief Justice, 'I wonder whether a repeat rapist, faced with an automatic life sentence, will not think it less risky to cut his losses by killing the only witness to his crime. He may then escape conviction altogether. If convicted of both rape and murder he still gets the mandatory life sentence.'

Finally, Lord Taylor said he disagreed with the government's proposals because he was convinced they would not work. He stressed again that what primarily deterred crime was the likelihood of detection.

His remarks seemed to make no impact on the government. When the White Paper appeared, the government's policy was seen not to have changed at all.

The White Paper

As far as 'honesty in sentencing' was concerned, the government stressed – as Michael Howard had done earlier – that its proposals to make prisoners serve virtually the whole term imposed by the court were not expected to mean offenders should serve longer in prison. No doubt anticipating that the Lord Chief Justice might be reluctant to issue a practice direction telling judges to take account of the abolition of parole, it said there could be a specific provision in the statute to that effect instead.[71]

Moving on, the government proposed that courts should be required to impose an automatic life sentence on offenders convicted for the second time of a serious violent offence or of a serious sexual offence, unless there were 'genuinely exceptional circumstances'. As expected, the trial judge would set the tariff to be served for retribution and deterrence. At the end of that period the Parole Board would decide if it was safe to release the offender.[72]

The White Paper also proposed that courts should be required to impose a mandatory minimum prison sentence of seven years on adult offenders who were convicted of drug-trafficking offences involving class A drugs and who had two or more previous convictions for similar offences. There would be a mandatory minimum of three years' imprisonment for domestic burglars with two or more previous convictions. In both cases the mandatory sentences would not apply if there were 'genuinely exceptional circumstances'.

The government's message was obvious. The public needed 'proper protection from persistent violent or sex offenders'.[73] Those who traded in human misery should get 'a very long prison sentence'.[74] Persistent burglars would be 'taken out of circulation for a long time'.[75] If this had already been the case, there would have been no need for legislation. It seemed that Michael Howard was saying he had to act because the judges could not be trusted to pass the right sentences.

'I don't accept that way of putting it,' he said early in 1997 in an interview for this book. 'I think that there has been a lessening of public confidence in the criminal justice system. I think it is of the utmost importance that public confidence should be sustained and, if possible, enhanced because the alternative is a vigilante system. When I looked at areas in which the public confidence could be increased, it seemed to me that you could enhance the protection of the public by targeting mandatory sentences on particular groups of criminals.[76]

That was not Lord Taylor's view. He had been hoping the government's plans would have been debated in the House of Lords while he was still well enough to speak there. As no debate was forthcoming Lord Taylor decided to organise one himself. It was to be the last occasion on which he spoke in public. He felt it was important for him, 'while still holding the office of Lord Chief Justice, to inform the House directly of the grave consequences' which he believed would follow if the government's proposals were implemented.[77]

Lord Taylor had a stark warning for the government:

> Never in the history of our criminal law have such far-reaching proposals been put forward on the strength of such flimsy and dubious evidence. The shallow and untested figures in the White Paper do not describe fairly the problems the government seek to address. Still less do they justify the radical solutions it proposes . . .
>
> Quite simply, minimum sentences must involve a denial of justice. It cannot be right for sentences to be passed without regard to the gravity, frequency, consequences or other circumstances of the offending. To sentence a burglar automatically to a minimum of three years' imprisonment on a third conviction is to take no account of whether he is before the court for only three offences or for thirty, no account of how long has passed between those offences, whether they involved sophisticated planning or drunken opportunism, and a host of other factors. To impose a minimum sentence of seven years on those convicted for the third time of trafficking in proscribed drugs will simply fill our prisons with addicts who sell small quantities to support their own addiction.[78]

Only six years earlier the Conservative government had firmly rejected moves to 'bind the courts with strict legislative guidelines'.

Ministers promised that 'the courts will properly continue to have the wide discretion they need if they are to deal justly with the great variety of crimes which come before them'. For that reason the government rejected 'a system of minimum or mandatory sentences for certain offences'. Why? Because 'this would make it more difficult to sentence justly in exceptional cases. It could also result in more acquittals by juries, with more guilty men and women going free unjustly as a result.'[79]

Lord Taylor drew attention to these powerful comments at the end of his final speech to the House of Lords. He said they were 'self-evidently wise, fair and just'. He asked the Lord Chancellor why 'every one of these propositions of government policy so recently propounded is now to be jettisoned and replaced by its exact opposite'.[80]

In reply, Lord Mackay said he understood the reason for the government's change in policy was 'the realisation of the extent to which actual crime results from persistent offending'. There was no question of the government scrapping the general principles of the 1990 White Paper. Yet although the Lord Chancellor dutifully read out his brief, he went out of his way not to associate himself with the views of his cabinet colleague: 'The Home Secretary, as the member of the government who has prime responsibility for policy relating to the criminal law, has a duty to do what he sees as necessary to protect the public from dangers which they perceive. . . The Home Secretary has the responsibility to put forward proposals which seem to him to be effective.'[81]

The real reason for the government's change of policy was obvious enough. Michael Howard disagreed with the approach taken at the time by his liberal-minded predecessor, Douglas Hurd.[82] He waited for what he no doubt saw as a decent interval before seeking to implement his own views.

Lord Mackay was hardly pledging unqualified support for Michael Howard. Nor was he particularly critical of Lord Taylor. One would have got little idea of this from a glance at two of the following day's newspapers: their reporters seemed to have been listening to a different speech. MACKAY: JUDGES ARE OUT OF TOUCH was the headline in the Daily Telegraph. MACKAY BLASTS SOFT JUDGES was how the Daily Mail put it.[83]

These headlines were supported by quotations attributed to the Lord Chancellor. In a front-page story by its chief political correspondent, the *Daily Mail* claimed Lord Mackay had told peers: 'I am bound to say that the Home Secretary's proposals received a general public welcome when they were announced. And some of those critics from whom we have heard today might reflect on that.'

The *Telegraph* quoted the Lord Chancellor as saying: 'We are not free to ignore public opinion. The proposals received a general public welcome when they were announced. Some of those critics from whom we have heard might perhaps reflect on that.'

The *Telegraph* described Lord Mackay's response as 'unusually forthright'. It would have been – if he had made it. What he did say was:

> We are not free to ignore public opinion. That particularly applies to the Home Secretary who is accountable to [the House of Commons]. The government of the day must take careful note of public expectations and concerns in framing their policies because the structure of law and order in a democratic society rests on the broad consent of the population to the way their safety and rights are safeguarded. I believe that these proposals received considerable support when they were made public.[84]

We can now see that the *Daily Telegraph* account was inaccurate in two respects. By leaving out the sentences between 'we are not free to ignore public opinion' and the Lord Chancellor's reference to public support the paper gave the impression that it was the judges who were ignoring people's views. It was on the basis of this false assumption that the paper's Home Affairs Editor constructed his opening sentence: 'Senior judges were accused by Lord Mackay, the Lord Chancellor, of being out of touch with public opinion . . .' That, in turn, inspired the misleading headline. In reality, Lord Mackay was referring to the Home Secretary. Even more remarkably, the phrase 'some of those critics from whom we have heard might perhaps reflect on that' was never spoken by the Lord Chancellor.

How is it that the two newspapers most sympathetic to the government could have quoted a remark the Lord Chancellor never made? How could they have both come up with an identical misquotation – 'general public welcome' instead of 'considerable support'? Indeed, where had words like 'soft' and 'out of touch' come from?

Contrary to popular opinion, the *Mail*'s chief political correspondent and the *Telegraph*'s home affairs editor do not make things up. They had indeed been listening to another speech. Somebody must have read them a draft of what the Lord Chancellor was going to say – or, rather, what their source hoped he was going to say. The Lord Chancellor's Department never supplied advance copies of Lord Mackay's closing speeches to reporters because he would usually amend them in the light of the preceding debate.[85] He no doubt did so on this occasion. His speeches often went through several drafts.

Who then gave the *Mail* and *Telegraph* a misleading account of the Lord Chancellor's speech? A good detective will look for motive and opportunity. In this case, both point firmly in the direction of the Home Office. It was the Home Secretary who stood to benefit from reports of this nature (LAW CHIEF BACKS HOWARD IN SENTENCING ROW was the *Mail* strapline, printed at the top of the page). It was also the Home Office which dealt with the drafting of Lord Mackay's speech (because he was answering for the Home Secretary's responsibilities, not his own). Although the Home Secretary may have known nothing about it, we may assume that someone working for him was responsible for spinning these two reporters a yarn.

In the rough and tumble of everyday politics it might not matter much that two national newspapers chose to report the most remarkable judicial criticism of a minister to be heard in the House of Lords for seven years[86] in a way that suggested the government had won the argument. This misreporting was balanced by the *Guardian*, which declared – in what purported to be a news story – that Mr Howard had suffered a 'persistent and devastating attack' which sealed 'his reputation as Britain's worst Home Secretary for nearly forty years'. What does matter is that the newspapers, and those in government who briefed them, were regarding the judges as fair game for this sort of treatment. It all helps belittle the judiciary in the eyes of the public.

Normally we cannot tell when those in government have briefed reporters against the judges. It is only when they are careless enough to put out a story which is demonstrably untrue that we may see the lengths to which they are prepared to go. There is another example of this, again involving the hapless *Telegraph*, in Chapter 4.[87]

Those who inspired these newspaper stories manifestly did not care about the damage they were doing to the judges. Lord Taylor ought not to have been surprised by this, although he certainly should have been worried. He should have realised that the Home Office would fight back when attacked. He should also have realised that Michael Howard had an acute sense of what was in the public's mind and that ordinary voters – understandably though misguidedly – shared the Home Secretary's assumption that judges were soft on crime. Before speaking out, Lord Taylor should have considered the risk that his speech might backfire.

The Crime Bill

The government published its clumsily named Crime (Sentences) Bill in October 1996. Mr Howard modestly described it as 'the biggest step change in the fight against crime this century'. Asked to explain what a 'step change' was, he said it meant a radical departure from the previous sentencing arrangements.

The serving judges kept their own counsel on the day the bill was published. It was left to Lord Donaldson, the former Master of the Rolls, to sum up the judicial mood. Plans to give repeat violent or sexual offenders automatic life sentences would 'produce injustice, gross injustice in particular cases'. Lord Donaldson pointed out that 'The second offence, or indeed both offences, might have been committed under gross provocation, perhaps in a domestic context.' Even so, the judge would have to pass a life sentence. 'The negative effect would be that judges would be no longer able to do their job, which is to see that the criminal gets his just deserts, to see that the punishment fits the crime, taking account of the circumstances of the crime and the circumstances of the offender.'[88]

It was remarkable to hear these comments from a judge who was considered so sympathetic to the Conservatives that he was denied promotion to the Court of Appeal while the 1974–9 Labour government was in power.[89] Lord Donaldson had at first been reluctant to give an instant response to the bill, although eventually he was persuaded not to let the judges' case go by default. As he no doubt feared, his remarks dragged the judiciary deeper into the political quagmire.

The Crime Bill itself was much as expected. Clause 1 obliged judges to pass a life sentence on anyone convicted of a serious offence for the second time. Serious offences included attempted murder, manslaughter, causing grievous bodily harm with intent, rape, attempted rape and armed robbery. Clause 2 required judges to pass a sentence of at least seven years on anyone convicted of a third offence of trafficking in class A drugs (such as heroin and cocaine). Clause 3 obliged the courts to pass a sentence of at least three years on anyone convicted of a third domestic burglary.

Then came the exceptions. All three clauses said that a court would not have to pass these sentences if it was 'of the opinion that there are exceptional circumstances which justify its not doing so'. In such cases, the judge would have to say in open court 'that it is of that opinion and what the exceptional circumstances are'. Exceptional circumstances were not defined in the bill.

Was this a loophole through which the judges might be able to escape passing the required sentences? Labour certainly thought so. The shadow Home Secretary, Jack Straw, argued that the bill represented a significant climbdown by Mr Howard. Mr Straw said: 'It appears that Mr Howard is to allow judicial discretion by the back door. It is clear that the Home Secretary has accepted our arguments that a wholly inflexible system would lead to injustice and more serious criminals pleading not guilty and walking free.'[90]

Needless to say, Mr Howard disagreed. The exception had been mentioned in the White Paper. In his view, it was not a loophole: once the legislation was on the statute book, he was sure the judges would respect the will of parliament and interpret it in the spirit intended. Should the judges choose not to do so he had a little warning for them: 'if the Attorney General takes the view that the sentence actually passed is unduly lenient, he will be able to use his powers to refer it to the Court of Appeal'.[91]

There are two comments to make on this particular threat. First, if a case is referred to the Court of Appeal it is the judges themselves who decide whether the sentence is too lenient. Second, if Mr Howard was confident that the Court of Appeal would increase unduly lenient sentences, why did he need this legislation in the first place?

His answer to the second question was that if a sentence were referred to the Court of Appeal it would be dealt with on the basis of the existing framework of sentencing. In his view, that framework needed to be changed by parliament to target those offenders from whom the public needed greater protection.[92]

The Lord Chancellor appeared to believe Mr Howard's 'exceptional circumstances' exemption would be enough to gain the judges' support. 'I think it enables them to deal justly with particular cases,' he said, 'while at the same time giving a very clear warning to anyone who's contemplating a crime of this kind what the result will be unless there are exceptional circumstances.'[93] If that was what he really thought, he was being more than a little naïve.

Mr Howard had his own ideas of what the clause might mean: 'Sometimes, someone appearing before a court gives the police exceptional help, which enables them to bring a number of other serious criminals to justice. That is an important factor, which I would regard as an exceptional circumstance justifying the passing of a sentence shorter than the minimum mandatory length.'[94]

However, the Lord Chief Justice put him right. When the courts had been told as recently as 1991 that they had to pass an immediate prison sentence on certain offenders unless there were 'exceptional circumstances'[95] they had put a narrow construction on the phrase. 'They have treated psychiatric problems, financial pressures, family difficulties, threats of suicide as not being exceptional,' said Lord Bingham, 'because in truth these are not exceptional.'[96]

Lord Bingham thought the phrase 'exceptional circumstances' did not meet the problem at all. He proposed a much broader exception: 'I think it would mitigate the difficulty if the Bill provided that a judge should not be obliged to pass a mandatory sentence if he considered it, in all the circumstances, unjust to do so. And I would expect him to have to state in court why he considered it unjust. But that would at least enable him to give effect to his sense of what the justice of the case demanded.'

The Master of the Rolls, Lord Woolf, said the state was taking powers which in the past had been regarded as those of the judiciary. 'They're taking them in a way which I don't think is entirely frank,' he said. The proposed legislation was not setting minimum sentences: it was setting actual sentences, because they had been pitched at so high a level that virtually no defendant could expect to get any more than the minimum. This was especially true in view of the 'levelling-down' of sentences prescribed in the bill: the courts were told to pass a sentence which corresponded to the term the prisoner would have served under the previous sentencing arrangements. 'That is a whole departure from our tradition with regard to the function of parliament and the function of the courts,' he said. In his view it was not unconstitutional, but it was a constitutional departure.

Lord Woolf did not think parliament was best qualified to determine what the sentence for a burglar should be. What's more, primary legislation would be needed to make any subsequent changes. 'How easy is it going to be,' he asked, 'for parliament to find the time to fine-tune sentences in the way they are fine-tuned through the court system?'[97]

The parliamentary process

The Labour party had chosen not to vote against the government's Crime Bill in the House of Commons. That fact was stressed by the Home Office minister, Baroness Blatch, when she introduced Mr Howard's bill in the House of Lords: 'It has the support of the elected chamber, and I hope that this house will consider our proposals on their merits and not on the basis of misplaced concern about the proper relationship between parliament and the judiciary.'[98] Quite what the minister meant by her last remark is not clear: she seemed to be suggesting that parliament was fully entitled to tell the judges what sentences they should pass. That was not in doubt: whether peers were wise to do so was another matter.

The bill that reached the House of Lords was broadly unchanged. There was now provision for prisoners serving sentences of more than two months to earn a discount of up to sixteen per cent of their sentence – a more generous provision than the one suggested at the time of Mr Howard's conference speech. The ending of a prisoner's automatic parole after he had served half his sentence was now balanced by a new clause requiring the court to impose a penalty equal to two-thirds of the sentence it would have considered appropriate if the offence had been committed immediately before the legislation came into effect.[99]

The Lord Chief Justice lambasted these proposals. His speech was all the more effective because of its calm, measured prose:

> First, the period of a sentence that a prisoner will not have to serve will be less clear and predictable than at present. Secondly, the overall period of control by supervision and licence will in all cases be shorter than at present. Thirdly, the invaluable provision for recall during the licence period will be lost. Fourthly, judgment on release of more serious offenders will no longer be made by the Parole Board and prisoners will remain in prison when their continued confinement serves no useful public purpose. Fifthly, the proposals for remission – a maximum of three days a month for those whose behaviour attains

the prescribed minimum standard and a maximum of three extra days a month for those whose behaviour has exceeded that standard – will prove incapable of fair operation.[100]

Lord Bingham then turned to the main provisions of the legislation. The automatic life sentence was 'irremediably flawed', he said. 'It is a cardinal principle of just sentencing that the penalty should be fashioned to match the gravity of the offence and to take account of the circumstances in which it was committed. Any blanket or scatter-gun approach inevitably leads to injustice in individual cases.'[101] It would also give rise to what the Lord Chief Justice called indefensible anomalies: a man who had sexual intercourse at the age of sixteen with a girl of twelve would be sentenced to life imprisonment if, in middle age, he intentionally caused serious injury in the course of a public-house brawl. A man convicted as a teenager of wounding with intent to cause serious injury would be sentenced to life imprisonment if, at the age of fifty, he returned home drunk and attempted to have intercourse with his wife against her wishes.

In Lord Bingham's view, the sentences for burglars and drug dealers were equally indiscriminate:

> It is one thing – and a very serious thing – to operate as a large wholesale supplier of heroin or cocaine. It is quite another to buy two ecstasy tablets at a party, one for yourself and another for a friend. Yet both fall within clause 2 of the bill. It is one thing – and again a very serious thing – to strip someone's home of its valuable contents, accompanied perhaps by terror to the householder or gratuitous and offensive vandalism. It is quite another to take a gallon of petrol from an outhouse or to reach through an open window and take a pint of milk. Yet both are domestic burglary within clause 3. A skilful professional burglar who avoids detection until he is brought to book on the same occasion for fifty domestic burglaries or a professional drug dealer eventually tracked down for the first time are not subject to the mandatory penalties. A feckless small-time burglar who is caught each time, or an addict dealing in small quantities at street level, is so subject. Anomalies of this kind are not the stuff of sound lawmaking.[102]

The Lord Chief Justice made his remarks from the cross benches. His wife watched from a side gallery; his predecessor Lord Taylor was among retired and serving judges who joined him in the debating chamber. Almost everything Lord Bingham said could be treated as neutral, non-political advice. However, the classical elegance of his peroration could not disguise the fact that it was a deeply political insult: 'If, as the century and the millennium slide to a close, our penal thinking is to be judged by the thinking which animates this Bill, then I, for one, will shrink from the judgment of history.'[103]

Lord Bingham's criticisms were echoed by Lord Woolf. The Master of the Rolls was afraid that the Crime Bill would prove to be an extremely expensive way of making the criminal justice system worse: 'First, it will result in injustice. Secondly, its proposals, if implemented, will have constitutional implications which are undesirable. Thirdly, it will damage the prison system. Fourthly, it involves profligate expenditure of public money. Fifthly, it will result in dishonest sentencing practices. Sixthly, it is unnecessary.'[104]

A third serving judge spoke in the debate: Lord Hope, a newly appointed law lord who had served as Lord Justice General, the Scottish equivalent of the English Lord Chief Justice.[105] He made it clear that, although the bill applied only to England, people from Scotland were at greater risk of receiving life sentences than English criminals. That was because convictions for certain offences under Scottish law would qualify an offender for a life sentence if he then committed a serious offence in England and Wales. The problem arose because there were *more* qualifying offences in Scotland, including sodomy and attempted sodomy, the broad offence of lewd, indecent or libidinous behaviour, and the unusual offence of clandestine injury to women.[106] These offences might not be particularly serious and they were difficult to define because – like many Scottish crimes – they are non-statutory common-law offences. Lord Hope pointed out, with studied understatement, that it would have been 'wiser' to study the bill's implications much more carefully before it was introduced.[107]

In accordance with normal practice, the Crime Bill was allowed to proceed to its committee stage without a vote. There, during the bill's detailed consideration, Lord Bingham finally got his way. He spoke in favour of a Labour amendment which peers passed by a majority of eight votes. His predecessors Lord Taylor and Lord Lane were among those who supported the amendment. It provided that courts would not have to impose a mandatory sentence of three years or seven years if there were factors which would make 'the prescribed custodial sentence unjust in all the circumstances'. Ministers were forced to accept the amendment when peers threatened to stop the Crime (Sentences) Act becoming law before parliament was dissolved for the 1997 election.[108]

An active judiciary

Lord Taylor's attack on Michael Howard's sentencing proposals was not the first occasion on which he had criticised the government's proposals. In 1993, he said government plans to cut eligibility for legal aid were 'draconian cuts' and 'wrong in principle'.[109] Obviously this was a matter on which he felt the judges were entitled to comment, even though it debarred him from any involvement in the Law Society's subsequent, unsuccessful, application for judicial review. While that case was being heard, he was asked[110] whether it was proper for the Lord Chief Justice to criticise the policies of an elected government, especially when those policies might have to be reviewed by the courts. Lord Taylor conceded that it was difficult to say how far a judge, even a senior judge, should become involved in such matters. However, he continued:

> whilst a judge must obviously be entirely independent of party politics, and indeed political issues which don't concern the law, I think that the Lord Chief Justice and the Master of the Rolls ought to have views and ought to make them known on matters which affect the administration of justice. Accordingly, I think it is right that I should be able to express a view for example on legal aid: what is clear is that having expressed one it would be quite wrong for me to sit on the case which is now before the courts. If you are asking: am I becoming political by addressing these issues, I see my membership of the House of Lords as being precisely for the purpose of enabling me to go and speak in the Lords on a debate which affects the administration of justice.

Is that really why the senior judges, the Lord Chief Justice and the law lords, are made members of the House of Lords? Lord Mackay had no doubt about it. Judges who were members of the House of Lords – the law lords and other senior judges – received a writ of summons to 'attend and give their counsel on matters in discussion'. It was 'entirely appropriate for members of the judiciary who are also members of the legislature to exercise their responsibilities as legislators', provided they said nothing to undermine their impartiality in the eyes of those who might appear before them.[111]

In reality, the judges are only members of the House of Lords because of a constitutional accident. In 1873 parliament passed the Supreme Court of Judicature Act to abolish the House of Lords' jurisdiction in respect of English appeals. Gladstone's Liberal government fell in February 1874, before the statute had come into effect, and its implementation was subsequently suspended by parliament for two years. In 1876, before the provisions of the Judicature Act dealing with the House of Lords had come into operation, they were repealed by the Appellate Jurisdiction Act. The official explanation for this change of heart was that 'public, professional and parliamentary opinion' had swung back in favour of the Lords' ancient jurisdiction.[112] According to a leading legal historian, the judges were reinstated only as the result of a battle by a group of disreputable backbench Tory MPs who were fighting to prop up the power of the hereditary peers.[113]

We saw earlier in this chapter how Lord Justice Rose was ridiculed by the Home Secretary for criticising Mr Howard's sentencing proposals. Speaking some months later, Lord Justice Rose said it was highly undesirable that judges should become embroiled in political controversy. He then put forward a remarkable proposition: 'One of the features of the criminal justice system at the moment has been how comparatively little difference there is between the main political parties in relation to, for example, sentencing. Some have thought that the judges therefore have a particular role to play in pointing out dangers which others are not pointing out.'[114]

Lord Justice Rose seemed to be suggesting that if there was an ineffective parliamentary opposition, perhaps because Labour wanted to appear just as tough as the Conservatives, it was then up to the judges to take on the opposition parties' traditional role. This is a slippery constitutional slope. We shall see more examples of judicial activism – as it is called – in the next chapter.[115]

The senior judges are excluded from party politics by what one writer has described as a 'cordon sanitaire'.[116] All full-time judges are disqualified from membership of the House of Commons.[117] Perhaps strangely, the rule does not apply to part-time judges, such as Recorders and magistrates; indeed magistrates are asked to declare their political allegiances before being appointed. The full-time judiciary would consider that an impertinent and unjustified enquiry, but the government argues it is needed to ensure that 'the political inclinations of magistrates on each bench broadly reflect those of the local community'.[118]

Some judges go to considerable lengths to avoid accusations of being partisan. Lord Justice Brooke took care not to sit in judicial review cases involving a certain prominent cabinet minister who happened to be his brother, Peter Brooke MP. Because Peter Brooke represented the Cities of London and Westminster, his brother Henry would not hear applications involving major organisations based there.[119]

Other judges appeared willing to go to court. When the *Independent* suggested in 1996 that a High Court judge had not disavowed the political views he once held it was obliged to publish a prominent apology for saying he was 'politically partisan'.[120]

According to the text-book writers, 'the superior judiciary are required by custom to avoid partisan controversy'.[121] As we have seen earlier in this chapter, that view is shared by the senior judges. Whether they observe it is another matter.

Drawing the line

Lord Mackay said it was one thing to take sides in a party political controversy, quite another thing to speak about a subject on which one had very considerable experience. He gave as an example Lord Taylor's disagreement with parts of the Criminal Justice Act 1991, which in Lord Taylor's opinion set arbitrary and unworkable restrictions on the discretion of the judge to sentence an offender to prison.[122] The Lord Chancellor said the public were entitled to hear the judges' views on issues such as these, provided the judges acknowledged, as Lord Taylor clearly did, that the ultimate decision was one for parliament.

Expanding on these remarks in a subsequent lecture, Lord Mackay said it was up to individual judges to decide whether to intervene in public discussions. He accepted that this might mean they would disagree in public with the government of the day. In his view: 'provided that they are able to do so without putting their impartiality at risk in the cases that come before them, or the confidence of the parties concerned in that impartiality, it is proper that they should contribute to debate on subjects where their expertise may be particularly valuable.[123]

Labour's Lord Chancellor-in-waiting seemed to think Lord Mackay had drawn the line fairly. Lord Irvine of Lairg QC was firmly of the view 'that in relation to the administration of justice and in relation to sentencing, where the expertise of the judges is obvious, they are well entitled to express their views and seek to influence parliament'. Lord Irvine then drew what he saw as an important distinction.

Speaking in the House of Lords in the summer of 1996, he sought to distinguish between 'judicial participation in public controversy of a political nature and the judges' participation in public controversy concerning the effective administration of justice'. In Lord Irvine's view, 'the judges would be wise to confine themselves to controversy about the administration of justice. If they engage more extensively in political controversy, they risk undermining public confidence in their political impartiality.'[124]

The shadow Lord Chancellor made these remarks in a debate he had initiated on 'judicial participation in public controversy' and 'the relationship between the judiciary, the legislature and the executive'. Lord Irvine accepted that there was a fine line to be drawn between judges commenting on topics such as sentencing and the administration of justice – which he thought they were well entitled to do – and judges commenting on political controversy – which he considered risky. However, his attempt to draw that line led him into deep waters. As he was forced to admit: 'The debates about legal aid, maximum and minimum sentences and the size of the prison population all concern the administration of justice. But at the same time they are issues of deep political controversy.'[125]

The problem with what Lord Irvine had to say is that there is a large area of overlap between controversy of a political nature and controversy concerning the administration of justice. The three topics he mentioned – legal aid, sentencing and the prison population – certainly 'concern the administration of justice'. Nevertheless, as he frankly acknowledged, they are also politically controversial. Indeed, virtually every aspect of the administration of justice is politically controversial these days: even if the political parties share broadly common objectives in a particular area, there will always be those who feel the government of the day should be spending more money on it. If the judges talk about legal aid, sentencing or prison – which Lord Irvine would allow them to do – then by his own definition they are also talking about 'matters of deep political controversy' – which he believed might lead to the risk of undermining public confidence.

Pressed on the issue, Lord Irvine said he was clear in his own mind about where the line should be drawn. Like the proverbial elephant, it was easy for him to recognise but difficult to describe:

it depends much more on tone and context than subject matter. In some circumstances, Lord Irvine might have considered it perfectly proper for a senior judge to make dignified comment on matters of political controversy. In others, a more junior member of the bench might have harmed the judiciary's reputation.

Lord Browne-Wilkinson, a senior law lord, said the judges were not getting politically involved. What was happening was that politics were being drawn into the law, not the other way round. Judges had always spoken publicly about sentencing policy and the technicalities of the law. 'What has happened is that "Law and Order" appears to have entered into the political arena,' he said, 'presumably on the basis that it gets votes.' Lord Browne-Wilkinson thought it was not wrong for those with expertise in a field to express a view simply because politicians had chosen to make it a political battleground.[126]

The senior judges themselves are in no doubt about their right – perhaps even their duty – to make their views widely known. During the same debate, Lord Woolf said that judges had given public lectures on the law for many years. He suggested this was a 'desirable and constructive practice'. The Master of the Rolls pointed out that 'the law lords themselves now[127] have the power to set aside decisions given in the past by which they no longer feel the public are served.' If they can do that, he said, 'surely it cannot be objectionable in the course of a lecture to identify an area of the law which many would say needs re-examination and suggest that, in the course of the ordinary development of the law on a case-by-case basis, a change might take place.' Lord Woolf added that it was not only the 'higher judiciary' who could be trusted to give lectures.[128]

Lord Mackay strongly agreed that it was 'absolutely fundamental that judges and other lawyers should be able to participate in discussion of developments in the law'.[129]

It was not the first time the judges had tried to draw the line between what was acceptable and what was not. In October 1993, Lord Woolf himself had made a speech in which he appeared to be suggesting that Michael Howard's newly-minted 'prison works' policy was 'short-sighted and irresponsible'.[130] That embroiled him (together with several other judges) in something of a battle with the Home Office.[131] In the light of this uncomfortable experience, Lord Woolf offered his own advice to the judges. It was essential, he thought, that the Heads of Division – the four most senior judges[132] – should 'explain the steps which are being taken to fulfil the judicial programme' and talk about 'matters which are of interest to the public on which they are in a special position to speak with authority because of the offices which they hold'. Apart from the Heads of Division (and, presumably, the law lords) Lord Woolf thought judges 'should exercise more circumspection before speaking in public'. Then came the exceptions:

> Judges are constantly in demand to give public lectures and they cannot avoid doing so from time to time. In addition, there are programmes on the media with which judges need to become involved so the public can understand how the judiciary works. There can also be situations where they are in a special position to make a contribution to a debate and then they should do so. They should however still avoid, so far as is possible, being involved in controversy because to do so can undermine the rule of law.

Again we see the fundamental contradiction: the judges should contribute to a debate when they are in a special position to do so, but they should try to avoid controversy. Clearly there are topics that are purely political and have no direct association with the administration of justice: interest rates, for example, or European Monetary Union. Clearly there are other topics that involve the administration of justice but have little to do with party politics: whether judges should wear wigs, for example, or whether the courts should be televised.[133] Nevertheless, there is a much larger area in the middle where the two overlap.

The judges themselves realise how difficult it is to draw the line on matters such as sentencing. In 1996, Lord Justice Kennedy said: 'On the whole, I think judges would prefer not to say anything about sentencing policy, but they do become very concerned if a proposal on the face of it appears to be heading towards a situation in which they will be obliged to act unjustly, as between for example one defendant and another.' Questioned further, Lord Justice Kennedy said judges should avoid entering the public fray. 'It's a mistake for judges who, in the end, are supposed to operate the system to become embroiled in what the system should be. They should not be in the forefront of political argument.'[134] This was wise advice.

It was left to Lord Bingham to give a definitive ruling. Senior judges, he said, could give their views on matters directly pertaining to the administration of justice. Retired and serving judges who were members of the House of Lords could speak on issues directly related to their professional expertise. Lord Bingham thought it should not prove too difficult in practice to decide where legitimate observations on the administration of justice ended and political controversy began:

> Lord Denning's [1949] Hamlyn Lectures *Freedom under the Law*, although the subject of objection by [the then Lord Chancellor],[135] and Lord Taylor's recent observations on sentencing practice, fell on the right side of the line; letters written by Mr Justice Stephen criticising the government's policy on India [during the nineteenth century], Lord Hewart's famous book *The New Despotism* [published in 1929] and the letter written to *The Times* [in 1954][136] by Mr Justice Lloyd–Jacob about the hydrogen bomb, one might feel, fell on the wrong side of the line.[137]

It was understandable that Lord Bingham did not wish to criticise his predecessor, who at that time was gravely ill. Even though he was – as he said – slightly less blunt in his use of language,[138] Lord Bingham made it clear that he shared Lord Taylor's concerns on sentencing policy. 'I very much hope that the Home Secretary and parliament will leave the judges with their sentencing discretion,' he said. For the reasons his predecessor had already given, Lord Bingham thought the interests of justice were served by allowing judges as far as possible to tailor the sentence to the facts and circumstances of individual cases. The judges were in a uniquely good position to judge these, he thought. Lord Bingham explained why he would be speaking about Mr Howard's proposals when they reached the House of Lords. He thought it was 'an appropriate thing for senior judges to contribute the benefit of their experience on matters directly lying within their field of experience.' In his view, sentencing 'undoubtedly' came within this definition: he did not regard it as a political issue.

In saying that sentencing was not a political issue, Lord Bingham was redefining the term. True, there was a measure of consensus between Labour and the Conservatives over Michael Howard's bill as it passed through parliament, but that was entirely for political reasons connected with the forthcoming election. It is also true to say that sentencing was not a *purely* political issue: it was clearly part of the administration of justice. It was political nevertheless.

That was apparent from a speech made by a former Conservative minister during a House of Lords debate on Mr Howard's Crime Bill. Lord Tebbit said he had been 'concerned to hear on the radio and in press reports in the past few days the views of a number of judges on the bill'. In his view, it was

> a great pity that so many judges have followed the rather unfortunate example of Judge Pickles, who could not resist talking into any microphone put in front of him.[139] I believe that the standing of the judiciary has been damaged by an excessive entry into the political (and not, I hasten to add, the party political) field, not least because, once they enter this field, it opens the way to criticism of judges.

Lord Tebbit said he understood the 'resentment' some judges had shown towards the sentencing proposals. He pointed out that a number of politicians had 'at times resented the extension of the doctrine of judicial review in the way that has happened in recent years'. He then made a telling admission: 'As a result of those happenings, especially that of judges speaking so much in public outside this house, I find myself, having almost all of my life regarded it as entirely improper for politicians to criticise the judicial conduct of judges, now doing so; and not too infrequently, I fear, in my role as a tabloid journalist.'[140] A stronger incentive for judicial reticence would be difficult to find.

Even though sentencing is part of the administration of justice, it is not the unique province of the judiciary: parliament is fully entitled to deal with it by way of legislation. Whether Mr Howard's proposals were wise is a matter of opinion. Views may vary, but the judges' views are of great weight. On this topic, they were right to speak out. Lord Bingham's approach, more restrained than Lord Taylor's, was none the less effective for that: his message was obvious, even if his tone was less shrill. It was not clear whether anyone in government was prepared to listen.

The judicial image

We have just encountered what we may call Tebbit's third law of motion: that when a judge criticises a politician, he experiences an equal but opposite criticism in return. In the same debate, Lord Tebbit also managed to suggest that the judges were soft on crime and out of touch with the views of ordinary people: 'I suspect that there are a good many people . . . in tower blocks in the decayed inner-urban areas who, if they had heard our debate so far today . . . would be inclined to say "It's all right for them. They don't suffer crime in the way we do."'[141]

Those criticisms had already been dismissed by Lord Nolan, the law lord appointed by the Prime Minister to chair the Committee on Standards in Public Life. 'The truth of the matter,' he said in a lecture delivered towards the end of 1996, 'is that up and down the country, on every working day, hundreds of cases involving the liberty of the subject are being tried fairly and competently, in open court, by judges and juries and this gets no publicity at all, for the simple reason that good news of this kind does not sell newspapers.'

In Lord Nolan's view, much of the responsibility for the poor publicity which judges received lay with the judges themselves. 'The legal profession in general and the judges in particular have always been bad at cultivating the art of public relations,' he said. However, Lord Nolan noted, 'in recent years judges have increasingly come to recognise the need to anticipate the public reaction to controversial decisions and to cater for it in their judgment – or even, in extreme cases, by holding a press conference.' The judges had recognised, late in the day, that this criticism had reached a level that imperilled the confidence of the public in the judicial process, and it must therefore be countered.

Lord Nolan seemed to be calling for some sort of judicial public relations officer. Others have made similar suggestions. In 1993, the Attorney General, Sir Nicholas Lyell, visited the Commonwealth Law Conference in Cyprus. He was struck by the degree to which some courts, particularly those in Canada and Australia, had tried to develop a good working relationship with the media. Their aim was to make sure that important judgments were both accessible and comprehensible to the media – and therefore to the public. Sir Nicholas discovered that some courts had even appointed their own press officers: the Canadian media relations officer had the job of giving reporters off-the-record briefings on the Supreme Court's most important judgments to make sure they were understood correctly by those who might not have any legal experience or training.

In a paper delivered the following year,[142] Sir Nicholas wondered whether there were lessons to be learned. Was it sufficient for the courts to let their judgments 'speak for themselves'? 'I have in mind the fact that even a detailed written judgment is open to misunderstanding on the part of non-lawyers. Equally, a journalist may seek to give particular emphasis to just one aspect of a judgment which seems especially newsworthy and, in doing so, may well fail to give a balanced account of the judgment as a whole.' The Attorney General put forward no specific proposals. He hinted that he would like to see more done to make the decisions of the courts more readily accessible to the public at large, but nothing came of it. This was hardly surprising: his remarks were little noticed at the time, perhaps because his own department did not acquire its first press officer until more than two years later.

Sir Nicholas Lyell's comments deserve closer consideration by the judiciary. Judges still have much to learn about the black arts of media manipulation.[143] At present, they are offered assistance from the Court Service press officers – which for all practical purposes means the Lord Chancellor's Department press office. Staff there are more than willing to help the judges, but they are well aware that they are employed to serve the Lord Chancellor, whose agenda may be different. If the judges have anything controversial to say, they should not rely too heavily on Court Service press officers for confidential advice.

The Lord Chief Justice (alone among the judges) has a Private Secretary.[144] Yet he too is on temporary loan from the Lord Chancellor's Department, and he knows his prospects of promotion depend on impressing senior staff there rather than the Lord Chief Justice.

The effect of all this is that the judges have no impartial source of advice on media relations. Although judicial independence is a cornerstone of our constitution the judges themselves depend on civil servants for key advice. Lord Bingham was well aware that the Lord Chancellor's Head of Information (and her deputy) were helping to run the news conference he gave in October 1996. He may well have wondered why press officers from three other government departments – the Home Office, the Attorney General's Department, and the Crown Prosecution Service – were lurking behind the cameras at the back of the room. Was it so that they could issue instant rejoinders in the event of judicial criticism? An independent press officer might have advised him that even though it was customary for government press officers to invite colleagues from other departments, these officials had no right to attend his news conference.

It would be valuable for all concerned if the judiciary acquired their own independent media relations officer. At the very least, such a person would let reporters know when important judgments were about to be delivered – something done already by press office staff at the European Courts in Luxembourg and Strasbourg.

Should a press officer provide summaries of judgments or give off-the-record briefings to reporters? If these were to have any value, the press officer would need a fair degree of legal training. The Head of Information at the European Court of Justice in Luxembourg[145] is a barrister. The press officer at the European Court of Human Rights is not legally qualified, but after a barrage of hostile publicity in the British media during 1995 one of its staff lawyers was appointed to handle media relations.

Journalists are rightly wary of press officers. They are paid to serve their employers, not the press. Press officers are expected to neutralise or minimise bad publicity while maximising favourable coverage. They are often expected to keep journalists away from primary sources of information. Even so, an independent, legally qualified, court press officer would be a useful person to have around the courts of England and Wales. He or she could draw attention to decisions that might otherwise be missed, set the record straight when judges were misreported and make sure that non-specialist journalists understood what was going on. This has become particularly important now that PA News, the main national news agency in Britain, does not have enough specialist staff to cover the higher courts. However, a press summary is no substitute for the judges' words. Nothing must be done to make it harder for reporters to read the judge's sentences.

3

The Theatre of War: Judicial Review

The courts are now trying to play party politics and it is high time they came out of their courtrooms and stood for election if this is the game they want to play.

David Wilshire MP (Conservative) (1996)[1]

Far from seeking to usurp the functions of parliament, the judiciary is here ensuring that the will of parliament is carried out.

Lord Taylor, Lord Chief Justice (1996)[2]

The proper constitutional relationship of the executive with the courts is that the courts will respect all acts of the executive within its lawful province, and that the executive will respect all decisions of the courts as to what its lawful province is.

Lord Justice Nolan, appeal judge (1992)[3]

The battleground

Any trial of strength between the judiciary and the executive will be fought most fiercely on the battleground of judicial review. In the hands of the judges, judicial review can be a rapier missile, ruthlessly striking down unlawful ministerial decisions. Ministers still have the ultimate weapon: so long as they can persuade parliament to overturn adverse rulings they have nothing to fear. They can even threaten to spike the judges' guns. However, it is not always easy for governments to obtain the legislation they seek.

What judicial review is not

Judicial review has become so popular that people sometimes imagine it is a remedy for all ills. This confusion is compounded by the writings of some journalists. Thus a recent story on the front page of the *Sunday Times*[4] began: 'A woman suffering from a terminal illness is seeking a judicial review of the law so that doctors can end her life without fear of being prosecuted for murder. Annie Lindsell, 45, a businesswoman, will this week consult two of Britain's top human rights lawyers in her attempt to change the law, which bans assisted suicide. She claims it infringes her rights.' This is legal nonsense, as no doubt Ms Lindsell would have been told by even the most junior human rights lawyer. The clue is in the phrase '*a* judicial review'. Lawyers do not use the indefinite article because 'judicial review' is the name given to the remedy ('the applicant seeks judicial review of the minister's decision') and not a description of the hearing.

The level of public ignorance demonstrated by this report is telling nevertheless. Ms Lindsell fondly imagined that the judges have it within their power to overrule or perhaps sidestep an act of parliament that provides up to fourteen years imprisonment for complicity in suicide[5] (or, as she apparently thought, murder). The two *Sunday Times* journalists who reported her words presumably shared that ignorance: they certainly succeeded in spreading it further. As we shall see in this chapter, the courts have not been shy about curbing the wilder excesses of government ministers. Yet not even the most interventionist of judges would seek to replace the clear words of an act of parliament with a licence to kill.

How judicial review works

Judicial review is judge-made law. Because it has grown up over the years, there is no handy statute defining its scope. A recent book on judicial review, which does not even attempt to refer to all the reported cases, runs to more than a thousand pages.[6] What follows now is only the merest summary.

Judicial review is a way of overturning a decision taken by a public body that has exceeded or abused its powers. The judges maintain that they are not concerned with the merits of the decision, merely with the way in which the decision-maker has reached it. Their job is to make sure that someone who is given a discretion by parliament – often a minister – keeps to the rules.

Ministers might reasonably point out that those rules are generally made by the judges. As we shall see, they sometimes suspect judges of looking for a way of declaring a decision unlawful if they happen not to agree with it.

Broadly speaking, in cases where judicial review is available the courts will insist that a public body acts reasonably, fairly and within its powers. We shall look at each of these requirements in turn.

Reasonableness

If a decision is challenged as *unreasonable* the court must decide whether the power under which a decision-maker acted has been improperly exercised.

The courts have been enforcing reasonableness for at least 400 years. In 1598 the Commissioners of Sewers had the power to levy charges for repairing river banks. They tried to make one adjacent landowner pay for some repairs instead of dividing the cost among all those who benefited. The courts said this was unreasonable: 'The commissioners ought to tax all who are in danger of being damaged . . . equally, and not him who has the land next adjoining to the river only . . . and notwithstanding the words of the commission give authority to the commissioners to do according to their discretions, yet their proceedings ought to be limited and bound within the rule of reason and law.'[7]

Although the requirement of reasonableness has an ancient pedigree, the leading academic Professor Sir William Wade says 'the cases in which it was invoked were few and far between' until the *Padfield*[8] case opened a new era in 1968.[9] But when lawyers talk of a minister or public body acting unreasonably, they are usually referring to the tests mentioned in a case decided twenty years earlier. This case gave its name to the concept of '*Wednesbury* unreasonableness', which is perhaps a little harsh on those who live in that particular part of the West Midlands: in the *Wednesbury* case itself, the court found that the local council had behaved perfectly reasonably.[10]

Writing in 1994, Mr Justice Sedley said it was typical of the 'ahistoricism' of lawyers that they treated *Wednesbury* as a landmark when it was no more than an off-the-cuff judgment in which the Master of the Rolls 'rehearsed a number of doctrines which had been perfectly familiar to the Victorian judges who devised and developed them, and proceeded to refuse relief in a case which today might well be regarded as disclosing an abuse of power.'[11] Two years later Mr Justice Sedley noted that the word 'Wednesbury' was being used as little more than an expletive (as in the phrase 'My Lord, this was Wednesbury unfair').[12]

Nevertheless, the famous case of *Associated Provincial Picture Houses v. Wednesbury Corporation* offers a good introduction to the idea of unreasonableness in the law. This is how the concept was explained by Lord Greene, then Master of the Rolls:

> A person entrusted with a discretion must, so to speak, direct himself properly in law. He must call his own attention to the matters which he is bound to consider. He must exclude from his consideration matters which are irrelevant to what he has to consider. . . Similarly, there may be something so absurd that no sensible person could ever dream that it lay within the powers of the authority. Lord Justice Warrington[13] . . . gave the example of the red-haired teacher, dismissed because she had red hair. This is unreasonable in one sense. In another it is taking into consideration extraneous matters. It is so unreasonable that it might almost be described as being done in bad faith; and, in fact, all these things run into one another.[14]

In 1984, Lord Diplock, who was nearing the end of his career as a highly respected law lord, chose to reformulate the grounds for judicial review. He was giving judgment in what is commonly referred to as the *GCHQ* case.[15] Instead of referring to unreasonableness, Lord Diplock used the term *irrationality* as a test of whether a decision should be overturned. By an irrational decision he meant one which was 'so outrageous in its defiance of logic or of accepted moral standards that no sensible person who had applied his mind to the question to be decided could have arrived at it'.[16]

This seems a large hurdle to jump, but the courts do not have much difficulty in finding examples of irrationality. As Professor Wade says, 'This is not because ministers and public authorities take leave of their senses, but because the courts in deciding cases tend to lower the threshold of unreasonableness to fit their more exacting ideas of administrative good behaviour.'[17]

Although Lord Diplock's reformulation is attractive, the term 'irrational' is best avoided. Very few decisions are truly irrational. If a decision is bad in this sense it is more likely to be because the decision-maker acted improperly in some other way: he has acted in bad faith, he has unjustifiably discriminated against someone or his decision is unduly oppressive.[18] These actions are much better described as 'unreasonable'.[19]

Fairness

The courts will strike down a decision as *unfair* if the decision-maker has not followed the correct procedures. The requirement of reasonableness, just mentioned, deals more with the substance of a decision. The concept of fairness relates to the way in which it is taken. Broadly speaking, those affected by a decision should normally be given a proper opportunity to influence its outcome.

This aspect of judicial review deals with issues such as the requirement to consult, to hear representations and to hold hearings.[20] It also protects what are called 'legitimate expectations': if a decision-maker has induced in someone who may be affected by the decision a reasonable expectation that he will receive or retain a benefit – or that he will be granted a hearing before the decision is taken – then the courts will not allow that expectation to be summarily thwarted.[21]

These principles can be traced back to the so-called rules of 'natural justice'. There are two rules:

nobody can be a judge in his own cause[22] (which means adjudicators must be disinterested and unbiased); and
a court must always 'hear the other side'[23] (in other words, it must hear a person's defence).

Though ancient, and widely followed, these principles are in no sense 'natural'. However, they do form the basis of the modern law.

In the *GCHQ* case, Lord Diplock recategorised the failure to act fairly as *procedural impropriety*. He used this strange phrase to make it clear that a tribunal which failed to observe procedural rules laid down by parliament would be subject to judicial review, even if it had not acted unfairly in a particular case. Though a little less accurate, 'fairness' or 'procedural fairness' are likely to be better understood than Lord Diplock's phrase.

Lawfulness
It is a fundamental principle of judicial review that a public body may not exceed its powers, that it must not act *ultra vires*. An administrative decision is *unlawful* if

it contravenes or exceeds the terms of the power which authorises the making of the decision; or
it pursues an objective other than that for which the power to make the decision was conferred.[24]

Lord Diplock reformulated this as a duty to avoid *illegality*. By that he meant that a decision-maker must understand correctly the law that regulates his or her power to make decisions and give effect to it. To most people, acting illegally means committing a crime – breaking the criminal law. It is therefore better to speak of a duty not to act unlawfully.

Proportionality

Lord Diplock also suggested a fourth ground for judicial review, *proportionality*. To satisfy this test a decision-maker must ensure that he maintains a balance between the aims of his policy and any adverse effects it may have: in other words, he should not use a sledgehammer to crack a nut. At the time Lord Diplock was speaking the test was not yet established in English law. Nevertheless, in a recent asylum case (considered in more detail later)[25] Lord Justice Neill spoke of the minister's duty to 'strike a balance'. At one point the judge said: 'In my judgment a court is only entitled to intervene where the interference with the other rights is disproportionate to the objects to be achieved.'[26]

The criterion of proportionality seems to be gaining ground. Mr Justice Laws has said (outside court) that he thinks the principle 'ought now to be regarded as a separate head of challenge'.[27] If that becomes the law the judges will have fashioned for themselves a powerful weapon. It would give them much greater powers to second-guess ministers and to strike down decisions on their merits.

Perhaps for that reason, Labour's Lord Chancellor-in-waiting was against it. According to Lord Irvine of Lairg QC, introducing proportionality as a ground for judicial review would enable courts to review the merits of a decision on the basis of a standard that is much lower than *Wednesbury* reasonableness. He feared it would 'involve the court in a process of policy evaluation which goes far beyond its allotted constitutional role'.[28] In other words, judges would be meddling in politics. In a democratic society, he said, compromises between competing interests must be resolved by parliament – or, if parliament so decides, by ministers. There spoke a man who confidently expected he would soon become a member of the government.

Judicial activism

It is essential to grasp how much judicial review has developed since the early 1960s. Before then, judges were doing little to control the executive: a minister's word was effectively law. As recently as 1959,

Professor Stanley de Smith – one of the first academics to study the subject – could say: 'One characteristic of judicial review in English administrative law that strikes foreign observers is that it is so seldom invoked.'[29] As Professor Sir William Wade said:

> During and after the Second World War a deep gloom settled on administrative law, which reduced it to the lowest ebb at which it had stood for centuries. The courts and the legal profession seemed to have forgotten the achievements of their predecessors and they showed little stomach for continuing their centuries-old work of imposing law upon government . . . [Administrative law] relapsed into an impotent condition, marked by neglect of principles and literal verbal interpretation of the blank-cheque powers which parliament showered on ministers.[30]

Sir William Wade was Professor of English Law at Oxford University from 1961 to 1976 and at Cambridge University from 1978 to 1982. His assessment was endorsed by the Master of the Rolls, Lord Woolf, and by Jeffrey Jowell, Professor of Public Law in the University of London. They wrote: 'In the 1950s, judicial self-restraint appeared to have won a decisive victory over judicial activism . . . In a number of leading decisions over the years judges voluntarily curbed their own power to review administrative action.'[31]

A creative judiciary
Over the past three decades, as Lord Woolf and Professor Jowell freely acknowledged, the judges' role has become far more creative. Among the reasons they suggested for this judicial activism were:

> an increase in awareness of the more impressive performance of courts in the United States, France and some Commonwealth countries;
> a judicial willingness to adopt a more purposive approach to the interpretation of statutes;
> the indirect influence of academic literature on practitioners;
> the resourcefulness of individual judges;
> consumer pressure against public bodies which had previously seemed immune from accountability or control.[32]

To these we may add two more factors. The first has been the influence of Sir William Wade himself on the judges. Professor Wade did more than anybody to bring together the sources of judicial review and develop them into a coherent legal framework. Even the phrase 'judicial review' must have sounded unfamiliar in

1961, when he published the first edition of his *Administrative Law* – a modest volume in comparison with the massive seventh edition which appeared in 1994. Professor Wade used the term in 1961 to contrast judicial review with a system of appeals, but he entitled his key chapter 'Judicial *Control* of Administrative Powers', a phrase which no doubt his readers would have understood better. At the time he was writing, administrative law was (he said) 'still in dire need of analysis'.[33]

Some of the current High Court judges were students when Professor Wade's influential book was published; a few, no doubt, attended his lectures at Oxford. They will have noted his insistence that 'government under the rule of law demands proper legal limits on the exercise of power'. They will also have seen that even in 1961 he dismissed the doctrine that a minister is responsible to parliament alone – still today the government's automatic response to an adverse court ruling – because it would not lead to sufficient control over the huge number of administrative decisions then being made:

> Administrative justice demands some regular, efficient, and non-political system of investigating individual complaints against the powers that be. This is exactly what ministerial responsibility does not provide . . . Parliament cannot possibly control the ordinary run of daily government acts except by taking up occasional cases which have political appeal . . . Some quite different kind of organisation is needed if the merits of innumerable discretionary decisions are to be kept under proper review.[34]

Professor Wade was calling on the courts to develop a sophisticated system of judicial review. Few writers have the satisfaction of seeing their demands granted so quickly and so effectively. There has been a spectacular growth in judicial review: in 1980, there were 491 applications to the courts, compared with 3,293 applications in the first ten months of 1996 alone.

Redressing the political balance
The second reason for increased judicial activism is that the electorate chose to give one party some eighteen years of uninterrupted political power. Despite what were presumed to be their natural conservative inclinations, it seems that many judges felt it was up to them to redress the political balance. Speaking as shadow Lord Chancellor, Lord Irvine of Lairg recognised that 'the consequences of the "democratic deficit", the want of parliamentary control over

the executive in recent years, have been, to an important degree, mitigated by the rigours of judicial review'.[35] Mr Justice Sedley wrote with commendable frankness that 'modern public law has carried forward a culture of judicial assertiveness to compensate for, and in places repair, dysfunctions in the democratic process.'[36]

There is clear support for this analysis of the judges' role from Lord Woolf himself. Speaking in 1994, he drew attention to the 'dramatic nature' of the changes that had occurred in the area of judicial review. Lord Woolf candidly admitted that these changes had been influenced by the political situation in Britain. 'It is one of the strengths of the common law that it enables the courts to vary the extent of their intervention to meet current needs, and by this means it helps to maintain the delicate balance of a democratic society.'

In Lord Woolf's view, this 'favourable' picture was not confined to Britain: in many areas the English judiciary were often simply following a path marked out by courts abroad. It was apparent from his remarks that he welcomed the ability of the judiciary to assist those who sought judicial review: they included 'the immigrant, the disabled, investors, parents of children in the care of local authorities, corporations as large as ICI and the trade unions'.[37]

An even more explicit acknowledgement that the judges abhor a political vacuum came from Lord Mustill, one of the most independent of the law lords, at the end of a powerful dissenting judgment he gave in 1995. It was in a case about compensation for criminal injuries.[38] First, Lord Mustill explained the 'peculiarly British conception of the separation of the powers'.

> Parliament has a legally unchallengeable right to make whatever laws it thinks right. The executive carries on the administration of the country in accordance with the powers conferred on it by law. The courts interpret the laws, and see that they are obeyed. This requires the courts on occasion to step into the territory which belongs to the executive, not only to verify that the powers asserted accord with the substantive law created by parliament but also that the manner in which they are exercised conforms with the standards of fairness which parliament must have intended.

So far, so good. Lord Mustill said that concurrent with this judicial function parliament had its own means of ensuring that the executive, in the exercise of its delegated functions, performed in a way which parliament found appropriate. He was presumably thinking of the daily questions to ministers and the powerful Commons select committees. 'Ideally,' he said, 'it is these latter methods which should be used to check executive errors and excesses; for it is the task of parliament and the executive in tandem, not of the courts, to govern the country.' Recently, however, he added:

> the employment in practice of these specifically parliamentary remedies has on occasion been perceived as falling short, and sometimes well short, of what was needed to bring the performance of the executive in line with the law, and with the minimum standards of fairness implicit in every parliamentary delegation of a decision-making function. To avoid a vacuum in which the citizen would be left without protection against a misuse of executive powers the courts have had no option but to occupy the dead ground in a manner, and in areas of public life, which could not have been foreseen thirty years ago.

The judges are well aware of what they are doing. Some of them have expressed concern. Another senior judge[39] accepted that parliament had failed to control the executive properly and could not be relied on to spot badly drafted legislation (such as the Criminal Justice Act 1991, which had to be amended within a few months of coming into effect).[40] He also accepted that opposition to the government in parliament had been inadequate. 'But,' the judge insisted, 'that does not entitle the judges to set themselves up as an opposition. In the ultimate analysis we live in a democratic society in which we elect our legislators, not the judges.'

Writing in 1994, Professor Wade took it for granted that the development of judicial review was a good thing. Decisions of the courts are 'the only defences against abuse of power', he maintained.[41] Nevertheless, he also felt the need to answer those who might believe a developed system of administrative law made it difficult for governments to act efficiently. 'Intensive government will be more tolerable to the citizen, and the government's path will be smoother, where the law can enforce high standards of legality, reasonableness and fairness,' he said. 'Provided that the judges observe the proper boundaries of their office, administrative law and administrative power should be friends and not enemies. The contribution that the law can and should make is creative rather than destructive.'[42]

That view was shared by Lord Woolf. 'We must try to get the message across to the government and its supporters that judicial review is not something they should regard with disfavour.' He realised this was 'hugely optimistic', but he felt no minister would deliberately act unlawfully.[43] He was, perhaps, being deliberately over-generous to ministers. Ten years earlier, he himself had drawn attention to a change in standards among public bodies large and small. 'It used to be the case that, if the legality of a course of action was in doubt, it was not adopted. Now it appears to be [be]coming a case of anything is permissible unless and until it is stopped by the courts.'[44]

Too big for their wigs?
As Lord Woolf was the first to acknowledge, governments do not share his sanguine view of judicial review. Although ministers are usually cautious about attacking the judiciary in public, they sometimes speak off the record to trusted reporters. An article published in the summer of 1995 certainly reflected the private views of one senior member of the government.[45] Writing in the *Spectator*, Boris Johnson thought he understood why ministers were being overruled so often: the judges were frustrated politicians, and Labour politicians to boot.[46]

In the past, he noted, these judges would have served as MPs while toiling at the bar:

> But the days of F. E. Smith, of the great lawyer-politicians, are gone. Partly this is because the lawyers cannot face the personal exposure entailed. As [one eminent] QC puts it, 'I don't want to spend my life with people asking me questions about every strange woman I'm seen with.' Mainly though, I suspect, it is because the financial rewards for staying in their pleasant, Oxbridge-college-style inns are irresistible next to the pathetic salaries of MPs. And so, having been raised to the bench, and having made their pile as barristers, I suggest that they are trying to have their cake and eat it. They rejoice in the fancy new grounds for judicial review being imported from Europe – whether a measure is 'proportionate', whether it conforms to 'legitimate expectation' – and, yes, some of them relish the chance to engage in the political process.

As reported by Boris Johnson, politicians believed the judges were substituting their own discretion for the discretion of ministers. In his article, he quoted Mr Justice Sedley's reference to the judges repairing the dysfunctions of the democratic process and Lord Woolf's remarks about helping to maintain the delicate balance of a democratic society.[47] Boris Johnson took these comments to mean they thought that 'when a political party has been in office for too long, and the culture of opposition has declined, then it is up to the judges to volunteer resistance.'

Whether or not that was what these judges were implying, they would not have been the first to recognise it. In the summer of 1993, the distinguished lawyer and historian, Professor Robert Stevens, said that the judges were 'politically quite sophisticated'. He suspected they were 'concerned when they see government appearing to flounder: they have moved into that vacuum as you would expect from people who are very talented, perhaps more talented than the other branches of government'.[48] Professor Stevens noted that, after 1979, Britain had 'a radical government of the right with a Labour party, soon to be led by Michael Foot, appearing to lurch to the left. There was a vacuum of power in the centre and, consciously or not, the judiciary began to move into it.' If this was not apparent at the time, that may have been because until 1987 the Lord Chancellor was Lord Hailsham, a man protective of the traditional role of judges who insisted on the continuation of the Kilmuir rules on silence.[49]

At the same time as Professor Stevens was speaking, the present Lord Chief Justice suggested that the constitutional balance was tilting towards the judiciary. Lord Bingham said 'the courts have reacted to the increase in the powers claimed by the government by being more active themselves', adding that this had become all the more important at a time of one-party government.[50]

That remark was attacked as 'unwise' by Lord Irvine, the shadow Lord Chancellor. Speaking in the House of Lords, he said the 'judges should never give grounds for the public to believe that they intend to reverse government policies which they dislike . . . It suggests to ordinary people a judicial invasion of the legislature's turf.'[51]

It suggested as much to some Conservative MPs as well. Sir Ivan Lawrence, a leading barrister who tried criminal cases part-time as a Recorder, suggested at the beginning of 1996 that there were 'some judges, maybe a new breed of judges, who think that there is a greater role which the judges should be playing in society than they have been playing in the past: that is why some judges are coming dangerously near to stepping over the boundary of restraint.'[52]

Speaking at around the same time, Lord Bingham said the judges were 'most emphatically not' becoming more political. 'It is an absolutely cardinal principle,' he said, 'that one's private views are of no relevance whatever to the decision one makes, which is a purely legal judgment as to whether the minister has or has not exercised his powers lawfully.'[53] But he then admitted that judicial review was changing:

First, the procedures have altered so as to make it somewhat easier for members of the public to come to the court and seek to challenge a ministerial or public decision of some sort or another. Secondly, I think that the judges have become slightly less reluctant to hold that a decision is unlawful. During two world wars, the courts were rightly conscious of the need not to impede the war effort and obstruct those who were straining every nerve to try and prevent a national disaster. For the middle years of this century the courts, on the whole, were very respectful of government and very reluctant to interfere. I think to some extent that has weakened.[54]

Other judges have gone further. One said privately that they had a duty to speak out at a time when the parliamentary opposition was trying, for electoral reasons, to avoid controversy. In an unguarded moment Lord Taylor seemed to hint that judges thought carefully about the policy implications of what they were doing. In evidence to the Commons Home Affairs Committee, he said much was being made of the extent to which the judiciary was prepared to use judicial review to overturn government decisions. He then said: 'We are very careful not to go too far.' As examples, he referred to unsuccessful attempts to overturn the Maastricht treaty on European unity and the Anglo-Irish agreement of 1994. In those cases, he said, the judges would say these were matters for parliament, and they would stand off. He distinguished these examples from cases where 'some minister or some civil servant has exceeded his powers'.[55]

One reading of these remarks is that the judges were careful not to get involved in 'political' decisions. Another meaning may be that they were cautious about getting involved in the most serious decisions, especially those with an international element. Either way, it suggests they were well aware of the political realities.

As Lord Chief Justice, Lord Bingham expressed the traditional view. Judicial review was not a novel phenomenon, as could be seen from the Latin names of the principal remedies.[56]

> No constitutional democracy governed by the rule of law could function without it. Far from challenging the authority of parliament, as is sometimes suggested, judicial review buttresses the authority of parliament by ensuring that powers conferred by parliament are used as parliament intended. Nor does it involve any usurpation of ministerial authority. Judges are concerned with the lawfulness of administrative decisions, not their wisdom or advisability.[57]

Lord Woolf also insisted that the courts did not get involved in policy considerations: 'I do really think that we don't get involved in considering the merits of a policy. Certainly, I can only speak for myself. I know the rules of judicial review, I don't cheat on them and I don't think any of my colleagues do.[58]

Lord Bingham maintained that judges were not concerned with the policy merits of a decision, merely its lawfulness. It was something they often said: he was not sure what critics made of it. 'They may perhaps regard it as a meaningless incantation; or as an unconvincing attempt to camouflage an illegitimate agenda, like a sadistic Victorian schoolmaster saying "I don't want to do this"; or as evidence of the judges' ability to delude themselves. I can only assert that the judges mean what they say.'

Of course, Lord Bingham added, judges had their own views on the issues under review; very often they reached judicial decisions which ran counter to those views. 'I can assert with complete confidence,' he said, 'that my private views have not influenced my judicial decisions and the same is, I know, true of my colleagues.'[59]

We may have little difficulty in accepting that the judges do not act in a party-political way: they are not the sort of people who would support a policy simply because it has been adopted by a political party. We must accept that they are telling the truth when they say they do not look at the merits of a decision before considering its lawfulness. That said, they are not machines. Deciding a case means choosing between alternatives. Each will have some legal validity; each will have been supported by one of the advocates who argued the case. If the alternatives are of equal strength the judge would be less than human if he or she did not veer, however subconsciously, towards the option which seemed closer to what seemed to be the justice of the case.

If they go no further than this, the judges cannot be faulted; indeed, they deserve our praise for seeking to reach a just result. The time to worry is when we think the judges are ignoring a persuasive argument because they dislike its consequences.

Lawful or right?

The orthodox view, as we have just seen, is that in judicial review the court is concerned only with whether a decision is lawful: it is not the judges' job to decide whether the decision was the right one. The leading academic in the field of judicial review argues that this should not deflect the judges from what he sees as their task.

There are, of course, many cases in which judges have to decide whether a decision was right on its merits: criminal appeals, for example. However, all rights of appeal are created by statute. It is up to parliament to decide whether there should be an appeal in any given circumstances. Judicial review, on the other hand, is the exercise of the court's power to decide whether or not action is lawful. It is a fundamental principle that powers must not be exercised beyond their true limits.[60]

Yet as Professor Wade frankly acknowledged, 'the distinction between "merits" and "legality" is not in fact so rigid'. One reason for this, he said, was that the courts interpret acts of parliament as only authorising action which is reasonable or has some particular purpose. In this way – crucially – its merits decide whether it is lawful. The judges will infer such a limitation from the statute even if there is no such provision in the text. As he explained:

> The judges have been deeply drawn into this area, so that their own opinion of the reasonableness or motives of some government action may be the factor which determines whether or not it is to be condemned on judicial review. Although in principle the dichotomy between legality and merits is still observed, the dividing line becomes blurred. The further the courts are drawn into passing judgment on the merits of the actions of public authorities, the more they are exposed to the charge that they are exceeding their constitutional function.[61]

Nevertheless, said the campaigning professor, 'unless the courts are prepared to act boldly in this direction, they can give but feeble protection against administrative wrongdoing'. As we have seen, it is not just an excess of authority which makes an administrative act unlawful. An 'improper motive or a false step in procedure' have the same effect. Professor Wade said that 'unless the courts are able to develop doctrines of this kind, and to apply them energetically, they cannot impose limits on the administrative powers which parliament confers so freely'.

Reading these words, ministers may wonder whether the courts will allow them to govern. Surely they have been given the authority of parliament to exercise their discretion in the way they see fit?

Professor Wade has a devastating response:

> If merely because an act says that a minister may 'make such order as

he sees fit', or may do something 'if he is satisfied' as to some fact, the court were to allow him to do as he liked, a wide door would be opened to abuse of power and the rule of law would cease to operate. It is a cardinal axiom, accordingly, that every power has legal limits, however wide the language of the empowering act . . . Although lawyers appearing for government departments often argue that some act confers unfettered discretion, they are guilty of constitutional blasphemy. Unfettered discretion cannot exist where the rule of law reigns.[62]

The judges have frequently shown that they are not prepared to allow ministers unfettered discretion. They find ever-more ingenious ways of getting round the unambiguous words of a statute. The individual citizen may have reason to be grateful. At the same time, the nation as a whole may wonder whether the judiciary is running out of control.

Parliament must have intended . . .

As we have seen, the courts interpret acts of parliament as only authorising actions that have some particular purpose – the purpose they assert parliament 'must have intended'. Usually it is impossible for anyone to show that the judges' interpretation was wrong. Occasionally, though, parliament can tell the courts just what it really did intend. The results may not be entirely pleasing to the judiciary.

In the summer of 1996 the courts had to consider two asylum cases. The first concerned a young woman who had escaped from Zaire and arrived in Britain. She was taken straight to an immigration centre, where she claimed asylum. Until February 1996, she would then have been able to claim certain social security benefits. As a result of the chillingly titled Social Security (Persons from Abroad) Miscellaneous Amendment Regulations 1996, certain types of asylum-seekers lost the right to claim income support. They included people who failed to claim asylum immediately on arrival in the United Kingdom and people who were appealing against the refusal of asylum – a substantial proportion of asylum-seekers.

The Zairean woman, known only as *B*, argued that the Social Security Secretary Peter Lilley had acted beyond his powers (in Latin, *ultra vires*) in making the new regulations. She said they were therefore unlawful. That was because they left asylum-seekers with what Lord Justice Simon Brown was to describe as 'a bleak choice': whether to remain in the United Kingdom destitute and homeless until their claims were finally decided or whether to abandon their claims and return to face the very persecution from which they had fled.

Supported by the Joint Council for the Welfare of Immigrants, B's lawyers argued that Mr Lilley's power to make social security regulations, widely drawn though it admittedly was, could not have been intended to interfere with a person's fundamental human rights or that person's right to claim asylum under the Asylum Act of 1993.

By a majority, the Court of Appeal agreed.[63] Two appeal judges denounced the regulations in exceptionally strong terms. Lord Justice Simon Brown said they rendered the rights of asylum-seekers 'nugatory':

> Either that, or the regulations necessarily contemplate for some a life so destitute that to my mind no civilised nation can tolerate it. So basic are the human rights here at issue that it cannot be necessary to resort to the European Convention of Human Rights to take note of their violation . . . I would hold it unlawful to alter the benefit regime so drastically as must inevitably not merely prejudice, but on occasion defeat, the statutory right of asylum-seekers to claim refugee status . . .
>
> For the purposes of this appeal . . . it suffices to say that I for my part regard the regulations now in force as so uncompromisingly draconian in effect that they must indeed be held *ultra vires* . . . Parliament cannot have intended a significant number of genuine asylum-seekers to be impaled on the horns of so intolerable a dilemma: the need either to abandon their claims to refugee status or alternatively to maintain them as best they can but in a state of utter destitution. Primary legislation alone could, in my judgment, achieve that sorry state of affairs.

Lord Justice Simon Brown was supported by Lord Justice Waite. For him, the 'stark question' that had to be answered was whether 'regulations which deprive a very large number of asylum-seekers of the basic means of sustaining life itself have the effect of rendering their ostensible statutory right to a proper consideration of their claims in this country valueless in practice by making it not merely difficult but totally impossible for them to remain here to pursue those claims'. In his view that was exactly what the regulations did.

Was it right for Lord Justice Simon Brown to have used such strong words when giving judgment? Shortly afterwards, the Lord Chancellor said that in past cases the law lords had acknowledged the importance and the sensitivity of the 'interface between the legislature and the judiciary'. Lord Mackay said it was wise for both judges and legislators to approach this interface with caution, 'and to be careful and moderate in their language when they do so'.[64] On the other hand, if Lord Justice Simon Brown had not spoken in such forthright terms, it would have been difficult for him to justify his conclusion that the Secretary of State had exceeded his powers.

It is worth looking again at the judge's remarks. He said 'parliament cannot have intended' asylum-seekers to choose between refugee status and destitution. Ministers disagreed: they said their policies had been endorsed by healthy majorities in both houses of parliament. Mr Lilley then created a rare and valuable opportunity for all students of judicial review. He decided he would ask parliament to reverse the Court of Appeal's ruling by passing new primary legislation. That way, we could find out exactly what parliament wanted to happen – and what it presumably had intended a few months earlier.

Meanwhile, the same three judges had delivered another powerful judgment on asylum law. This time, the question for the court was whether what Lord Justice Simon Brown called the 'utter poverty and resourcelessness affecting certain asylum-seekers' as a result of Mr Lilley's social security regulations was capable of bringing them within the categories of specially vulnerable people entitled to priority housing. All three judges decided it was.[65] True to form, Lord Justice Neill said the task was merely 'applying the ordinary principles of statutory interpretation'. So, in effect, did Lord Justice Simon Brown, although his use of the highly-charged phrase quoted above creates a different impression.

Within hours, that decision was attacked by the chairman of the House of Commons Select Committee on Home Affairs. Sir Ivan Lawrence QC MP said it was a 'great pity that some members of the judiciary go out of their way to show how out of touch they are with the British people's feelings'. He said they could 'quite easily remedy the situation by not making political statements and by doing something to contain the burgeoning power of judicial review'.[66]

Mr Lilley went ahead with his plans to overturn the first asylum decision but parliament proved a little less accommodating than the minister had supposed. The House of Lords carried an opposition amendment to the Asylum and Immigration Bill allowing asylum-seekers three days to claim refugee status. That would have been enough to allow *B* the income support she needed. The Lords' amendment was reversed by a majority of twenty-one when the bill returned to the House of Commons.[67] The House of Lords tried again: they passed a fresh amendment which would once more have allowed asylum-seekers three days' grace. That too was rejected by the House of Commons, this time by a majority of fourteen votes.[68] The Asylum and Immigration Act 1996 passed into law unscathed.

It follows from these votes that if Lord Justice Simon Brown had been able to ask parliament whether it intended a significant number of genuine asylum-seekers to be impaled on the horns of what he called 'so intolerable a dilemma', the answer would have been 'yes'. MPs voted twice to do just that; peers, albeit reluctantly, then accepted the view of the democratically elected chamber.

It might have been thought the judges would have found it a little harder to use the 'parliament must have intended' fig leaf in the future. Far from it. Within a few months, they were at it again.

This time asylum-seekers' lawyers had spotted a handy provision in the National Assistance Act of 1948. Broadly speaking, the act obliges local councils to provide temporary accommodation for people in need of care and attention. That provision was still in force, unaffected by the 1996 legislation.

Could it be used by destitute asylum-seekers to obtain accommodation from local authorities? Yes, said Mr Justice Collins in the High Court.[69] Surely parliament had made it clear less than three months earlier that refugees who failed to claim asylum immediately on arrival in the United Kingdom should not get housing or social security benefits? No, said the judge. Michael Beloff QC, representing the three London boroughs who would have to pick up the bill, argued that parliament had clearly intended to deprive asylum-seekers of access to public assistance of any sort: parliament had decided that truly draconian measures were needed to deal with the increasing problem of bogus applicants.

Not so, said Mr Justice Collins. If that was what parliament meant, it could have said so in clear terms. In the absence of any reference to the National Assistance Act in the 1996 legislation, an inference could be drawn that parliament intended it to be available for asylum-seekers to use.

Mr Justice Collins concluded that the 1948 act did require local councils to provide help for asylum-seekers. He explained that he did not regard this conclusion as in any way frustrating the will of parliament in passing the 1996 legislation:

I find it impossible to believe that parliament intended that an asylum seeker, who was lawfully here and who could not lawfully be removed from the country, should be left destitute, starving and at risk of grave illness and even death because he could find no one to provide him with the bare necessities of life.

Clearly parliament intended that, unless they applied on entry, asylum-seekers should find it very difficult to exist in this country. No doubt, it was hoped that the bogus would thereby be deterred from coming or forced to return whence they came. But if an entrant faced the dilemma and decided that he had to stay, because to return would court persecution, I am sure that parliament would not have intended that he must nonetheless be left to starve.

It is after all likely that genuine claimants will stay here since they have real fears of persecution if they return. But if parliament really did intend that in no circumstances should any assistance (other than hospital care) be available to those asylum-seekers, it must say so in [clear] terms. If it did, it would almost certainly put itself in breach of the European Convention on Human Rights and of the Geneva Convention [on refugees] and that is another reason why I find it unlikely that the safety net has been removed.

This was a brave and decent judgment. It demonstrated humanity and compassion. For all that, it was deeply disingenuous. *Of course* parliament had intended asylum-seekers to starve if they had the temerity to remain here. That was the whole point of the Social Security (Persons from Abroad) Miscellaneous Amendment Regulations 1996. *Of course* parliament had intended asylum-seekers to lose housing and social security benefits. That was the whole point of amending the Asylum and Immigration Act 1996.[70] Parliament had made its intentions perfectly plain. It may not have used the clear words Mr Justice Collins demanded to see; he was therefore fully entitled to reach the conclusion he did. Nevertheless, he knew well enough what parliament had in mind. In the last paragraph quoted above, he virtually admitted it. He can hardly have been surprised to find the Home Office was 'disappointed' with his judgment. The government – and the local authorities which had to pay for accommodation – were equally disappointed to find Mr Justice Collins' judgment upheld on appeal in February 1997 in a court headed by Lord Woolf.

Dabbling in politics?

It is not only the politicians who think judges sometimes dabble in politics. Judges themselves think they do. In one recent case, a judge accused his colleagues of 'an unwarrantable intrusion . . . into the political field and a usurpation of the function of parliament'.[71] If the judges cannot agree among themselves on where to draw the line, the politicians may be forgiven for thinking the judges are moving it about to suit themselves.

Compensating victims

The remarks just quoted were made in a case of some importance. In 1964, the government set up a scheme to compensate the victims of violent crime. Although parliament agreed to fund the Criminal Injuries Compensation Scheme, it was not set up under any statutory authority; instead, *ex gratia* (or voluntary) payments were made under prerogative powers. The scheme rumbled along happily enough for nearly a quarter of a century. Eventually, in 1988, parliament passed legislation to put the informal compensation scheme on to a statutory basis. However, the legislation did not all come into effect on the day it was passed by parliament. Like many statutes, the Criminal Justice Act 1988 provided that it should 'come into force on such day as the Secretary of State may by order . . . appoint'. The minister was allowed to bring different parts of the act into force at different times.

The Criminal Injuries Compensation Board, which administered the scheme, was not really ready for the new arrangements: it hoped to shift its backlog first. At its request, nothing was done to bring the statutory scheme into effect for several years.

Along came Michael Howard. Faced with the rapidly rising cost of paying compensation, he decided to introduce a new scheme. Payments would be made on a 'tariff' basis – £1,000 for a sprained ankle, for example, and a maximum of £250,000 for paralysis in all four limbs. There would no longer be any additional compensation for loss of earnings or medical care, which had pushed some individual claims above £1 million.

The new scheme was also going to be non-statutory, at least to begin with. What about the recent legislation? Mr Howard simply announced that 'the provisions in the 1988 act will not now be implemented'.[72]

Could he do that? Eleven trade unions thought not. Their members had benefited under the old scheme; they would be worse off if the government's changes went through. They sought judicial review. The Fire Brigades Union was the first on the list, and so the case is known by that union's name.[73]

The unions' argument[74] was plain enough. The Home Secretary was under a statutory duty to bring the provisions in the 1988 act into force. If he had a good reason for delaying implementation it was within his discretion to do so, but he could not frustrate the will of parliament by saying that the statutory scheme would never be brought into effect.

That argument was dismissed by two judges in the High Court. The unions tried again in the Court of Appeal: this time they won on the main issue by a majority of two to one. The Home Secretary appealed to the House of Lords and lost by three votes to two.

Speaking for the majority in the House of Lords, Lord Browne-Wilkinson accepted the Home Secretary was not under any duty to bring the provision into effect at any particular time. Yet, in his view, the minister did not have a discretion to decide *whether* the provision should come into force. To suppose that the executive could decide at will whether or not to make parliamentary provisions a part of the law was, he thought, constitutionally dangerous: it flew in the face of common sense. For Michael Howard to say, as he had, that the provision would *never* be brought into force was therefore unlawful. 'It would be very surprising,' said Lord Browne-Wilkinson, 'if, at the present day, prerogative powers could be validly exercised by the executive so as to frustrate the will of parliament expressed in a statute.'

Lord Lloyd agreed that the statute conferred 'a power to say when, but not whether'. Lord Nicholls also agreed: Mr Howard had 'disabled himself from discharging his statutory duty in the way parliament had intended'.

The remaining two law lords profoundly disagreed. Lord Keith, at that time the senior law lord, said parliament had never intended the courts to decide whether the provision should be brought into force. Such a decision was 'of a political and administrative character'; it was quite unsuitable for review by a court of law. Any failure by the Home Secretary to do so could be called into question only in parliament: interference by a court would be 'a most improper intrusion' into parliamentary affairs.

Lord Keith added that because the Home Secretary did not owe the public any duty to bring the provision into force he could not be in breach of his duty to the public if he announced he would not be

doing so. He concluded: 'I am clearly of opinion that the [unions']
case fails on a proper application of the rules of statutory construction
and of the principles which govern the process of judicial review. To
grant the [unions] the relief which they seek, or any part of it, would
represent an unwarrantable intrusion by the court into the political
field and a usurpation of the function of parliament.'

Lord Mustill agreed. 'If there is no duty to bring the relevant
provisions into force,' he said, 'there can be no breach of duty
simply by announcing in advance that the non-existent duty will
not be performed.' He then delivered a profound warning. In the
absence of a written constitution much sensitivity was required of
the parliamentarian, administrator and judge if the delicate balance
of unwritten rules evolved over the years was not to be disturbed.
In a clear reference to what the unions had claimed, he said that
'some of the arguments addressed would have the court push to
the very boundaries of the distinction between court and parliament
established in, and recognised ever since, the Bill of Rights 1688.[75]
Three hundred years have passed since then, and the political and
social landscape has changed beyond recognition. But,' said Lord
Mustill, 'the boundaries remain; they are of crucial significance to
our private and public lives; and the courts should . . . make sure
that they are not overstepped.'[76]

For all that, Lord Keith and Lord Mustill were in the minority and
so it was back to the old tariff-based scheme. Not for long, though.
The government introduced new legislation a month later.[77] Major
concessions were made to buy off critics in parliament,[78] but in the
end the government got most of what it wanted. Governments
usually do.

Child B

In the case of 'Child B' a judge was again accused of adjudicating
on the merits instead of the law.[79] Jaymee Bowen was a ten-year-old
girl suffering from leukaemia whose father wanted Cambridge Health
Authority to pay for what would have been her third course of
chemotherapy. The health authority said that, faced with all the
other demands on their resources, they could not afford to fund
expensive treatment that would ultimately be futile. In March 1995,
the girl's father asked the High Court to overturn the authority's
decision. Mr Justice Laws appeared deeply moved by the little girl's
plight and ordered the authority to think again.

Within a few hours the health authority went to the Court of Appeal, which rapidly overturned the judge's ruling. While not directing his remarks directly at anyone in particular, the then Master of the Rolls, Sir Thomas Bingham, seemed highly critical of the approach Mr Justice Laws had taken. Sir Thomas stressed that – 'contrary to what is sometimes believed' – the courts were 'not arbiters as to the merits in cases of this kind'. He added: 'we have one function only, which is to rule on the lawfulness of decisions. That is a function to which we should strictly confine ourselves.'[80] The Master of the Rolls gave no indication of whether he thought Mr Justice Laws had strayed outside that function.

The Pergau Dam decision

The *Pergau Dam* case was not one where the judges disagreed. However, it shows how the courts are prepared to come close to making decisions which may be regarded as political.

The World Development Movement is a non-partisan pressure group that campaigns to improve the quantity and quality of British aid to foreign countries. It seeks to ensure that Britain's aid budget is used to best advantage for the relief of poverty and for development work in needy countries.

An applicant for judicial review must show he has sufficient 'standing' (in Latin, *locus standi*) to bring an application. The rule is designed to exclude busybodies. Under what Lord Justice Rose described as 'an increasingly liberal approach to standing on the part of the courts during the last twelve years'[81] the World Development Movement was allowed to bring an application for judicial review even though none of its members had a direct personal involvement in the decision they were challenging. Commenting later, Mr Justice Sedley said that in opening their doors wider to applicants who had nothing personally to gain, the courts were moving towards 'a principled system of invigilation of the legality of government action'.[82]

The action in this case was a decision by the Foreign Secretary, Douglas Hurd, to give Malaysia £234 million in overseas aid so it could build a hydro-electric power station on the Pergau river. Some of the money was to come out of a fund provided under the Overseas Development and Co-operation Act 1980, which allows assistance to be provided 'for the purpose of promoting the development or maintaining the economy of a country or territory outside the United Kingdom'.

The court accepted that development had to be economically sound to fall within the definition laid down by parliament. However, the World Development Movement argued that the Pergau Dam project was not a sound development: there were cheaper ways of producing electricity in Malaysia. The court agreed. Although the government had to consider a number of wider political issues, the Foreign Secretary could not be allowed to exceed the powers given to him by parliament. Since Mr Hurd had done so, he was found to have acted unlawfully and his decision was quashed.

Speaking later, Mr Justice Sedley revealed that ministers had not consulted the government's own lawyers before deciding to give Malaysia the money. 'In an earlier period it is almost certain that the issue . . . would not have reached the courts,' he said; 'if its legality had been thought doubtful it would have been modified or dropped.'[83]

The Bulger case

As Sir William Wade said, 'unfettered discretion cannot exist where the rule of law reigns'. A good example of that principle in action could be seen in the Bulger case.[84] Jon Venables and Robert Thompson were both aged ten-and-a-half when they murdered two-year-old James Bulger in 1993. It was a truly horrific crime, 'an act of unparalleled evil and barbarity' as the trial judge called it. The toddler was abducted from a Merseyside shopping centre and, as the judge said, 'battered to death without mercy'.

Once the boys had been convicted of murder Mr Justice Morland had no choice but to sentence them to detention during Her Majesty's pleasure. In accordance with normal practice, he was then asked to give the Home Secretary his private view on 'the actual length of detention necessary to meet the requirements of retribution and general deterrence for the offence'. Mr Justice Morland said it should be eight years. The Lord Chief Justice was then asked for his view. He said 'the minimum period for punishment and deterrence should be ten years'. The Home Secretary thought they were both wrong. Michael Howard said the period the boys ought to serve 'to meet the requirements of retribution and deterrence' should be fifteen years. As Lord Woolf was to say later, this involved the Home Secretary 'publicly being in significant disagreement with the judiciary which could only tend to undermine the public confidence in the criminal justice system'.[85] Not for the first time, one might add.

The two judges and the Home Secretary were dealing with what is generally known as the *tariff* – the penal element of the sentence. This is the minimum period of punishment an offender can expect to serve: he may be detained longer, perhaps much longer, if he is still a danger to the public. In a case such as this, the Parole Board begins a review three years before the tariff is due to expire. The board then comes to a view on whether it is safe to release the prisoner and the Home Secretary decides whether he should be allowed out of prison on licence.

Venables and Thompson sought judicial review of the Home Secretary's decision to set a tariff in their case. Adults, they said, were given tariffs because they were sentenced to life imprisonment for murder. The sentence of detention during Her Majesty's pleasure, they argued, was different: it was unlawful to set a tariff in the case of a child.

High Court

The first application for judicial review was made to the High Court in April 1996.[86] Two of the brightest and youngest QCs in the country appeared, both specialists in prisoners' rights: David Pannick for the Home Secretary and Edward Fitzgerald for Venables. David Pannick argued that detention during Her Majesty's pleasure was just like a life sentence for an adult murderer: parliament had given the Home Secretary a broad discretion in deciding how to treat young murderers and it was well within the minister's powers to conclude that punishment was an appropriate policy. Moreover, the Home Secretary was not bound to follow the minimum periods set by the judges.

For Venables, Edward Fitzgerald argued that children were different from adults in the eyes of the law and the sentence of detention during Her Majesty's pleasure was designed to protect society while reforming and rehabilitating the offender. The boys' lawyers said that even if it was right to set a punishment period the Home Secretary should not have increased the tariff; he should not have taken account of public opinion as expressed by 21,000 readers of the *Sun* who sent in coupons from the paper; and he should not have acted without psychiatric or social-inquiry reports.

Giving judgment in May 1996,[87] Lord Justice Pill and Mr Justice

Newman concluded that Michael Howard had acted unlawfully; as a result, they set aside his decision. The judges said the Home Secretary could not treat children detained during Her Majesty's pleasure in the same way as adults sentenced to life imprisonment for murder. They explained that a tariff was acceptable in a murder case because 'the true and judicially imposed tariff is life' and the Home Secretary was entitled to grant remission by setting a lower tariff. As there was no judicially imposed tariff involved in detention during Her Majesty's pleasure, there was no period to shorten. There was a distinction between detention and imprisonment.

The judges added the Home Secretary had every right to form an initial and provisional view of the length of detention required by punishment and deterrence. What he could not do was to fix a fifteen-year tariff for a child of ten or eleven, as he could for an adult. It was the minister's duty to keep the length of detention under regular review as the child grew older.

This was a powerful judgment. Even more striking was the reaction of the Home Secretary. Michael Howard was clearly furious at the ruling, which he said flew in the face of judicial practice and precedent. 'Let us not forget that this was an appalling crime which deeply shocked the nation,' he said. 'This novel decision is quite remarkable. The power I exercised was given to me by parliament. It has been exercised four hundred times without challenge since 1983.' Mr Howard said that if parliament had wanted the power changed it could have used any of the six Criminal Justice Bills which had been before the legislature over the past ten years. Mr Howard concluded: 'This government believes in the rule of law and the supremacy of parliament. We intend to appeal and we shall, if necessary, legislate so that the will of parliament may prevail.'[88]

It is common enough for unsuccessful applicants to complain when they are refused judicial review. Nevertheless, ministers can be expected to show restraint when the courts give them guidance on the public performance of their duties. Michael Howard's remarks deserve some analysis.

Mr Howard said it was 'an appalling crime'. That fact is beyond dispute, but it could not justify unlawful behaviour by the Secretary of State.

Mr Howard said the power had been 'exercised four hundred times without challenge since 1983'. This was not the point. Although the policy had been introduced in 1983, it was not until ten years later that Mr Howard publicly announced that children detained during Her Majesty's pleasure would be treated in the same way as adults convicted of murder. That was in 1993, the year Venables and Thompson were convicted.

Mr Howard said parliament could have used any of the six Criminal Justice Bills of the past ten years to change the law. This is true in constitutional theory but not in practical politics. At no time during the passage of these bills was parliament asked to consider the sentence of detention during Her Majesty's pleasure. Unless some unexpected crisis forces an issue on to the public agenda, the chances of backbench pressure persuading governments to bring in unintended legislation are remote.

Mr Howard said the government 'believes in the rule of law'. If this phrase means anything at all, it must mean the government accepts that judges decide whether the minister has exercised his discretion properly in an individual case, not the minister himself.

Mr Howard said the government believes in 'the supremacy of parliament'. Again, this does not mean the supremacy of ministers.

Mr Howard said 'we shall, if necessary, legislate so that the will of parliament may prevail'. This is just a snub to the judges. As we have seen, they consider it their job to ensure that the will of parliament *does* prevail. What they did not believe is that Mr Howard followed it. It was also an attempt by Mr Howard to have his cake and eat it. What he was saying was that if he didn't get the answer he wanted from the courts, he would try to get it from parliament instead.

Court of Appeal

The Home Secretary went to the Court of Appeal and found his case being heard by the newly appointed Master of the Rolls, Lord Woolf, sitting with two Lords Justice of Appeal. David Pannick and Edward Fitzgerald took them through the arguments.

Judgments were delivered in July 1996.[89] In the hope that the public might understand the difference between a review and an appeal, Lord Woolf began with a reminder of what the High Court had decided earlier in the summer. He stressed that it had not found against the Home Secretary because it disagreed with the length of the tariff: 'it did so because it considered that as a result of the tariff being fixed at a period as long as fifteen years . . . the Home Secretary was preventing himself from exercising the discretion to release the applicants conferred on him by parliament as the law by statute required.'

106

Lord Woolf thought that detention during Her Majesty's pleasure was indeed a separate and different sentence from the mandatory sentence of life imprisonment for murder. In the former there was a discretion to extend the length of a sentence; in the latter there was a discretion to bring the sentence to an end.

He then set out the way in which Venables and Thompson had challenged the Home Secretary's decision. Conveniently, their application for judicial review can be seen as fitting into the three categories listed earlier in this chapter:

lawfulness: was the Home Secretary's policy in imposing a punishment tariff unlawful because it conflicted with his statutory discretion to release young offenders?

reasonableness: if the tariff policy was lawful then had it been applied too inflexibly so that it unlawfully fettered this discretion?

fairness: was irrelevant material (such as the public petitions) unfairly taken into account? Was information wrongly kept from the boys? Was information which should have been obtained not taken into account?

Answering these questions, Lord Woolf found that the policy of setting a tariff *was* lawful: punishment had a role to play, even for young offenders. But turning to application of this policy, it appeared 'totally unreasonable' to postpone the first review of a young offender's case for a period which under the Home Secretary's self-imposed rules could be as long as seventeen years. Even putting off a review of Venables and Thompson's case for twelve years – the effect of a fifteen-year tariff – was 'unacceptable'.

Moving on to deal with the question of fairness, Lord Woolf said it was clear that the Home Secretary had taken into account petitions from 250,000 members of the public as well as the coupons sent in by readers of the *Sun*, all of which had urged him to fix a higher tariff than the one set by the judiciary. Lord Woolf said he regarded this as a departure from the standards of fairness required of someone exercising a discretion of this kind. 'The petitions may or may not have been conducted fairly,' he said. 'We do not know . . . While the Home Secretary is not confined in his consideration of the tariff to the material which a court would regard as relevant, he should at least bear in mind when performing a role similar to that of the courts how the courts perform that role. A court would regard it as quite improper for this type of material to be put before it . . . Indeed to run a campaign designed to increase the punishment in a particular case could amount to an interference with the due administration of justice.'

Lord Woolf dismissed the Home Secretary's appeal and told him to reconsider the case. He went on to call for a fresh look at how cases such as this were dealt with in general. This might at first appear dangerously close to dabbling in politics, but the Master of the Rolls explained that parliament had created a flexible sentence of detention and 'by a series of policy decisions that flexibility has in relation to these cases all but disappeared . . . This does not accord with what parliament has laid down,' he said. 'Nor does it result in this case in a just result.'

Lord Justice Hobhouse and Lord Justice Morritt agreed with Lord Woolf that Mr Howard's appeal should be dismissed because of the way he had gone about reaching his decision. One judge was critical of the fact that Michael Howard appeared to have been influenced by a 'hopelessly unscientific poll from members of the public'. The other judge criticised Mr Howard for not getting hold of the papers and reports that a judge would have seen. Both judges agreed that he had reached his decision in a way that was procedurally unfair. In a classic statement of the requirements of public law, Lord Justice Hobhouse said: 'The Secretary of State must . . . adopt fair procedures, inform himself of and take into account the relevant circumstances, exclude what is irrelevant and, here, have regard to his full statutory discretion.'

Where the two judges disagreed with the Master of the Rolls (and the High Court) was on the meaning of the sentence being served by Venables and Thompson. In their view, detention during Her Majesty's pleasure *was* effectively the same as a life sentence. It provided for punishment: it was not 'solely preventative and reformatory'. On this point they found for the Home Secretary.

This time Mr Howard's reaction to the judgment – according to *The Times*, his twelfth defeat at the hands of the judiciary – was understandably more muted. 'We won on the substantial question on which we lost in the court below,' he said. 'We have lost on one other point, and we will appeal that to the House of Lords.'[90] Mr Howard was saying that the court had found he was right in his understanding of the sentence the boys were serving and wrong in the way he had gone about deciding how long they should serve.

If Mr Howard's response was restrained, that of *The Times* itself was not:

> The Home Secretary has acted as he has in the Bulger case, and provoked judicial displeasure, only because the judges themselves have failed. The erosion of public confidence in the justice system owes more to a series of over-lenient sentences than to any of Mr Howard's actions. He is right and the judges are wrong, and nowhere more so than the tragic Bulger case . . .
>
> Mr Justice Morland, the judge at the trial of the killers, Venables and Thompson, described their crime as an 'act of unparalleled evil and barbarity' . . . But Mr Justice Morland failed to match the stringency of his words with the severity of his sentence . . . Only when Mr Howard insisted on a tariff of fifteen years was natural justice seen to be done.[91]

Natural justice? Why is fifteen years more 'natural' than ten? Or eight? And why did *The Times* suppose the boys would have been let out after eight or ten years anyway? Surely the leader-writer realised they had been sentenced to an indefinite term of detention?

As the former Master of the Rolls, Lord Donaldson, had to explain to *The Times*, the Court of Appeal did not deal with the question of whether the tariff was too high or too low.[92] Nor did the appeal judges criticise the Home Secretary for taking account of public revulsion at the nature of the crime. 'What they criticised and criticised strongly was his taking account of organised attempts to influence his judgment.' Lord Donaldson said that to accept such action as a proper exercise of judicial power could not possibly improve confidence in the criminal-justice system. It would be a move towards substituting the rule of the mob.[93]

The prisons fiasco

It would be wrong to assume that Michael Howard *always* lost in the courts: sometimes the judges even came to his rescue. That was what happened as the result of a bizarre decision in August 1996 which trod the narrow line between farce and fiasco.

The Prison Service is run as an 'executive agency', supposedly at arm's length from the Home Office. During the early part of 1996 its officials had been studying a series of judicial review applications brought over the past fifteen years by prisoners serving concurrent (or overlapping) sentences. The courts had been asked to consider the effect of legislation which said that 'the length of any sentence of imprisonment' must be reduced by time the prisoner has spent in custody awaiting trial.[94] In effect, there was one question before the courts in each of these cases:

A defendant is arrested for burglary *A* and remanded in custody for six months. He is then released on bail. While he is on bail he commits burglary *B*. He is arrested and remanded in custody for a further six months. At his trial he is convicted of both burglaries and sentenced to one year's imprisonment on each, to run concurrently. He has spent a total of one year in custody awaiting trial. Should the defendant therefore be released immediately?

In each case the court's answer was 'no'. The court decided that such a defendant is entitled to the full credit of twelve months in respect of burglary *A*, but as he has served only six months on remand in respect of burglary *B* he still has six months to serve.

That approach meant interpreting 'any sentence of imprisonment' in the statute to refer to each individual sentence imposed by the court – not the total produced by several concurrent sentences. Otherwise, in the example just given, there would have been just one twelve-month sentence and the prisoner would have been let out immediately because he had already spent a year in custody.

As far as prisoners serving concurrent sentences were concerned, the position seemed clear. However, early in 1996 the Prison Service began thinking about how this interpretation of the statute should apply to inmates serving *consecutive* sentences (one after another). Under the existing arrangements, the sentences were added up and the prisoner had any time spent on remand deducted from the total. Therefore, if a defendant who had spent six months on remand was sentenced to two twelve-month sentences, to be served one after the other, he would end up serving eighteen months.[95]

As we have seen, the courts had said 'any sentence of imprisonment' must refer to an individual sentence, not the total. If so, then in the example above the defendant must surely have been entitled to six months' remand time taken off *each* sentence. In that case, he should serve only a year, not eighteen months.

The Prison Service spent the early part of 1996 thinking about this knotty problem. Eventually, they took advice from an in-house lawyer working for the Home Office. He advised the Prison Service that they were right to think prisoners serving consecutive sentences should have time spent on remand deducted from each of their sentences.

Oh dear, said the Prison Service. That means we have prisoners in custody who should have been released months ago. We had better let them out quickly: if we keep them any longer, they'll sue us. As a result, in the middle of August, the Director General of the Prison Service, Richard Tilt, sent new instructions to every prison. Governors were told to recalculate sentences for inmates serving consecutive sentences and release those who should no longer be in prison. Over just a few days, 541 bemused prisoners walked out of jail earlier than they had expected to leave. On average, they were released three months early, although two of them were released two-and-a-half years before their sentences were due to expire.

All this came as a complete surprise to the Home Secretary. At first, he thought there was nothing he could do about it. Then, as his 'prison works' slogan appeared to be crumbling into ruin, he realised desperate measures were needed. He called in David Pannick QC.

Mr Pannick took one look at the problem and decided that if the Home Office lawyer was saying all these prisoners had to be let out immediately he was talking nonsense. On the strength of this advice Mr Howard immediately suspended all further releases. He then invited any prisoner who was expecting early release on the Prison Service version of the law to challenge him in the courts.

An inmate from Doncaster obligingly agreed to lend his name to the enterprise and the case came quickly to court. For the Home Secretary, David Pannick argued that deducting remand time from each sentence would produce 'absurd' consequences:

> Two defendants are arrested and charged jointly with five burglaries. Prisoner *A* has absconded in the past and is therefore remanded in custody. Prisoner *B* has no previous convictions and gets bail. At their trial a year later, they are both convicted and sentenced to one year for each of the five burglaries, to be served consecutively. Prisoner *A* has a year deducted from each of his sentences and walks free. Prisoner *B* has to serve five years. He is overheard saying that next time he won't be asking for bail.[96]

Mr Pannick said this was such an absurd situation that the courts should not accept it unless they were compelled to do so by the plainest of statutory language. The judges agreed. Lord Justice Simon Brown was worried by the possibility that the courts were interpreting 'any sentence of imprisonment' to mean 'the total period' when dealing with consecutive cases and 'each individual sentence' when dealing with prisoners serving concurrent sentences. He accepted that the Prison Service view was 'powerful and logical . . . at first blush'. Nevertheless, it could not be allowed to stand; any inconsistency would have to be sorted out later by another court.

Michael Howard was no doubt grateful to the courts for getting him out of a hole. He appeared not to have doubted that the judges would behave properly, but such was the climate in which the courts were having to operate that Lord Justice Simon Brown felt the need to stress, at the outset of his judgment, that 'political considerations have not the least part to play in this case'. A few years previously, such a remark would have been considered superfluous.

Lord Justice Simon Brown's judgment led straight to an unfortunate sequel for Mr Howard. As he had expected, there was a challenge from prisoners serving concurrent or overlapping sentences.[97] Now that the courts had said 'any sentence of imprisonment' must refer to the total period in custody when dealing with consecutive sentences, surely it must mean the same when dealing with sentences served concurrently?

The judges, headed this time by Lord Bingham, had to agree. Until now, they said, courts had misunderstood the relevant statutes. Some prisoners had suffered injustice as a result. The prisoners who had brought their cases before the courts should be released early. Others would also be set free.

Again, there was no direct criticism of Michael Howard. Yet the court had an obvious message for the Home Secretary:

> The principle that a prisoner's release date should be beyond dispute, and that the provisions governing it should be easy to apply, is of great importance, for reasons both of fairness and good administration. It is not, on any showing, a test which the present provisions meet. They are not clear to the courts, or the legal profession, or prisoners or (it would seem) the prison authorities. They are certainly not simple. It appears that defendants are remaining in prison when the sentencing court did not intend that they should.

The judges called for a new act of parliament to make the law clear. They hoped this would be treated as a high priority. In fact, Mr Howard already had amending legislation before parliament.[98] How quickly it might become law would depend more on politics than on policies.

Political leanings

By 1997 the judges had spent the best part of eighteen years deciding whether to overturn the decisions of Conservative ministers. Would they do the same with a Labour government?

Lord Woolf was sure that a change of government in 1997 would make no difference to the courts' approach. He recalled the Labour governments of the 1960s and the 1970s when Lord Denning was presiding over the Court of Appeal. During the last Labour administration Harry Woolf was 'Treasury Devil', the independent barrister who appeared in court for the government in the most important judicial review cases. He remembered it as a period of confrontation: the courts took a very forceful line whenever Labour ministers tried to exceed their powers.[99]

That view was shared by Lord Bingham:

> What people forget is that when there was last a Labour government in power it was of course Labour ministers who were making decisions, being challenged in the courts and sometimes challenged successfully. Over the last seventeen years for obvious reasons all the decisions have been made by officials and ministers in this government. But that could change and it's not the product of political hostility in any way, it's simply that challenges are made to the lawfulness of decisions and conduct and occasionally those challenges succeed.[100]

Speaking the following month, Lord Nolan – the law lord heading the Committee on Standards in Public Life – said judges were less political than they had been in the past. 'In the first half of the century,' he said, 'there were certain instances of barrister-MPs being appointed by their Prime Minister straight to the Court of Appeal.' The convention that the Attorney General was entitled to appointment as Lord Chief Justice if a vacancy arose was not abolished until after the Second World War.[101]

Lord Bingham pointed out that in countries like the United States it would not be regarded as an abuse to pack the judicial bench with 'appointees of a certain political persuasion or known political views'. Yet since 1945 there had been virtually no evidence of any appointments not being made on the basis of perceived merit.[102]

'Even as late as the 1980s,' said Lord Nolan, 'the idea that the courts were staffed by "Tory judges" still gained some currency.' He referred to an opinion poll conducted at the height of the miners' strike of 1984–5 which suggested that, since June 1969, the number of people who thought the judges were influenced by the government in power had risen from 19 per cent to 43 per cent, while those who thought the judges were independent had dropped from 67 per cent to 46 per cent.[103] However, said Lord Nolan, 'that strike, and the earlier history of the Industrial Relations Court, had placed the judges, through no fault of their own, in the unenviable position of enforcing deeply unpopular laws upon a number of trade unions and their members. The judges were thus portrayed, unfairly, as allies of the Conservative government. Those days seem a long way away now.'

Lord Nolan said the relative absence of industrial strife had taken the judges out of the firing line. There was no serious suggestion of party-political bias on the part of any of them, nor should there be. 'The legal profession knows its judges pretty well, and I can think of no appointment to the bench which has been attributed to political motives.'[104]

Despite all the difficulties Conservative ministers had with judicial review, no Labour politician could expect to find the English judiciary a soft touch. By 1997, the most that could be said was that the judges were more balanced, or neutral, in their political views than they had ever been before. As we shall see in Chapter 4, that did not deter them from creating new law.

4

Laying Down the Law

The deep and . . . underlying truth seems to be that judges, however subconsciously, desire to retain or obtain for the judiciary problems more fit for executive decisions . . . In recent years . . . it has been difficult for the State to obtain justice from the judges of the High Court.
Sir Claud Schuster, Permanent Secretary to the Lord Chancellor (1929)[1]

Given the will [to intervene], the judiciary has picked up the ball and run with it regardless of whether or not written rules gave it the right to do so. It no doubt tells us something about Britain and its pragmatism that this is how both rugby football and modern judicial review originated.
Mr Justice Sedley, High Court Judge (1994)[2]

The view from on high

Three days before it was confirmed that Lord Bingham of Cornhill was to be appointed Lord Chief Justice of England, he delivered a major speech on the subject of personal privacy.[3] He pointed out that although countries like France and Germany have laws to protect people's privacy, there was no such right in England. In his view, there should be one. Lord Bingham said the new law he was proposing 'must be narrowly drawn, to give full effect to the right of free speech and the public's right to know. It should strike only at significant infringements, such as would cause substantial distress to an ordinary phlegmatic person.'

During his lecture Lord Bingham considered – and dismissed – all the arguments against legislating for a right of privacy. The last of these was that the matter was best left to the courts, which could work out appropriate safeguards on a case-by-case basis. Unfortunately, he believed, the prospects for creative law-making were discouraging.

That was evident from a case brought in 1990 on behalf of the television actor Gorden Kaye,[4] who had been photographed by a journalist while in hospital, heavily sedated and recovering from

115

severe head injuries. The Court of Appeal felt there were no grounds for preventing a newspaper from publishing these pictures. Three judges, of whom Lord Bingham was one, regretted that there was little they could do to protect Mr Kaye's privacy.

That decision had been attacked at the time by a number of commentators, including Lord Lester QC. He noted that the American courts had developed a right of privacy on a case-by-case basis, deriving the principles from a number of nineteenth-century English decisions – as indeed Lord Bingham had recognised. Lord Lester believed the Court of Appeal could have followed their lead in the Gorden Kaye application:

> It could have drawn on Lord Keith's observations in the *Spycatcher* case,[5] suggesting the existence of a common law right of privacy. It could also have referred to the guarantee of a right of privacy in article 8 of the European Convention on Human Rights as a source of accepted moral standards in an area where the common law is developing and where the courts should endeavour, if possible, to declare the common law to accord with convention rights and freedoms. The Court of Appeal could have developed a right of privacy using the line of cases on the right of confidentiality . . . and by extending the cases on private nuisance beyond narrow proprietary interests.[6]

Apparently stung by this criticism, Lord Bingham used his 1996 lecture to discuss ways in which the judges could extend the existing law to help those whose privacy was threatened. 'If the judges are, on a case-by-case basis, to extend the protection available under the existing law,' he said, 'it seems clear that this will be done not by introducing a law of privacy so called but by enlarging the boundaries of existing causes of action' (in other words, extending existing rights to sue). He pointed out that some judges had already started down that road: Mr Justice Laws (of whom we shall hear more later in this chapter) had said that publishing an unauthorised telephoto picture of someone 'engaged in some private act' would be just as much a breach of confidence as publishing a stolen diary.[7]

This, said Lord Bingham, was certainly one way forward. It might be the best way, he thought. He had 'some unease about appropriating causes of action to purposes quite alien to their original object, but this is how the law has developed in other fields and it does have the advantage that rules are forged in the furnace of everyday experience'.

Lord Bingham's preference was for 'legislation, which would mean that the rules which the courts applied would carry the imprimatur of democratic approval'. But if, for whatever reason, legislation was not forthcoming, he thought 'it almost inevitable that cases will arise in the courts in which the need to give relief is obvious and pressing; and when such cases do arise, I do not think the courts will be found wanting'.

Did this mean the judges were threatening to step in where parliament had feared to tread? As we shall see, some people thought so.

Their fears were hardly allayed when another leading judge happened to deliver a remarkably similar lecture just a day later.[8] Lord Hoffmann, a reforming law lord, noted that 'the right of privacy does not command majority support'. Even so, that did not mean it should not be protected. 'On the contrary,' he said, 'the individual's right to dignity and respect is essential to a civilised community.'

Then Lord Hoffmann also seemed to argue in favour of judicial law-making: 'If the English judges were to decide that the lack of a right to privacy represented a gap in the law, there are ample materials to hand to enable such a right to be constructed . . . I do not think that one can expect such a right to be created by a majority decision in parliament. But that makes it all the more important that it should be recognised at common law.'

This judicial activism clearly worried Lord Irvine of Lairg QC. Speaking shortly afterwards from the opposition front bench in the House of Lords, Labour's Lord Chancellor-in-waiting drew attention to 'recent extra-judicial statements that if parliament does not legislate a law of privacy then the judges will invent – or perhaps I should say develop – one'. He thought 'statements that judges can invent or make a law protecting privacy, where there is no consensus for it, sound to ordinary people uncomfortably like a judicial threat to legislate'. In his view, it was for parliament to decide whether self-regulation of the press should be replaced by a law of privacy:

> The general understanding of English law is that it does not recognise a generalised right to privacy. Should the judges make one? Only, I would say, if there were a clear community consensus that way. If there is no such consensus – and I am sure there is none – then I say that if the judges invented a law of privacy they would seem to be taking sides. The result would be to imperil their major asset: their reputation for impartiality . . . I say that the judges should think hard

117

before they don the mantle of moral leadership through their judgments according to law.[9]

This drew an immediate response from the new Master of the Rolls. Lord Woolf told the House of Lords that it was a desirable and constructive practice for judges to give lectures. Nevertheless, it was important that what they said should not be taken out of context. He then continued with a devastating put-down: 'If my noble friend Lord Irvine of Lairg will forgive me in this respect, I would say that he was in error in focusing upon one or two lectures and extracting from those lectures a sentence here or there which did not give a true representation of the content of the lecture as a whole.'

Lord Irvine understood this to be a reference to a lecture he gave in 1995 criticising a lecture Lord Woolf had given in 1994;[10] he denied having quoted Lord Woolf out of context.[11] In fact, Lord Woolf had in mind the two lectures given a few days earlier by Lord Bingham and Lord Hoffmann. Lord Woolf did not consider his fellow judges were threatening to thwart or supplant parliament. This interpretation was shared by the Lord Chancellor: Lord Mackay said he did not regard Lord Bingham's remarks as an indication that judges would create legislation. 'As I understand it,' said Lord Mackay, 'he says that if a particular case arises in which a remedy is obviously required as a pressing matter the courts will not be found wanting in granting it.'[12]

What are we to make of Lord Irvine's criticism of Lord Bingham? The leading barrister David Pannick QC would soon be eligible for a judicial appointment: he had no fears about attacking the man who might have to decide when Mr Pannick should join the High Court bench. 'To criticise judges for making a "threat to legislate" or for showing "moral leadership" when deciding hard cases,' David Pannick said, 'is fundamentally to misunderstand the nature of the judicial function . . . When judges are asked to decide a novel question about the right of the individual plaintiff to personal privacy, they are entitled to draw on principles to be found in the law of trespass, breach of confidence and the European Convention on Human Rights. Such reasoning by analogy, with principles being derived from existing case law, is as old as the common law itself.'[13]

Asked whether he was threatening to supplant the right of the executive to put proposals to parliament, Lord Bingham himself stressed that he had given 'one hundred per cent weight to the democratic process'; he had said he thought the most effective way of dealing with the matter 'would be by legislation which would carry the imprimatur of democratic approval. But I then said that if there were no legislation I thought the probability was that very hard cases would arise in which the court would feel that protection should be given to a plaintiff. That is, I think, what would happen.'[14]

Nevertheless, as every lawyer knows, once the courts start providing remedies in cases where none has previously been granted they are indeed making law. Each change may be marginal, but over time a series of marginal developments can result in a complete reversal of the status quo. That seemed to be what Lord Bingham had in mind. As he made clear subsequently, he was not saying the judges should set out to change the law overnight. However, on one reading of his lecture he did seem to be saying that the judges could – and should – develop the law over a period of time *with a particular policy objective in mind*.

Asked specifically[15] whether this was the case, Lord Bingham made no attempt to deny it:

> I expressed the view that there is a right to a measure of privacy. It would be surprising if there were not. After all, we have signed up to the International Covenant on Civil and Political Rights[16] which recognises a right of privacy, and we have also signed up to the European Convention on Human Rights which also does that.[17] Both of those instruments and the law at large also recognise, as a right of the utmost importance, a right of free expression. The difficult question is: where does free expression end and a right to privacy begin? That is bound to be a very difficult borderline, but what I was suggesting was that the law should recognise both those rights and not just one of them.

It is one thing to say what the law should be. It is quite another thing to say that the courts will make it so. As we have seen from Lord Irvine's comments, that sort of thing still makes parliamentarians anxious. Surely judicial law-making should come as no surprise to them?

Making the law

Judges have been making new law for at least 700 years. For most of that time, they tried to hide this uncomfortable fact from the public: they called judge-made law the common law, as if to suggest it has always been with us, permanent and unchanged.

In order to disguise the reality of the law-making process, legal writers of the eighteenth and nineteenth centuries maintained that the common law consisted of ancient customs and usages that had been made known by the judges. According to this analysis, the judges' job was to expound, declare and publish the law; their decisions were not sources of law but simply evidence of what the law had always been. But, as the Lord Chancellor Lord Mackay explained in 1996, 'this theory notably fails to explain the fact that the rules of equity are known to have been judge-made, and indeed that the names of the Lord Chancellors responsible are known in many cases. Practically the whole framework of the modern law of tort and contract was constructed by the judges in a conscious policy of moulding and adapting the principles of the common law in response to the changing usages of society.'[18]

Apart from creating the modern law of negligence, the judges also developed most of our administrative law: the principles of judicial review we explored in Chapter 3. In the graphic words of Mr Justice Sedley, 'law spends its life stretched on the rack between certainty and adaptability, sometimes groaning audibly but mostly maintaining the stoical appearance of steady uniformity which public confidence demands.'[19] Sir Stephen Sedley, one of the most original thinkers to be appointed to the High Court bench in recent years, went on to give some stark reminders of the way courts reflect the views of society at any given time:

> How and why is it that the same American constitution in 1896 legitimated racial segregation in public services[20] and then in 1954 forbade it?[21] How does it come about that not dissimilar abortion laws have in recent years been struck down by Canada's Supreme Court as too restrictive[22] and by Germany's Constitutional Court as too permissive?[23] On our own patch, how did it come to be self-evident to the Court of Appeal in 1925 that it was perfectly all right for an education authority to sack married women teachers on the ground that their duties lay at home[24] or, in 1948, that it was perfectly all right for Wednesbury Corporation to use its cinema licensing powers to stop young people going to the pictures on Sundays?[25]

As Mr Justice Sedley explained, the courts do not ignore the decisions established in earlier cases: they simply adapt a 'centuries-long culture of reasoning and principle' to meet the needs of a new generation.

The great Scottish jurist Lord Reid said in a much-quoted lecture:

There was a time when it was thought almost indecent to suggest that judges made law – they only declare it. Those with a taste for fairy tales seem to have thought that in some Aladdin's cave there is hidden the common law in all its splendour and on a judge's appointment there descends on him knowledge of the magic words 'open sesame'. Bad decisions are given when the judge muddles the password and the wrong door opens. But we do not believe in fairy tales any more.[26]

As Lord Reid explained, nobody now denies that the judges make law. What is difficult for them to decide is how far they should travel down the law-making road.

It is worth recalling that Lord Irvine thought the courts should not develop a new law of privacy – or, presumably, any other law – unless there was a 'clear community consensus' on the issue. The Lord Chancellor, Lord Mackay, also thought there should be clear limits on the courts' law making powers:

The primary function of law making rests with parliament, the supreme law making body. The government, the executive branch, must act within the law and the courts must apply and give effect to it. The role of the courts in developing the common law should not be underestimated; but that role is developing principle, not creating wholly new law. Statute is the supreme source of law, and in any conflict between the common law and the clearly expressed will of the legislature in an act of parliament, the act must prevail. But even here the function of the courts is by no means purely mechanical: they must construe and apply these acts and, in doing so, they may rely on historical common law principles of interpretation and application.

Lord Mackay drew attention to the first occasion on which the courts had effectively overturned an act of parliament. In the *Factortame* case, the law lords held in July 1990[27] that the Merchant Shipping Act 1988, which was passed to stop 'quota-hopping' by Spanish fishing vessels, was contrary to European law and therefore invalid. The English judges had sought advice from the European Court of Justice in Luxembourg; in reaching their decision, the law lords were simply applying the judgment they had received.

Lord Mackay rejected the suggestion that the European Court had applied law of a 'higher order which dilutes or reduces the sovereignty of parliament'. On the contrary, he said European Community law[28] had authority in the United Kingdom *because* of an act of parliament – the European Communities Act 1972:

The *Factortame* decision rests on the basis that the Merchant Shipping

Act had to be read in the context of the European Communities Act, which expressly provided that all other statutes should be construed and have effect subject to the provisions giving community law primacy in our legal system. That was enough, in the absence of a clear provision in the 1988 act overriding the 1972 act, to reverse the rule that, in a conflict between two acts of parliament, the later takes precedence. Accordingly the English court correctly proceeded on the basis that parliament did not intend to override community law in passing the Merchant Shipping Act.

Lord Mackay said it was open to parliament expressly to override the 1972 act and, if it did so, the courts would be bound to give effect to this, even though that might be a breach of obligations under the community treaties. That, said the Lord Chancellor, would be a problem for the government and parliament to deal with, rather than the courts.[29]

European law has led to a more subtle change in the way the English courts view legislation. Community treaties are drafted in more general terms than acts of parliament: as a result, our own judges have become more accustomed to dealing with points of principle rather than specific decisions. Francis Jacobs sits at the European Court of Justice as an Advocate General – an officer of the court who delivers a reasoned opinion which assists the judges when they decide the case. He thought the judges' experience in interpreting European law must have had some impact on the way they applied English law. 'English judges are saying that when they are interpreting a text now it's a fallacy to believe that there is simply a question of taking a text and mechanically applying it,' he said. 'The court has to look at the purpose of the provision and apply it in accordance with the purpose.'[30]

The former Master of the Rolls Lord Denning was well known as an early supporter of this 'purposive' approach to the law – the attempt to discover the purpose of an act of parliament, or at least what Lord Denning believed the purpose should have been. What then did he think a judge should do with a statute whose text did not appear to deal with the case before him? Writing in what was to become his much-parodied style, Lord Denning said the judge should ask himself the following question: 'If the makers of the act had themselves come across this ruck in the texture of it, how would they have straightened it out? He must then do as they would have done. A judge must not alter the material of which it is woven, but he can and should iron out the creases.'[31]

This homely metaphor offers little to help the judges. It assumes that that they can divine parliament's intention from the material they have in front of them. The reality is different. Filling a gap in the law is not just a matter of ironing out the creases: the judge must sometimes tailor a new garment to cover a litigant who arrives naked in the courtroom. That garment may be fashioned in traditional style, virtually indistinguishable from those worn by others. On the other hand, it may be entirely new, setting a trend to be copied or spurned according to the vagaries of fashion. Only the judges can decide.

The conflict between the creative, purposive approach and the more traditional, legalistic view can be seen in a case from 1950. Lord Denning found himself against Lord Simonds, who was soon to become Lord Chancellor in Churchill's post-war government. It was still a bleak time for judicial activism: as Mr Justice Sedley put it, 'the legal literalism of Lord Simonds, which has become a byword for narrow formalism, was no more than part of an entire mood of legal minimalism which left the Chancery Division with a shortage of work and put the Bar into a numerical decline that was not reversed until the late 1960s'.[32]

Giving judgment in the Court of Appeal, Lord Denning said:

We do not sit here to pull the language of parliament and ministers to pieces and make nonsense of it. That is an easy thing to do, and it is a thing to which lawyers are too often prone. We sit here to find out the intention of parliament and of ministers and carry it out, and we do this better by filling in the gaps and making sense of the enactment than by opening it up to destructive analysis.[33]

When the case reached the House of Lords Lord Simonds made his disapproval of Lord Denning's approach very clear. In the most scornful of tones, he insisted that 'it would not be right for this House to pass unnoticed the propositions which the learned Lord Justice lays down for the guidance of himself and, presumably, others'.

Turning to Lord Denning's assessment of the judicial role, Lord Simonds was equally dismissive: 'it is sufficient to say that the general proposition that it is the duty of the court to find out the intention of parliament – and not only of parliament but of ministers also – cannot by any means be supported. The duty of the court is to interpret the words that the legislature has used; those words may be ambiguous, but, even if they are, the power and duty of the court to travel outside them on a voyage of discovery are strictly limited.'

Lord Simonds reserved his greatest scorn for Lord Denning's policy of 'filling in the gaps': He said: 'It appears to me to be a naked usurpation of the legislative function under the thin disguise of interpretation. And it is the less justifiable when it is guesswork with what material the legislature would, if it had discovered the gap, have filled it in. If a gap is disclosed, the remedy lies in an amending act.'[34]

Analysing these approaches, Lord Lester of Herne Hill QC conceded that Lord Simonds was 'entirely right to be concerned to prevent the unelected independent judiciary from usurping the legislative function'. However, Lord Lester said it was 'no usurpation but a proper judicial function for judges to interpret legislation in accordance with its true purpose'.[35]

Who then is to say what the 'true purpose' of the legislation is? Since 1992, when the case of *Pepper v. Hart*[36] was decided, the courts have been able to resolve cases of ambiguity, obscurity or absurdity by looking up what the minister said in *Hansard* while the legislation was going through parliament. They may also refer to White Papers.[37] What should be done if there is no legislation on the subject? When should the courts intervene?

The law lords step in

The House of Lords, as the highest appellate court in the United Kingdom,[38] is often asked to change the law; sometimes it agrees.[39] The law lords will sometimes step in if they feel there is clear public agreement on how the law should develop. On other occasions they will act, with some reluctance, precisely because there is *no* consensus and therefore no prospect of parliament acting.[40] Either way, they are likely to be criticised for developing the law in a particular direction without the agreement of parliament and the public. Some cases will help illustrate the approach taken by our most senior judges to the dilemmas they face.

Marital rape

For more than 250 years the law allowed a man to rape his wife. Sir Matthew Hale's *History of the Pleas of the Crown*, published in 1736,[41] said: 'the husband cannot be guilty of a rape committed by himself upon his lawful wife, for by their mutual matrimonial consent and contract the wife hath given up herself in this kind unto her husband which she cannot retract.' This was regarded as an accurate statement of the law until after the Second World War. Gradually, however, the courts started allowing exceptions to it. A man could be found guilty of raping his wife if there was a non-cohabitation order in force; or a decree nisi; or a non-molestation undertaking; or a deed of separation. What if none of these existed?

In October 1989 a married woman from Leicester left home with her four-year-old son and went to live with her parents. She told her husband[42] that as a result of their matrimonial problems she intended to seek a divorce. Less than a month later her husband forced his way into her parents' house and attempted to have sexual intercourse with her against her will. He was charged with rape.

Despite 250 years of history, Mr Justice Owen bravely ruled that such a charge was possible in law. Of course, he tried to pretend that he was doing nothing new:

> I accept it is not for me to make the law. However, it is for me to state the common law as I believe it to be. If that requires me to indicate a set of circumstances which have not so far been considered as sufficient to negative consent [to intercourse] as in fact so doing, then I must do so. I cannot believe that it is part of the common law of this country that where there has been withdrawal of either party from cohabitation, accompanied by a clear indication that consent to sexual intercourse has been terminated, that that does not amount to a revocation of that implied consent.

On the basis of that ruling, the husband pleaded guilty to attempted rape. Despite that plea, he was entitled to challenge the judge's ruling in the Court of Appeal. This he proceeded to do.

The Lord Chief Justice, Lord Lane, carefully assembled a particularly 'strong' (in other words, large) court to hear the man's appeal. Apart from Lord Lane himself, it included the President of the High Court Family Division (Sir Stephen Brown) and three senior Lords

Justices of Appeal. If they were going to do something radical, there would be strength in numbers.

These judges had no need for fairy stories. 'We take the view,' they said, 'that the time has now arrived when the law should declare that a rapist remains a rapist subject to the criminal law, irrespective of his relationship with his victim.' They proceeded to declare it so.

The 'idea that a wife by marriage consents in advance to her husband having sexual intercourse with her whatever her state of health or however proper her objections' was, they said, a 'fiction'. By that, the judges meant that the wife – whether she knew anything about it or not – was deemed to consent to intercourse. In the court's view, a fiction was a 'poor basis for the criminal law' and it was 'no longer acceptable'.

Surely it was up to parliament rather than the judges to change the law? Indeed, the government had already asked its advisers at the Law Commission to look at the whole issue of marital rape and recommend changes. No, said the judges: 'this is not the creation of a new offence, it is the removal of a common law fiction which has become anachronistic and offensive and we consider that it is our duty having reached that conclusion to act upon it.' So they did: marital rape was established as a crime.[43]

Just to make the position absolutely clear, the Court of Appeal granted the husband, known by his initial as R, permission to appeal to the House of Lords. The law lords obligingly upheld his conviction. 'The common law is . . . capable of evolving in the light of changing social, economic and cultural developments,' said the senior law lord, Lord Keith. 'Hale's proposition involves that by marriage a wife gives her irrevocable consent to sexual intercourse with her husband under all circumstances . . . In modern times any reasonable person must regard that conception as quite unacceptable.'[44] In November 1995, the European Court of Human Rights unanimously dismissed a claim by R that his conviction amounted to a breach of article 7 of the Human Rights Convention, which prohibits retrospective criminal legislation.[45]

The English judges' rulings were widely welcomed; no rapists came forward to argue against them. In due course, the judgments were put on to a statutory footing.[46] This was unnecessary, but it served to remind the courts that parliament still felt it had some role to play in the law-making process.

Building society
Sometimes the judges go even further. In 1992, the law lords had to decide whether the Woolwich Building Society was entitled to £6.7 million in interest on tax which the courts had already decided should not have been paid.[47] As the law then stood, a person who paid tax under a mistake of law could not get it back unless he was acting under duress – even if the Inland Revenue had exceeded its powers in claiming it. What the law lords could not agree on was whether, in the words of Lord Browne-Wilkinson, they should 're-interpret the principles lying behind the authorities so as to give a right of recovery in those circumstances'.

Three of the law lords decided they could do so: Lord Goff, Lord Browne-Wilkinson and Lord Slynn were with the Woolwich. The two Scottish judges – Lord Keith and Lord Jauncey – said that changing the law should be left to parliament.

Speaking for the majority view, Lord Slynn said he found it unacceptable in principle that the common law should provide no remedy for a taxpayer who had paid tax demanded under an invalid regulation and held free of interest pending a decision of the courts. Lord Goff went even further, dismissing the objection that the law lords were being asked to 'overstep the boundary which we traditionally set for ourselves, separating the legitimate development of the law by the judges from legislation'. He added:

> Although I am well aware of the existence of the boundary, I am never quite sure where to find it. Its position seems to vary from case to case. Indeed, if it were to be as firmly and clearly drawn as some of our mentors would wish, I cannot help feeling that a number of leading cases [in the House of Lords] would never have been decided the way they were. For example, the minority view would have prevailed in *Donoghue v. Stevenson*;[48] our modern law of judicial review would never have developed from its old, ineffectual origins;[49] and *Mareva*[50] injunctions would never have seen the light of day. Much seems to depend on the circumstances of the particular case.[51]

There were a number of factors which impelled Lord Goff to recognise 'the justice underlying Woolwich's case'. He went on: 'the first is that this opportunity will never come again. If we do not take it now, it will be gone forever. The second is that I fear that, however compelling the principle of justice may be, it would never be sufficient to persuade a government to propose its legislative recognition by parliament; caution, otherwise known as the Treasury, would never allow this to happen.'[52]

What? The courts would have to step in *because* parliament feared to tread? This wasn't just ironing out the creases; it was weaving a whole new fabric. Far from saying, in Lord Denning's words, 'we are here to find out the intention of parliament and carry it out', Lord Goff seemed to be saying he had a pretty good idea of what parliament would do and he was determined to do the opposite.

Sexually transmitted debt

Another clear example of the law-making process at work was the case of *Barclays Bank Plc v. O'Brien*, decided by the House of Lords in October 1993.[53] It was the first time the law lords had considered the phenomenon of 'sexually transmitted debt'.[54] Bridget O'Brien had agreed to mortgage her family home in Slough after her husband told her she would be guaranteeing a business debt of £60,000 for a few weeks. In fact, Mr O'Brien's company soon owed Barclays Bank more than £150,000 and Mrs O'Brien then realised she had pledged the house, which was in joint names, to cover the whole of her husband's overdraft. Nobody had advised her to seek legal advice before signing the mortgage, although the bank had intended to warn her of the risks. Barclays then sought to sell her home to recover the money it was owed.

The law lords' judgment was given by Lord Browne-Wilkinson. As a former Chancery judge he was perhaps more used to channelling the streams of equity into deserts which the common law had left parched and barren; he certainly had no hesitation in shaping the law to fit what he saw as the needs of modern society.

Lord Browne-Wilkinson began bluntly enough by outlining the 'policy considerations' that lay behind his decision. The concept of the ignorant wife leaving all financial decisions to her husband was outmoded, he said, but the practice did not yet coincide with the ideal. In many marriages it was still the husband who had the business experience and the wife who was willing to follow his advice. Such wives could reasonably look to the law for some protection when their husbands had abused the trust put in them. On the other hand, it was easy to allow sympathy for a wife who was threatened with the loss of her home at the suit of a rich bank to obscure the important public interest: if small businesses were to grow bigger, banks should be able to lend safely on the security of the matrimonial home.

The whole of the modern law on this subject had been derived from a decision in 1902 which Lord Browne-Wilkinson decided was built on unsure and possibly mistaken foundations. He concluded that the law lords should 'seek to restate the law in a form which is principled, reflects the current requirements of society and provides as much certainty as possible'.[55] In his view, if a woman offered to guarantee her husband's debts, the bank should warn her – in person and without her husband present – of the risks she was taking on. That principle would apply to all couples, married or single, heterosexual or homosexual, whenever there was a risk that one party had been guilty of undue influence or misrepresentation.[56] Unless that was done, the debt could not be enforced. The law lords agreed, and that became the law. Mrs O'Brien kept her house.

The law lords fear to tread

It would be wrong to assume that the law lords always agree to change the law. If public opinion is not of one voice, they may be reluctant to impose a solution. As Lord Reid once said, 'where parliament fears to tread, it is not for courts to rush in'.[57] Again, some examples will help to illustrate the judges' approach.

Private Clegg

In 1990, a soldier on duty at a military checkpoint in West Belfast opened fire on a stolen car. As a result, Karen Reilly, a passenger in the car, was killed. The soldier, Private Lee Clegg, stood trial for murder. He claimed he had opened fire because he thought the life of another soldier, Private Aindow, was in danger. Private Clegg said he thought Private Aindow had been hit by the car. However, the judge found that Lee Clegg had shot at the car after it had gone past him. It was already more than fifty feet down the road when Karen Reilly was hit. The judge also found that Private Aindow's injuries had been caused by another soldier stamping on him in order to make it look as if he had been hit by the car.[58]

On that basis, the judge rejected Private Clegg's claim that he was acting in self-defence. There was no evidence to support any other defence and he was convicted of murder.

The Northern Ireland Court of Appeal found no grounds for quashing his conviction. Nevertheless, giving judgment the Lord Chief Justice of Northern Ireland, Sir Brian Hutton, said it would have been much fairer if the judge had been able to convict Private Clegg of the 'lesser crime of manslaughter on the ground that he did not kill Karen Reilly from an evil motive, but because . . . he reacted wrongly to a situation which suddenly confronted him in the course of his duties'.[59]

Could the law lords change the law in this way? No, they all said, no matter how desirable such a change might be. Lord Lloyd said he was 'not averse to judges developing law – or, indeed, making new law – when they could see their way clearly'. That was the case even when questions of social policy were involved (such as in the marital rape case discussed earlier). In the *Clegg* case Lord Lloyd had no doubt the law lords 'should abstain from law making'. In his view, the reduction of what would otherwise be murder to manslaughter was essentially a matter for parliament.[60]

Little more than two years after he was convicted, Lee Clegg was released on licence in July 1995. His murder conviction seemed not to have damaged his military career: he was even promoted to lance corporal. In January 1997, the Northern Ireland Secretary, Sir Patrick Mayhew QC MP, referred Lee Clegg's case back to the Court of Appeal – 'in the light of new forensic evidence', as Sir Patrick put it.[61] Although the error is almost universally accepted, it was disappointing to see a former Attorney General misusing the word 'forensic' in this way.[62]

Doli incapax

In the summer of 1992 Merseyside police caught a twelve–year-old boy trying to steal a motorbike. As the law then stood, a child aged ten, eleven, twelve or thirteen was presumed incapable of criminal responsibility (in Latin, *doli incapax*) unless the prosecution could show the child knew what he had done was seriously wrong, and not just naughty. The magistrates decided the boy – who could not be identified – must have known what he had done was seriously wrong because he and his friend had done substantial damage to the motorbike with a crowbar and had run off when stopped by the police.

The boy's lawyers took the case to the High Court, arguing that these facts were not enough to prove that the boy knew his actions were seriously wrong. Mr Justice Laws reviewed past cases and concluded that the boy's lawyers were right: if a child were to be convicted there had to be 'clear positive evidence that the defendant knew his act was seriously wrong'. In his view, evidence of what had actually happened was simply not enough.[63]

That conclusion was not what anybody wanted. It meant this particular boy would have to be cleared, even though the judge said he had been 'caught in the act of a thoroughly dishonest enterprise'. It meant also that other children could escape criminal responsibility by simply refusing to say whether they knew that what they had done was seriously wrong.

For Mr Justice Laws, the only answer to this dilemma was to abolish the presumption that a child of this age was incapable of criminal responsibility. ('This presumption has no utility whatever in the present era,' he said. 'It ought to go.') The only question was whether the High Court had the power to abolish it.

There were three arguments against doing so.

First, it would mean the court was creating retrospective criminal law, criminalising something that the court reckoned was not an offence at the time the boy was caught. The boy in question, said Mr Justice Laws, would hardly have been relying on these rarefied arguments at the time of the crime and he would suffer no injustice if the presumption were abolished.

Second, the presumption was so old that 'it should only be changed by parliament or at least by a decision of the House of Lords'. The answer Mr Justice Laws gave to that one explains how he felt the judges should operate:

> Antiquity of itself confers no virtue on the legal status quo. If it did, that would assault one of the most valued features of the common law, which is its capacity to adapt to changing conditions. The common law is not a system of rigid rules, but of principles whose application may alter over time and which themselves may be modified. It may, and should, be renewed by succeeding generations of judges, and so meet the needs of a society that is itself subject to change. In the present case the conditions under which this presumption was developed in the earlier law now have no application. It is our duty to get rid of it, if we properly can.

Third, the court was bound by the doctrine of precedent: only the appeal courts could change the law. However, said Mr Justice Laws, in these circumstances the High Court was sitting as a court of appeal from the magistrates' courts; in criminal cases the only further appeal was to the House of Lords.[64]

The effect of all this was that – somewhat surprisingly – Mr Justice

Laws felt free to hold that the *doli incapax* rule 'was no longer part of the law of England'. Even more surprisingly, he persuaded a more senior judge who was presiding over the court to agree.[65]

The case went to the House of Lords. This time the boy's lawyers drew attention to a White Paper[66] in which the government had said specifically that it did not intend to change the *doli incapax* rule. Faced with this evidence, Lord Lowry said the presumption was still recognised as effective; he considered that the doctrine remained part of English law. 'To sweep it away under the doubtful auspices of judicial legislation' was, in his view, 'quite impracticable'.[67]

Lord Lowry reviewed a number of cases in which the House of Lords had shied away from judicial law-making (including the case of Private Clegg, just mentioned). He distilled five principles:

> If the solution is doubtful, the judges should beware of imposing their own remedy.
> Caution should prevail if parliament has rejected opportunities of clearing up a known difficulty; or has legislated while leaving the difficulty untouched.
> Disputed matters of social policy are less suitable areas for judicial intervention than purely legal problems.
> Fundamental legal doctrines should not be lightly set aside.
> Judges should not make a change unless they can achieve finality and certainty.

Applying these principles, Lord Lowry said Mr Justice Laws had been 'bold and imaginative'[68] – in other words, wrong – in saying the *doli incapax* presumption was no longer part of our law. This case was different from the marital rape case discussed earlier in this chapter. The case of *R* 'dealt with a specific act and not with a general principle . . . It was based on a very widely accepted modern view of marital rape and it derived support from a group of up-to-date decisions . . . And, in contrast to the present case, a definite solution could be, and was, achieved.'

What then was to happen to the Merseyside juvenile delinquent? The presumption was back where it started, and there was no evidence, apart from what had actually happened, to rebut it. The boy was therefore not guilty. A change in the law was clearly required, but the law lords felt they were not the people to make it. As Lord Lowry said, it was 'a classic case for parliamentary investigation, deliberation and legislation'.

It seems that by presenting parliament with an unpalatable result

Lord Lowry and his fellow law lords hoped to 'bounce' or shame the legislature into action. There was an uncharacteristic silence from the government. However, in March 1997 the shadow Home Secretary Jack Straw announced that a forthcoming Labour government would abolish the *doli incapax* presumption.

Judicial supremacism

In the past few years leading judges have begun to consider the limits on parliamentary sovereignty. In the past, it was said that parliament's powers were unlimited. Three of these judges are now not so sure.

Lord Woolf

As we saw in Chapter 3, the courts insist that a minister or other official who is entrusted with a discretion must exercise it fairly; if not, they will grant judicial review and quash the decision. In a lecture[34] he delivered at the end of 1994, at a time when he could never have expected that illness would create a vacancy in the post of Master of the Rolls, Lord Woolf said it was possible for the judges to justify this insistence by 'reading into' a statute an implied requirement that any powers conferred by the statute were to be exercised fairly and reasonably. Lord Woolf admitted he was 'far from sure whether in these circumstances the court is fulfilling an intention parliament actually possessed or . . . indulging in a fondness for fairy tales. However, if this gives the role of the court respectability, so be it.' Lord Woolf then referred to a case in which his fellow law lords had required the Home Secretary to follow new procedures when dealing with prisoners serving life sentences for murder.[70] He hoped the courts would act in the same way even if the minister had explicitly said in parliament that he was not intending to behave in a way that the courts would see as fair.

What happens, Lord Woolf then wondered, 'if a party with a large majority in parliament uses that majority to abolish the courts' entire power of judicial review in express terms? . . . Do the courts then accept that the legislation means what it says?'

Lord Woolf was sure that in practice this was unthinkable. It would never happen. Nevertheless, if it did, in his personal view the courts would *not* have to accept that the legislation meant what it said.

This was a startling conclusion. Lord Woolf justified it by explaining that he saw the courts and parliament as being partners, both engaged in a common enterprise involving the upholding of the rule of law:

> Our parliamentary democracy is based on the rule of law. One of the twin principles on which the rule of law depends is the supremacy of parliament in its legislative capacity. The other principle is that the courts are the final arbiters as to the interpretation and application of the law. As both parliament and the courts derive their authority from the rule of law so both are subject to it and can not act in a manner which involves its repudiation.

Lord Woolf said there had already been cases where the law had had to take a stand. He gave as an example a leading case from the late 1960s.[71] The Foreign Compensation Act 1950 said that decisions of a commission which allocated compensation to those who had lost property abroad 'shall not be called in question in any court of law'. Even though the intentions of parliament seemed entirely plain, the judges had decided that those unambiguous words could not exclude the jurisdiction of the courts.

Lord Woolf believed that parliament had not subsequently tried to challenge the reviewing powers of the courts.[72] 'However,' he said, 'if parliament did the unthinkable, then I would say that the courts would also be required to act in a manner which would be without precedent. Some judges might choose to do that by saying it was an unrebuttable presumption that parliament could never intend such a result. I myself would consider there were advantages in making it clear that ultimately there *are even limits on the supremacy of parliament*,[73] which it is the courts' inalienable responsibility to identify and uphold.' As if perhaps to minimise the significance of this revolutionary statement Lord Woolf said these limits were of 'modest dimensions': he believed any democrat would accept them. 'They are no more than are necessary to enable the rule of law to be preserved.'

Lord Woolf was not the only judge to suggest that parliament might not always hold the trump card.

Mr Justice 'higher-order' Laws

Mr Justice Laws is a judge to watch. In his role of First Junior Treasury Counsel – or 'Treasury Devil' – from 1984 until his appointment to the bench in 1992, he represented the government in a number of high-profile public law cases such as *Spycatcher*[74] and the IRA members' inquest in Gibraltar in 1988. In the summer of 1994 Sir John Laws delivered a lecture with the promising title of 'Law and Politics – No-go Areas for Judges?'[75] As befits a brilliant classical scholar, he began his talk with a detailed account of a sea battle during the Peloponnesian War in 406BC. In due course, he moved on to more modern times.

First, he examined the classic grounds for judicial review. As we saw in Chapter 3, these can be defined as unreasonableness, unfairness and unlawfulness. Unlawfulness was clear enough: no subordinate body could be allowed by the judges to exceed the powers granted to it by parliament. What, though, about the duties to act fairly and reasonably? Anticipating Lord Woolf perhaps, Mr Justice Laws pointed out that these requirements had been imposed on ministers by the judges. Before the 1960s it had not been thought that administrative bodies had to hear the other side of an argument.[76] Nor had it been thought that the courts would intervene if a minister thwarted the implied (though unstated) purposes of the legislation.[77] Mr Justice Laws pointed out that parliament had not suddenly decided, during the 1960s and the 1970s, that ministers should observe the principles of fairness and reasonableness: 'They are, categorically, judicial creations. They owe neither their existence nor their acceptance to the will of the legislature. They have nothing to do with the intention of parliament, save as a fig leaf to cover their true origins. We do not need the fig leaf any more.'

Even though the powers given by parliament were apparently unlimited, he said, ministers were required by the courts to act fairly and reasonably. Mr Justice Laws then went on to argue that for the survival of democracy there *must be* limits on what can be done by those who exercise political power. This led him to a striking conclusion:

> The constitution must guarantee by positive law such rights as freedom of expression, since otherwise its credentials as a means of honest rule are fatally undermined. But this requires for its achievement what I may call a higher-order law: a law which cannot be abrogated as other laws can, by the passage of a statute promoted by a government with the necessary majority in parliament ... The democratic credentials of an elected government cannot justify its enjoyment of a right to abolish fundamental freedoms.

This was heady stuff. Mr Justice Laws was well aware that his

135

argument would appear to some as 'a plea for judicial supremacism.' There was more to come:

> It is a condition of democracy's preservation that the power of a democratically elected government – or parliament – be not absolute. The institution of free and regular elections, like fundamental human rights, has to be vindicated by a higher-order law: very obviously, no government can tamper with it if it is to avoid the mantle of tyranny; no government, therefore, must be allowed to do so.

In the judge's analysis, parliamentary sovereignty is not derived from legislation: parliament cannot confer authority on itself. 'A higher-order law confers it, and must of necessity limit it.'[78]

Mr Justice Laws pointed out that in most countries these 'higher-order laws' were to be found in written constitutions. Britain did not have a constitution of this kind. In theory, therefore, a government could prolong its own life beyond the normal five years.[79] In practice, such undemocratic changes 'are or should be off limits for our elected representatives'.

Summing up, the judge accepted that parliament held political sovereignty but not what he called 'constitutional' sovereignty. The constitution for these purposes consisted of 'a framework of fundamental principles which include the imperative of democracy itself and those other rights, prime among them freedom of thought and expression, which cannot be denied save by a plea of guilty to totalitarianism.' It was the judges' duty to enforce these superior principles.

There was yet another judge prepared to venture down this hazardous road.

Mr Justice Sedley

Before he was appointed to the High Court bench, Stephen Sedley was one of England's most strongly independent-minded barristers. Since his appointment he has continued to contribute widely to public affairs, writing long articles for papers such as *The London Review of Books* and delivering elegant lectures on the future of law. During a lecture on human rights delivered in March 1995, Mr Justice Sedley mentioned, almost as an aside, that he had trouble with Mr Justice Laws' concept of a higher order law as the basis of human rights adjudication. He suggested that in England and other common law jurisdictions Dicey's doctrine of the sovereignty of parliament was giving way to 'a bi-polar sovereignty of the Crown in parliament and the Crown in its courts, to each of which the Crown's ministers are answerable – politically to parliament, legally to the courts'.[80]

Mr Justice Sedley developed these thoughts in a lecture the following year. As parliament cannot govern directly, he explained, it delegates 'enormous tranches of public power' to ministers. Because ministers can control the parliament to which they are theoretically subordinate, it is crucial to stress the fact that the executive is not sovereign. 'It is in parliament and the courts, each exercising a discrete though interdependent function of the state, the legislative and the judicial, that the sovereignties of the state reside.'[81]

So there we have it: three judges who were willing to challenge the traditional view that parliament can do anything it wants. The government naturally disagreed. However, its initial response was thwarted by the well-known cock-up theory of politics.

The government fights back

In December 1995, the political editor of the *Daily Telegraph* found himself with something of a scoop: 'Judges Warned to Keep in Line' was his front-page headline. His story, which *The Times* lifted without checking and used in its later editions, quoted extensively from a speech which the Lord Chancellor was supposedly making in the City of London that evening.

'The Lord Chancellor, Lord Mackay, is to take the unprecedented step of reminding judges that the courts are not superior to parliament', it said. 'He will warn them not to overstep their powers by using judicial review to challenge ministerial decisions.'

'Lord Mackay,' the *Telegraph* confidently predicted, 'will reject suggestions that the judges are biased or that they have taken a group decision to frustrate ministers at every turn. But he will stress that ministers are part of the elected government and must be allowed to propose policies as they think fit.' The story continued:

> Lord Mackay will also seek to clarify the scope of judicial review, where adverse decisions have increasingly been portrayed as a personal defeat for the minister involved. He will make it clear the courts are not overturning decisions on policy and administration, which can be made only by ministers accountable to parliament. The judges' role was to ensure that ministers were exercising their powers in accordance with

137

the law. It was not the decision that was being considered, but the way in which it was being made.

But, in a section which will be seen as a warning to the judges not to exceed their powers, he will reaffirm the supremacy of parliament to decide laws. He is expected to state that it is 'dangerous and mistaken' to argue that there is some form of authority in the courts that is superior to parliament. Rather it is the duty of judges to apply the law as parliament has enacted it – and the ultimate authority over the executive and the judiciary is parliament.[82]

This speech raises issues that are fundamental to this book. Unfortunately, it was a speech Lord Mackay never made. Indeed, he never had any intention of making a speech that night, in the City of London or anywhere else.

The Lord Chancellor had indeed been invited to a City dinner, but it had taken place the night before. Far from delivering a speech, he had simply made a few light-hearted comments before proposing a toast to the Lord Mayor. So where had this apparently well-documented story come from?

It turned out that when Lord Mackay was first asked to dinner in the City he understood that he was being asked to make a formal speech. He presumably thought it would be a good opportunity to respond to what the judges had been saying about supremacy. A draft was prepared and, in line with normal procedures, it was sent to other government departments for comment. The Conservative party chairman, Brian Mawhinney MP, got hold of the draft and leaked it, through a hapless Central Office press officer identified as Sheila Gunn, to the normally sympathetic *Daily Telegraph*. At some point during this process the story acquired the sort of 'spin' which no legal correspondent would ever have given it: what was intended as a carefully balanced speech was turned overnight into a blunt attack on the judiciary.

The paper got its own back on its source the next day. It headlined an opposition attack on Dr Mawhinney: the Labour Chief Whip had accused Conservative Central Office of 'crass behaviour' after the Lord Chancellor had 'had to clarify' a report in the *Daily Telegraph*. The story quoted a letter Lord Mackay had fired off to the paper, chiding it about its 'erroneous account' of a speech he did not make. The Lord Chancellor said:

I should like to take this opportunity to emphasise to you and your readers that I would never warn the judiciary 'not to over-step their powers by using judicial review to challenge ministerial decisions'. Judicial review is a process under which judges have to determine whether a particular decision is in accordance with the law. It is ultimately for parliament to decide what the law should be and, so long as ministers have fulfilled their legal obligations, the decision of parliament, in the form of legislation duly passed, must prevail.

I do believe it is mistaken to argue that there is some form of basic fundamental law which is superior to parliament and against which the decisions of parliament can be measured. But it must also be understood that the judges act, and must be allowed to continue to act, independently – of parliament, of the government, of the Lord Chancellor and of each other. Each judge decides the case before him or her on the facts and the law and in accordance with the judicial oath. This independence is something in which I believe absolutely and which neither the Lord Chancellor nor any other member of the government would ever seek to challenge.[83]

Eventually, Lord Mackay found an audience prepared to listen to his views on the role of the judiciary. He spoke in July 1996, apparently at short notice, to a select audience invited by the Citizenship Foundation, a pressure group which, among its other aims, encouraged a sense of civic responsibility among schoolchildren. No children were present on this occasion but a surprisingly large number of senior judges had turned up: they were strangely reticent when the Lord Chancellor invited comments or questions.

As expected, Lord Mackay used his speech to say that judicial review 'in no way undermines the sovereignty of parliament'. It was an important feature of our constitutional arrangements that the judges were independent from the executive. 'Judicial independence should, however, be firmly distinguished from any hint of judicial supremacism. Just as the independence of the judiciary is fundamental to our constitutional arrangements, so is the idea that the judiciary is bound by an act of parliament.' Lord Mackay repeated that he was 'not convinced by arguments, although eloquently advanced, that there exists a higher order of law comprising basic or fundamental principles against which the judiciary may measure acts of parliament and, if necessary, strike them down.'[84]

Labour joins in

Lord Mackay's rejection of both judicial supremacism and a higher order of law was apparently directed at the three judges whose views we have already considered in this chapter. Labour's senior legal affairs spokesman had already drawn attention to their views in a lecture about judicial review he had given to the Administrative Bar Association in the autumn of 1995.

In his lecture,[85] Lord Irvine of Lairg QC spoke of judges who had suggested that in certain purely domestic circumstances the courts might hold that statutes passed by parliament were invalid. He had in mind Lord Woolf, Mr Justice Laws and Mr Justice Sedley – as well as the President of the New Zealand Court of Appeal, Sir Robin Cooke (later Lord Cooke of Thorndon).

Lord Irvine had some firm words for those he clearly saw as upstart judges. First, he said, their views were 'contrary to the established laws and constitution of the United Kingdom and have been since 1688'. Parliament was supreme and the judges themselves had said they could not declare any of its acts invalid. Second, Lord Irvine thought it was inconceivable that the actions of any parliament in the foreseeable future would justify such interference by the judges. On the other hand, if democracy were under threat the judges could hardly hold back a revolution. Third, he said, 'the danger with any extra-judicial claim of right to review the validity of any act of parliament is that to many it smacks of judicial supremacism'. In his view, this would make it more difficult for a Labour government to incorporate the European Convention on Human Rights.[86] Fourth, such a claim could only be advanced if parliamentary decisions were 'inconsistent' with the fundamental tenets of a free democracy and therefore unworthy of judicial respect. Since the opposite was true, and parliamentary decisions had a greater claim to democratic support, the judges should exercise self-restraint when taking decisions.

Lord Irvine repeated his remarks the following year. It was 'unwise' for judges to say that 'in exceptional circumstances the courts may be able to hold invalid statutes duly passed by parliament. This causes ordinary people not only to believe that judges may have got over and above themselves but that perhaps they are exercising a political function in judicial review cases instead of simply upholding the rule of law.'[87]

Second thoughts?

Lord Irvine's comments about judicial supremacism did not go down well with his own supporters. As one experienced reporter wrote, 'his lecture . . . was interpreted as a call to judges to exercise greater self-restraint in using the procedure of judicial review. . . To hear the shadow Lord Chancellor urge caution and restraint in a speech that, as one QC said, "could have been made by Michael Howard" dismayed Labour lawyers.'[88]

These remarks appeared to have dismayed Lord Irvine. He insisted he was a firm supporter of judicial review.[89] A month later, he was even more explicit.

'In a sense I regret the use of the term judicial supremacism,' he told the editor of the *New Statesman*. 'I don't regret it in principle, because I meant what I was saying, but I regret the misunderstanding the expression caused. What I was addressing was not any decision ever taken by a judge in a judicial review case. I am a firm upholder of judicial review. I was discussing statements by certain judges extra-judicially[90] that circumstances could arise in which it would be right for the judges to strike down an act of parliament because it offended some notion of natural right.' These judges risked giving the impression 'wrongly, I believe, that in their judicial review function they may have a political agenda in which their decisions are arrived at because of their hostility to a particular act of parliament'.[91]

Bingham down to earth

The Lord Chief Justice seemed to think there was little point in a theoretical discussion of judicial supremacism. While he was Master of the Rolls, Lord Bingham had said that 'whatever political theorists – or even judges in their more speculative, off-duty moments – may opine, [the doctrine of parliamentary sovereignty] is not, as a matter of law, under threat.'[92]

Speaking as Lord Chief Justice five months later, he warmed to this theme. 'It is easy to pose speculative questions,' he said. 'Suppose parliament were to enact the anti-semitic laws of the Third Reich, what would the judges do then?' He accepted that questions such as these were a legitimate subject for debate: a learned profession could not be expected to eschew speculation. 'But debates of this kind have as much to do with day-to-day judicial decision-making as the theological controversies of mediaeval schoolmen with running the Mothers' Union.'[93]

On the face of it, this appeared to be something of a put-down for judges like Mr Justice Laws and even Lord Woolf. True, Lord Bingham said the questions they had raised were 'a legitimate subject of debate'. Nevertheless, he clearly felt they were irrelevant to the job of judging.

Indeed, Lord Bingham maintained it was 'preposterous' to suggest that the judges were in any way equivocal in their deference to parliamentary sovereignty: 'We have no extra-territorial ambitions. We have our work cut out to do our own job without wishing to do anyone else's. But we will seek to honour our ancient promise to do right to all manner of people, according to the laws and usages of the realm, without fear or favour, affection or ill-will. We seek no other role and can conceive of none prouder.[94]

Other judges were irritated by what Lord Woolf and his like-minded colleagues had been saying. One of them[95] – who asked not to be named – spoke for the vast majority of his brethren when he said that in the event of a conflict the judges should not have the power to set aside an act of parliament. 'All of them would take that view in the end,' he insisted, 'and any remarks to the contrary would have to be seen in the context of an assumption that legislation will be followed.'

According to this judge, parliament must be sovereign: 'It's hypothetical to ask what should be done if parliament were to say all men with red hair should be executed. That's a silly question. If parliament passes legislation, that's the law, and the judiciary has no business saying "No, it isn't".'

Responding to the controversy at the end of 1996, Lord Woolf said he stood by his comments, but he insisted they had been misunderstood. He pointed out that he had been thinking the unthinkable. His lecture had been given in memory of Professor F. A. Mann, a lawyer who had come to Britain as a refugee from Nazi Germany and who had seen what had happened to the judiciary there. 'All I was indicating was that there are some things which I don't think parliament can do,' Lord Woolf said. 'Parliament obtains its authority because it's the democratic institution established by the authority of our electoral system. If parliament were, for example, to do something which was totally inconsistent with what any proper-thinking member of the community would regard as acceptable in any way, then that would be a different position from what we have ever seen. In that context,' he insisted, 'we would have to stand up and be counted. But in relation to the ordinary role of judges up and down the land it is clear that for all practical purposes parliament is supreme.'[96]

How far should they go?

Sometimes then the judges hesitate to change the law. On other occasions, they have fewer doubts. Nobody seriously denies that the judges *do* make law (although they are sometimes understandably coy about admitting it when they think the general public may be listening). The only question which remains is when they *should*.

Lord Browne-Wilkinson, the law lord who decided the 'sexually transmitted debt' case discussed earlier in this chapter,[97] said it was difficult for the senior judges to decide when it was legitimate or necessary for the courts to intervene. The courts often adopted a self-denying ordnance, saying that, however little they liked the existing law, it was for parliament to change it. The trouble was that parliament seldom addressed such issues. 'We are left with deciding these issues because the democratic system – for very good reasons, very often – cannot tackle the problem: it has not got time, or the political inclination.'[98]

Here we see a judge justifying his intervention in the political process. As we saw earlier in this chapter, Lord Irvine believed the judges should make law only if there was a definite community consensus in favour of a particular change. This approach was in line with that taken by the judges in recent years. There was certainly a consensus in favour of making marital rape a crime: research by the Law Commission suggested that there were few who opposed it.[99] On the other hand, as we have seen, there was no consensus on whether the courts should make it easier to get a manslaughter verdict or a young child convicted.

Is this approach correct? Should the judges decide whether there is a consensus? Surely parliament is better placed to assess public opinion than a dozen (fairly)[100] elderly judges?

How far the judges should go down the law-making road is, like many of the questions in this book, easier to ask than to answer. To some extent, it will depend on the political complexion of the party in power and the political views of the person answering the question. Those who oppose the government of the day will call for a creative approach from the judges. Those who suspect the judges of leaning too far in the wrong direction will stress the democratic legitimacy of an elected parliament. What is important is that we should all understand what the courts are doing – what powers they have to make new law, and how they choose to exercise them. If we think they have gone too far, we can then protest. If necessary, we may then call on parliament to put matters right.

The judges were right to say that parliament is supreme. Yet they do not derive their authority from parliament alone and it was honest of them to admit that there were circumstances in which they might ignore legislation. Ultimately, the people would expect nothing less. As it is, we expect them to make law when parliament chooses not to. It should be principled rather than arbitrary, and it should tread the narrow line between unpredictability and injustice. If the people do not like it, their remedy lies in legislation.

The leading human rights lawyer Lord Lester of Herne Hill QC called Lord Goff's speech in the building society case (mentioned earlier in this chapter) a 'scholarly and principled judgment'.[101] However, can it really be principled to say the courts should act contrary to the presumed intentions of parliament? This must surely be an example of expediency rather than principle, however much we may sympathise with Lord Goff's ultimate aims.

Conversely, Lord Lester questioned whether it was right for the judges to make marital rape a crime even though the law commission was about to publish its report on the subject.[102] Why not? The Law Commission's proposals were hardly going to come as a surprise. If one supports judicial law-making in appropriate cases, one can hardly expect the courts to wait for parliament to act.

In general, however, Lord Lester welcomed what he saw as 'wise and courageous judicial law-making' through which the judges 'subtly altered the balance of power between the three branches of government'.[103] A very different view was taken by Professor Conor Gearty, a left of centre commentator at King's College London. For him, 'the judge's primary task is an interpreter of the words deployed by the people (through their representatives in parliament) to express their will.' That still left plenty of room for judicial creativity, but it had to be within a framework of parliamentary sovereignty.[104]

Professor Gearty was therefore perfectly happy with the *Pergau*

Dam and the Criminal Injuries Compensation Board rulings discussed in Chapter 3. Nevertheless, he saw a world of difference between cases such as these and the suggestion that the judges should be able to go one step further and substitute their will for that of parliament. This represented 'a mind-boggling claim to the exercise of pure, undiluted undemocratic power'. For him, a bill of rights would be just as bad. For Lord Lester, though, it would be just the opposite. It is this fundamental difference of opinion that forms the basis of our next chapter.

5

A Bill of Rights

Incorporating the convention

In his speech to the 1996 Bar Conference, the shadow Lord Chancellor, Lord Irvine of Lairg QC, reaffirmed the Labour party's 'firm intention' to incorporate the European Convention on Human Rights into domestic law. He noted that the Conservative government was 'implacably opposed'. Nevertheless, he insisted, 'we will do it.'[3]

It was the clearest indication yet of what may prove to be a major shift in the balance of power between the executive and the judiciary. A few weeks earlier, Tony Blair had said 'the case for . . . incorporation of the European Convention on Human Rights into British law is now generally agreed outside the Conservative party and even by some within it . . . Only the strange mentality of the modern Tory Bourbons could think it satisfactory to force British citizens to go to France to enforce their rights because their own courts are incapable of doing so.'[4] Bringing the Human Rights convention into the laws of the United Kingdom has been Labour party policy since 1993. Mr Blair's predecessor John Smith had spoken

146

in favour of incorporation,[5] and the policy was publicly confirmed later in the year.[6]

Incorporating the convention means allowing Her Majesty's judges to interpret and apply it. Labour's commitment to incorporation meant the party was willing to trust the judges. That, in turn, spoke volumes about Labour's perception of the judges as fair-minded and progressive. Lord Irvine said incorporation would 'involve a very significant transfer of power to the judges'.[7] Critics found it strange that a shadow Lord Chancellor who was concerned about judicial supremacism was willing to give the judges such powers. However, allowing the judiciary to enforce the European Convention on Human Rights may not amount to the far-reaching constitutional change that some people have feared – or desired.

The convention's origins

In 1949, the United Kingdom and nine other countries came together to found the Council of Europe. The new international body was part of a growing movement towards post-war reconciliation. With the scars of war still raw, the Council of Europe decided that one of its first tasks should be to draw up an international agreement on human rights. Supporters of incorporation often remind us that British lawyers played a key part in its preparation: Sir David Maxwell-Fyfe, who had briefly served as Churchill's Attorney General in 1945,[8] chaired the legal committee of the Council of Europe's Consultative Assembly and Sir Oscar Dowson, former senior legal adviser at the Home Office, was the main draftsman of the text.[9]

What is less well known is that Britain's involvement in the process served only to dilute it. Research conducted by the leading human rights lawyer and Liberal Democrat peer, Lord Lester of Herne Hill QC, reveals that Attlee's post-war Labour government was against giving individuals the automatic right to complain to a preliminary investigating body; it also wanted to limit the court's powers. Lord Jowitt, who was Lord Chancellor until 1951, said that anyone familiar with the English legal institutions would recoil from the original draft convention 'with a feeling of horror'. In a remark which still has some resonance today, he said he could not view with equanimity an 'appeal to a secret court composed of persons of no legal training, possessing the unfettered right to expound the meaning of seventeen articles which may mean anything, or – as I hope – nothing'.[10]

In the summer of 1950, the revised draft of the convention came before the Council of Europe Consultative Assembly. Many members were concerned about the weakening of the original proposals by the British government, but faced with the alternative of no agreement at all they gave it their reluctant support. The Foreign Secretary, Ernest Bevin, persuaded his cabinet colleagues that Britain should accept the new agreement for diplomatic reasons; he signed it at a meeting in Rome towards the end of 1950. So too did ministers from the other member states: there were now fifteen in all. Four months later, in March 1951, the United Kingdom ratified the Convention for the Protection of Human Rights and Fundamental Freedoms: it was the first country to do so. Others followed, and the European Convention on Human Rights – as it is more often called – came into force in 1953.[11]

As we have seen, the Committee of Ministers of the Council of Europe had decided that individuals should not have the automatic right to apply to, or 'petition', the European Commission on Human Rights (which was set up to investigate and filter alleged breaches of the convention). Ministers also agreed that member states would not have to accept the court's compulsory jurisdiction.

It took a Labour government to let people in Britain exercise these important rights. In December 1965, the Prime Minister, Harold Wilson, announced that the government had decided to accept the right of individuals to petition the Human Rights commission and the compulsory jurisdiction of the court for an initial period of three years. Surprisingly, as Lord Lester has noted, the issue was not discussed in cabinet or by a cabinet committee. There was not even any significant opposition from the Home Office.[12] Parliament was informed only after the decision had been taken.[13]

Since 1965 the United Kingdom has always renewed the right of individual petition, as it is called; sometimes, though, it has done so with great reluctance. In 1993, when the Council of Europe was discussing plans for a new, streamlined Human Rights court, the Home Office wanted to make the right of individual petition optional, while the Foreign Office said it should be mandatory. Eventually, when it became apparent that Britain would have been hopelessly outvoted, the Foreign Office view prevailed. When the new Court of Human Rights starts work – probably in 1999 – its doors will be open to all those who claim their human rights have been violated by a member state.[14]

Despite this commitment, in the autumn of 1995 British ministers seriously considered pulling out of the European Court of Human Rights. The government was furious with the European Court for deciding, by a bare majority, that Britain had been in breach of the Human Rights convention for allowing troops to kill three IRA terrorists who, in 1988, were planning to explode a bomb in Gibraltar. Following the decision, officials were asked to advise ministers on three options: leaving the Council of Europe; not renewing the right of individual petition; and lobbying for improvements. Ministers were persuaded that it would not enhance Britain's reputation if a country like Albania appeared more committed to human rights than the United Kingdom, and the government settled for the third option, reluctantly renewing the right of individual petition in 1995.[15]

Even so, early in 1997 elements within the Home Office still seemed to be fighting a rearguard action. The government organised a lobbying meeting at Wilton Park, the Foreign Office conference centre in Sussex. Judges and senior officials from the European Court of Human Rights were invited to discuss the form of the new streamlined court. According to accounts of the conference, the Home Secretary Michael Howard launched an outspoken attack on the Human Rights court for protecting terrorists and drug dealers. Guests at the conference were shocked by the tone of his remarks, which went far beyond the draft prepared by Home Office officials. It was thought that Mr Howard's intervention had undone months of careful campaigning by the Lord Chancellor for measured improvements in the court's structure.[16]

What the convention says

The European Convention on Human Rights was deliberately written in general terms: there is none of the detail to be found in an act of parliament. Almost fifty years on, it is still clear and refreshingly easy to read. The convention is divided into articles and most of the articles are further divided into two or more paragraphs: typically the later paragraphs limit the broad rights granted in the opening words. The following brief summary of the convention demonstrates this style of drafting.

Article 2 – Right to life
Everyone's right to life shall be protected by law. However, taking a life is permitted if it results from the use of force which is no more than absolutely necessary to defend someone from unlawful violence; or to make an arrest; or to quell a riot.

Article 3 – No torture
No one shall be subjected to torture or to inhuman or degrading treatment or punishment. (Unusually, there are no exceptions to this article.)

Article 4 – No slavery
No one shall be held in slavery or required to perform forced labour. This does not prohibit work done in prison or on proba-tion; military service; and work which forms part of normal civic obligations.

Article 5 – Liberty
Everyone has the right to liberty and security of person. No one shall be deprived of his liberty except when imprisoned; or when arrested; or when detained as an alcoholic or vagrant; or when awaiting extradition. Those arrested must be given reasons; they must be brought promptly before a court; and they must be tried within a reasonable time. They must be able to challenge the lawfulness of their detention by a court; if wrongly detained, they must be compensated.

Article 6 – Fair trial
Everyone is entitled to a fair and public trial (or civil hearing) within a reasonable time by an independent and impartial tribunal. Judgment must be given publicly but the press and public may be excluded where publicity would prejudice the interests of justice. Everyone charged with a criminal offence shall be presumed innocent and

allowed specified minimum rights (including free legal aid where the interests of justice so require).

Article 7 – No retrospective crimes
No one shall be held guilty of an act or omission which did not constitute a criminal offence under national or international law – or according to the general principles of law recognised by civilised nations – at the time when it was committed.

Article 8 – Family life
Everyone has the right to respect for his private and family life, his home and his correspondence. There are exceptions in the interests of national security, public safety and the economic well-being of the country; to prevent disorder or crime; to protect health or morals; and to protect the rights and freedoms of others.

Article 9 – Freedom of thought
Everyone has the right to freedom of thought, conscience and religion. Again there are exceptions in the interests of public safety; to protect public order, health or morals; and to protect the rights and freedoms of others.

Article 10 – Freedom of expression
Everyone has the right to freedom of expression. The exceptions cover such restrictions as are necessary in a democratic society in the interests of national security, territorial integrity or public safety; for the prevention of disorder or crime; for the protection of health or morals; for the protection of the reputation or the rights of others; for preventing the disclosure of information received in confidence; and for maintaining the authority and impartiality of the judiciary.

Article 11 – Freedom of assembly
Everyone has the right to freedom of peaceful assembly. Again there are restrictions in the interests of national security or public safety; for the prevention of disorder or crime; for the protection of health or morals; and for the protection of the rights and freedoms of others. Article 11 guarantees people the right to join a trade union unless they are members of the armed forces, police officers or civil servants.

Article 12 – The right to marry
Men and women of marriageable age have the right to marry and
found a family, according to the national laws governing the exercise
of this right.

Article 13 – Effective remedies
Everyone whose rights are violated must have an effective remedy
before a national authority.

Article 14 – No discrimination
Everyone is entitled to the rights set out in the convention without
discrimination on any ground.[17]

The first protocol
Some additional provisions were added in 1952. These include
the right to peaceful enjoyment of one's possessions (subject to
certain exceptions); the right to education in conformity with one's
parents' religious and philosophical convictions; and the right to free
elections.

Derogation
Article 15 contains a major let-out clause. It says that in time of
war or other public emergency threatening the life of the nation
any member state may derogate from its obligations under the
convention to the extent strictly required by the exigencies of the
situation. That means states can ignore the convention in extreme
circumstances. However, they are not allowed to derogate from
article 2 (right to life) except in respect of deaths resulting from
lawful acts of war. There must also be no derogation from article
3 (no torture), paragraph 1 of article 4 (no slavery) and article 7 (no
retrospective crimes).

The phrase 'threatening the life of the nation' has been given
a broad interpretation by the European Court of Human Rights.
Under the Prevention of Terrorism legislation it is possible for
suspected IRA and loyalist terrorists in the United Kingdom to
be held for up to a week without charge or court appearance. In
November 1988 the court held that this provision was inconsistent
with article 5.[18] A month later the government told the Council of
Europe that the United Kingdom would be availing itself of the right

of derogation from article 5. That derogation, in turn, was upheld by the court.[19]

What the convention does not say

Critics[20] complain that the European Convention is showing its age. It provides no right to obtain information from public bodies. There is no duty on the state to provide a fair hearing before extradition or deportation. Nothing is said about discrimination on grounds of a person's sexual orientation or disability. There is no protection as such for the environment. The convention makes no reference to data protection or children's rights.

Some of the rights granted by the convention are clearly inadequate. Police and troops may be justified in using lethal force to end a riot. The rights to privacy and freedom of expression are heavily restricted by the exceptions already mentioned.

To rectify these omissions Britain could draft its own, updated, Bill of Rights, perhaps based on the United Nations International Covenant on Civil and Political Rights which came into effect in 1976. This is what the Liberal Democrats seek to do. It is also apparently the Labour party's long-term intention,[21] but for the moment Labour's ambitions are limited to taking over and incorporating the existing European Convention on Human Rights.[22] It would be confusing to say the least if people had recourse to one convention in the British courts and another abroad. Nevertheless, the human rights group Liberty argued that incorporating the convention was no substitute for passing a domestic Bill of Rights.[23]

The European Court of Human Rights

The European Court of Human Rights is operated by the Council of Europe. In Britain there is little interest in the council's other responsibilities: few people are aware, for example, of the role it plays in bringing the former communist states into the democratic fold and preparing them for possible entry into the European Union. In other European countries these aspects of its work attract more media coverage than its responsibilities for upholding the European Convention of Human Rights.

The Council of Europe has its headquarters in the French border city of Strasbourg: it currently has forty member states, with more waiting to join. Universal confusion with the entirely separate European Union is compounded by the fact that the European Parliament currently spends one week in four lodging in the Council of Europe's debating chamber and offices – even though there is a perfectly good debating chamber adjoining the European Parliament's administrative offices in Luxembourg.[24]

Just across the river[25] from the Council of Europe offices in Strasbourg, the Human Rights court operates from a stark modern building designed by the British architect Lord Rogers of Riverside.[26] It was not so much his title that made him an appropriate choice to design the new court:[27] it was more that his fellow countrymen were among the best customers. As Lord Irvine said, 'Britain's reputation is that it is one of the most consistent transgressors of human rights in the Council of Europe.'[28] By the end of 1996, seventy-one British cases had been decided by the European Court of Human Rights. In forty-four of these cases the court had found at least one breach of the convention; there was no breach in the remaining twenty-seven cases.[29] Only Italy had a worse record – ninety-three breaches by the end of 1996 – and that was mainly the result of delays in the Italian legal system.

The government's view was that 'if account is taken of relative population sizes and the length of time the right of individual petition and jurisdiction of the court has been accepted here, we are about in the middle of the field'.[30] It is true that Britain has a larger population and has allowed the right of individual petition for longer than some other European countries (Italy granted it in 1973; France not until 1981) but this is hardly a record of which we can be proud.

The main reason why the court has found against Britain so often is that the Human Rights convention has not been incorporated into the three distinct legal systems of the United Kingdom.[31] That means people wishing to take advantage of the convention must take their claims to Strasbourg. Britain is alone among the major nations of Western Europe in not laying down in legislation the basic rights of its citizens while failing to give those citizens a direct means of asserting those rights through their own national courts.[32] How much better it would be, say critics, if our own courts could apply the convention themselves.

It is not necessarily true that incorporation of the convention would improve Britain's international record. As knowledge of the convention became more widespread, people would start bringing challenges in the domestic courts for the first time. Some of these would be rejected by the British courts and taken on to Strasbourg where, no doubt, some of them would be successful. On the other hand, many cases that currently go to Strasbourg would be resolved within the British courts.

How the convention operates

A brief and charming example may help to explain how the convention is applied by the Human Rights court.[33] English law is surprisingly relaxed about the names people choose for their children; people may normally change their names without any formalities. In France, the position is very different.

A French couple, M. and Mme. Guillot, decided to give their baby daughter the name 'Fleur de Marie' (after the heroine of Eugène Sue's novel *Mystères de Paris*). The local registrar of births refused to register the name as it was not listed in any calendar of saints' days.

The couple's appeal was dismissed by a local court, which ruled that a forename 'cannot . . . consist of a combination of two names linked by a preposition'. However, the court was prepared to accept the alternative name of 'Fleur-Marie'. Two further appeals were dismissed by the French courts.

The Guillot family complained that there had been a breach of article 8 of the Human Rights convention, which guarantees the right to respect their private and family life. The European Court noted that there was no mention of names in article 8. Nevertheless, the judges ruled that names were used to identify people within their families; the choice of a forename was a personal, emotional matter and it therefore did come within the ambit of article 8.

Even so, this did not mean there had been a breach of the convention. It was true that the girl would not be able to use the name 'Fleur de Marie' on official documents. She could, though, still be known by that name socially – as indeed she was. The French courts had considered it was in the girl's best interests for her names to be joined by a hyphen rather than a preposition; the Human Rights judges did not think the inconvenience complained of by the Guillot family amounted to a breach of her human rights.

There is one other lesson to be learned from this case. Fleur de Marie (as *we* shall call her, whatever French officialdom may say) was three and a half years old when her parents lost their third and final appeal in the French courts. She was not quite four when they lodged their application with the European Commission on Human Rights (which currently investigates cases before they can be heard by the court). By the time the court reached its decision, in October 1996, Fleur de Marie was thirteen.

The system does not normally operate as slowly as this: five years is more like the average. Officials fervently hoped that the new, streamlined court would work more quickly.

An unincorporated convention

By ratifying the convention in 1951, the British government undertook to observe its provisions. It is for the European Court of Human Rights at Strasbourg to decide whether there has been a breach of the convention in cases brought before it. Unlike decisions of the entirely separate European Court of Justice at Luxembourg, decisions of the Human Rights court do not have immediate effect within the United Kingdom. Whenever the European Court of Human Rights finds that there has been a breach of the convention in the British Isles, the government is obliged to see that domestic law is amended to the extent necessary to comply with the court's ruling. Any failure to make good the breach and prevent a recurrence amounts to a breach of the United Kingdom's obligations under international law and could lead, in theory, to Britain's expulsion from the Council of Europe. In practice, successive British governments have always complied promptly with the court's decisions – although sometimes to the minimum extent necessary.[34]

Because the European Convention is not part of domestic law, the courts have no power to enforce it directly. If United Kingdom legislation plainly conflicts with the enforcement of the convention then the courts must apply the domestic law until the European Court gives a ruling on the issue. Even so, as the Lord Chief Justice has pointed out, the Human Rights convention can have a significant influence over the laws of the United Kingdom in six ways:

Where a statute is ambiguous, the courts will presume parliament intended to legislate in conformity with the convention rather than in conflict with it.

Where the common law is uncertain, unclear or incomplete, the courts will rule, wherever possible, in a manner which conforms with the convention and does not conflict with it.

Where the courts are asked to construe a domestic statute enacted to fulfil a convention obligation, they will presume it was intended to meet that obligation.[35]

Where the courts have to exercise a discretion, they usually seek to avoid violating the convention.

Where the courts are called upon to decide what, in a given situation, public policy demands, they may have regard to the international obligations enshrined in the convention as a source of guidance on what British public policy requires.

When relying on European Community law (which is binding on the United Kingdom courts) the judges may find themselves applying the convention, as Community law includes laws derived from the Human Rights convention.[36]

That said, the European Convention on Human Rights has had only the most limited impact on domestic law. It is rarely invoked in court (except perhaps by devotees of the European Court such as Lord Lester) and even more rarely decisive.[37]

The effect of incorporation

The immediate effect of incorporation may be stated simply enough. If the European Convention were made part of domestic law then people who believed their human rights or fundamental freedoms had been violated could go to a court in the United Kingdom and argue that the convention should be applied. Whether their rights under the convention would prevail over other legislation would depend on which way parliament had chosen to incorporate the convention. If the British courts decided there had been no breach of the convention, claimants could still take their cases to the European Court.[38] These claimants might indeed have to do so if the British courts had been thwarted by immovable legislation. However, Strasbourg would become the court of last resort rather than the first port of call. The saving in time could be five years or more. The saving in lawyers' fees would be considerable.

157

More power to the judges?

We saw in Chapter 1 that Michael Howard was against incorporating the European Convention because he thought that doing so would make it more difficult to keep judges out of the political arena. Would incorporation give more power to the judges?

Lord Lester of Herne Hill QC, the British lawyer most closely associated with support for the Human Rights convention, said in 1993 that 'by enacting a modern Bill of Rights based upon the European Convention, parliament would guide the judges, by prescribing the proper limits of state power where fundamental human rights are at stake'.[39] Some supporters of incorporation seemed to think that means it would give the judges *less* power or discretion than they currently have. The newspaper columnist Polly Toynbee declared 'A Bill of Rights would secure essential principles to guide all future legislation, rules by which the courts would be bound in their interpretation of parliament's laws.'[40] Anthony Barnett of the constitutional pressure group Charter 88 stated that incorporation would restrict the way in which the judges exercised power: they would have greater powers but they would no longer be able to make up the constitution as they went along.[41] Professor John Griffith, formerly of the London School of Economics and author of a leading work called *The Politics of the Judiciary*,[42] asserted that the 'Charter 88 mob' were 'well known to be among the great misleaders of our generation'. He suggested a question for Polly Toynbee to consider: 'If a Bill of Rights would act as a restraint on judicial power, why are so many senior judges and so many QCs in favour of it?'[43]

Most opponents of incorporation think it would give the judges more power. These include a few on the left of the political spectrum as well as many on the right. Writing in 1991, Professor John Griffith said it was 'difficult to see how the welfare of the individual would be promoted' if the convention were incorporated with all its exemptions and interpreted by the judiciary of the day.[44] The columnist Melanie Phillips, while accepting that there was a 'democratic deficit', thought it seemed 'an extraordinarily perverse remedy to give a small, unelected and unaccountable group of judges the power to fetter the choices and decisions made by representatives elected by the people'.[45] Professor Conor Gearty of King's College London argued in a paper published by the Society

158

of Labour Lawyers that a Bill of Rights 'would empower the courts to strike down legislation passed by parliament. The effect would be thus to transfer the ultimate power in the community to the judges who by operating the Bill of Rights could dictate what the people through their political representatives could or could not do on any particular question.'[46] In a subsequent lecture, he repeated his view that entrenchment of the European Convention would enable the judges to substitute their views for those of parliament.[47] As we shall see, it all depends on what the legislation says.

Lord Irvine was well aware of the view that incorporating the European Convention would give more power to the judges. We have already seen[48] his criticism of judges like Lord Woolf for suggesting it might be possible to hold statutes invalid. In the same lecture, he noted that those who opposed incorporation of the convention were worried that it would mean a shift of power from an elected parliament to unelected judges. In a telling sentence, Lord Irvine declared: 'That objection, entertained by many along the political spectrum, can only be strengthened by fears of judicial supremacism.'[49]

His warning to the judges was clear: don't pull too hard on the reins or you'll frighten the horses. Lay off the judicial supremacism line; otherwise a Labour government will not get the parliamentary support it needs for incorporating the convention.

It seems plain enough that incorporating the convention would give the United Kingdom's judges more power. On the other hand, if fewer cases reach Strasbourg the judges there will have *less* power to shape our laws. Moreover, those judges who might take a creative approach to human rights law are probably the judges who are taking an innovative approach to the common law at the moment.

Methods of incorporation

People talk of incorporating the convention as if there were only one way of doing it. In fact, there are several; each of them offers a different degree of shift in the balance of power between the executive and the judiciary.

The difference lies in the level of *entrenchment* chosen by parliament. Entrenching legislation – metaphorically digging a trench round it to protect it from attack – is the process of making an enactment superior to ordinary legislation. Entrenching a law may also make it harder to repeal.[50]

Under the United Kingdom's unwritten constitution, even such basic laws as the Bill of Rights 1689 may be amended by a simple majority in parliament.[51] Until recently it was believed[52] that this principle made it impossible for legislation to be entrenched under our constitution: the sovereignty of parliament meant that no parliament could bind its successors and no court could set aside laws made by parliament. That view is now considered wrong.

The European Communities Act 1972 provided that community law should prevail over domestic law, including 'any enactment passed or to be passed'.[53] The United Kingdom's courts are now comfortable with the idea that European law from Brussels can trump pre-existing domestic legislation. There was originally some doubt over whether the European Communities Act – an act of parliament like any other – would succeed in reversing the normal principle of parliamentary interpretation: that a later statute will always override an earlier inconsistent one. In the event, it did. As Professor Sir William Wade said, with the words quoted at the start of this paragraph, 'parliament attempted to bind its successors and to subordinate all future legislation to community law. And the attempt has evidently succeeded.'[54]

This was demonstrated in 1990 by the famous *Factortame* case.[55] As we have seen in Chapter 4, the English courts took advice from the European Court of Justice and held that the Merchant Shipping Act 1988 – which was passed to stop 'quota hopping' by Spanish fishing vessels – was contrary to European law and therefore invalid.[56] This was the first time the courts had held that an earlier act of parliament had effectively invalidated a later one. The judges had effectively entrenched the 1972 legislation by holding that it was superior to the 1988 act. They had made the European Communities Act 1972 a law against which other legislation was to be judged.

This did not necessarily mean that the 1972 legislation was protected from repeal by a subsequent parliament, but it did give the 1972 law enhanced political status. It must surely be harder for a subsequent government to repeal a law to which the courts have attached such importance. The same status could be given to a new Bill of Rights.

There are at least four ways of incorporating the convention. They range from full entrenchment to no protection at all.[57]

Full judicial entrenchment: the United States
Under a system of full judicial entrenchment, the courts may strike down legislation that does not, in their view, comply with the fundamental law. If an act of parliament incorporating the Human Rights convention were entrenched it could trump inconsistent legislation enacted before or after the fundamental law was passed. Needless to say, this arrangement gives the supreme court considerable powers. We may see it operating in the United States of America and it has been used in a number of the new Commonwealth countries, including some with Westminster-style parliamentary systems. These countries all have written constitutions.

It should still be possible under our unwritten constitution to entrench human rights legislation in the United Kingdom in the same way as we have done with European Community law. But, as Professor Michael Zander said, this prospect 'ignores political realities. Given the current negative British attitude towards Europe it seems exceedingly unlikely that any foreseeable future Labour government would be prepared openly and avowedly to give the jurisprudence of the European Convention on Human Rights the same status as that of Community law.'[58] It seems we shall have to look elsewhere.

The 'notwithstanding clause' procedure: Canada
The next option would be a system of judicial entrenchment which parliament could override in clearly defined circumstances. Normally, parliament would have to act with its eyes open: a clause in any subsequent legislation would say it was to apply 'notwithstanding' (or despite) the fact that it contravened the human rights laws. This system was introduced in Canada in 1982: the courts were given wide powers under the Canadian Charter of Rights and Freedoms. As supreme law, this charter prevails over all existing and future legislation. Yet the charter also allows the federal parliament or provincial legislatures to declare, for five-year renewable periods, that specific legislation should be given effect 'notwithstanding' a contrary provision in the charter. Such a system could give citizens a reasonable level of protection.[59] As we shall see, it no longer seems the most likely option for the United Kingdom.[60]

161

Limited judicial entrenchment: Hong Kong
It is possible to pass a Bill of Rights which is not entrenched but still has some overriding status: the courts are told to follow it where they can although it can be modified by subsequent legislation. An example of this is the Hong Kong Bill of Rights Ordinance 1991. This allows the courts to strike down pre-existing legislation that is inconsistent with it. The ordinance also says that subsequent legislation should, if possible, be interpreted consistently with the Bill of Rights. If such an interpretation is not possible then the courts must obey the new laws: they have no power to declare subsequent legislation ineffective. This hybrid option preserves parliamentary sovereignty, but it gives judges the difficult task of deciding whether the clear words of an earlier statute have been repealed by the broad language in a bill of rights.

Merely an interpretative tool: New Zealand
Finally, it is possible to give a Bill of Rights no special status at all. The New Zealand Bill of Rights 1990 requires the judges to interpret statutes consistently with its provisions where possible, although it gives the judges no power to override any enactment passed before or since.[61] This is obviously the weakest possible form of protection: some commentators see it as 'little more than a symbolic gesture'.[62] Even so, it is the method of incorporation most likely to be adopted in the United Kingdom. We shall see later in this chapter what effect it would have.

Attempts at incorporation

The human rights lawyer, Lord Lester, made the first plea for incorporation of the European Convention as long ago as 1968.[63] Various backbench peers and MPs have supported legislative attempts to incorporate the convention,[64] the latest of which was a bill put forward by Lord Lester himself in 1996. A bill designed to incorporate the European Convention is often called a 'bill of rights', although the measure may have a slightly different name (for example, Human Rights Bill).

These bills have followed a common theme, though the wording has varied over the years. Bills introduced regularly between 1975 and 1981 by the Liberal peer, Lord Wade, provided that the convention should 'have the force of law, and shall be enforceable by action in the courts of the United Kingdom'. The convention was to prevail over previous enactments; it was also to prevail over subsequent enactments unless parliament stated to the contrary.

In spite of the Kilmuir rules,[65] a serving judge proposed during a public lecture in 1974 that there should be an entrenched bill of rights in the United Kingdom.[66] The judge was Lord Justice Scarman. In 1985 Lord Scarman, by then a law lord, announced that he would be introducing his own bill in the House of Lords with the aim of incorporating the convention. Lord Scarman saw nothing improper in introducing a bill on which he might eventually have to rule in his capacity as a judge: he said it was an excellent tradition that on matters dealing with the proper development of the law the law lords participated in the legislative process.[67]

Like previous measures Lord Scarman's bill also provided that the convention should have the force of law in the United Kingdom. Again, the convention was to prevail over previous legislation; again it was to override any subsequent enactments unless it was expressly excluded. This type of legislation seems closest to the Canadian model described above.

Lord Scarman's bill was eventually taken through the House of Lords by the Conservative peer Lord Broxbourne,[68] but it failed to get past the House of Commons. A similar measure introduced in 1986 with all-party support by the Conservative MP, Sir Edward Gardner QC, was also blocked by the government. The 1986 bill provided that the convention was to prevail over any subsequent act of parliament unless infringing the convention was unavoidable in order to give effect to the new legislation. This was broadly in line with the Hong Kong model.

In 1994, Lord Lester introduced his own Human Rights Bill. With the support of the senior judiciary and the Labour party it was passed by the House of Lords in May 1995[69] but once more it failed to get past the Conservative majority in the House of Commons.

Under Lord Lester's 1994 bill the convention was to be 'incorporated into the law of the United Kingdom', and 'given full legal effect in accordance with this act'. In its initial wording, the bill proposed that the convention should prevail over legislation passed *after* it had come into force.[70] Lord Lester argued that 'This legislative mandate for the courts to set aside inconsistent primary legislation would not have undermined the pure doctrine of parliamentary supremacy; it would have remained open to a future parliament to have repealed or amended the Human Rights Bill.' In other words, he was saying, the Human Rights Act would have had the same status as the European Communities Act 1972 now has.[71]

This all proved too much for the law lords on whom Lord Lester relied for support. He conceded that the clause 'would have been perceived as enhancing judicial power and limiting the actual, if not the theoretical, powers of parliament.'[72] In the end Lord Lester was persuaded to tone down his proposals, bringing them more into line with the New Zealand Bill of Rights. The amended version of his bill provided that 'so far as the context permits, enactments (whenever passed or made) shall be construed consistently with' the Human Rights convention. Lord Lester also withdrew a clause that would have obliged public bodies to compensate people whose human rights had been violated. As a result, he admitted that his bill had become 'more a mouse than a lion'. He hoped – in vain, as he had to accept – that this would give it a better chance of getting through the House of Commons.[73]

In 1995, Lord Browne-Wilkinson told the House of Lords that he was profoundly in favour of Lord Lester's bill. There was no disagreement over the fact that everyone in the United Kingdom enjoyed the rights set out in the European Convention. There was no disagreement over the fact that those rights should be enforceable. The only disagreement was over whether – as he put it – 'the rights of Englishmen[74] should be capable of enforcement in an English court and that Englishmen, enjoying those rights, should not be turned away from the English courts which say they have no power to act'. He made it plain that he and his fellow judges would welcome incorporation 'as conferring the basic right to which all Englishmen are entitled, namely to have their rights determined within this country and not outside it'. Lord Browne-Wilkinson denied that the moves would amount to 'empire building' or an attack on parliamentary sovereignty.[75]

Subsequently, Lord Browne-Wilkinson expressed reservations about having the power to overturn legislation. He agreed that if his fellow judges were given that responsibility they would become much more involved in the political process than ever before. That was because they would then be looking at the inherent merits of parliamentary legislation, rather than the way in which it had been expressed: 'That is the American experience. Therefore, as in America, you would find each generation of politicians, when in power, seeking to get their boys on to the Supreme Court, something which singularly does not happen at the moment. That, I think, is quite a dangerous thing.'

Lord Browne-Wilkinson suggested a much less extreme way of achieving the same effect: 'That is to say simply that, so far as possible, parliament is to be taken not to have intended to infringe the Convention on Human Rights, and that, so far as possible, the law should be construed so as to give effect to those Convention rights.'[76] This was of course what Lord Lester eventually proposed in the bill that Lord Browne-Wilkinson supported.

Many judges are worried about the risks involved in being drawn into politics. To take just one example, Lord Justice Ward, newly appointed to the Court of Appeal, said he did not want to become a constitutional court. He thought that incorporating the convention would give judges power to apply indiscriminately what were, after all, vague but important principles and use them to override what might otherwise be the clear intention of parliament. Why did that worry him? 'Because I think that it brings us even further into what is increasingly seen – wrongly, I often fear – as a battle between the judges and parliament. I don't particularly like being embroiled in that battle. I don't see us being in battle one with the other. We have different functions and I don't believe that our constitutional position is enhanced by making me all-powerful.'[77]

The Master of the Rolls Lord Woolf said he would certainly reserve to parliament the ability to override an incorporated convention, if it declared expressly that it was doing so. If it did not, there should be at the very least a strong presumption that it meant to observe the convention. He thought the judges should be conservative in this area because otherwise they would be drawn into issues that were highly political. That should be avoided as far as possible.[78]

Lord Lester deliberately reflected the judges' concerns in the latest version of his bill, published in October 1996.[79] It was broadly in line with the New Zealand model, the weakest form of incorporation. It was also broadly in line with Labour party thinking: on these issues the two opposition parties were working together. Under Lord Lester's bill, the European Convention[80] was to have effect 'notwithstanding any rule of law to the contrary'. That presumably meant that it was to override any inconsistent provisions of the common law. The bill then said: 'Whenever an enactment can be given a meaning that is consistent with [the European Convention], that meaning shall be preferred to any other meaning.' That apparently allowed the convention to be overridden by unambiguous language in any statute passed before or after the Human Rights Act had become law. The only saving grace was that the government would have had to alert parliament whenever it put forward legislation which might override the convention; it would also have to explain why it was doing so. As drafted, Lord Lester's bill could not have been invoked against private individuals or corporations: it would apply only to acts done by ministers or public bodies.

There was no possibility that Lord Lester's proposals could become law before the 1997 General Election. Yet his bill was a realistic attempt to sum up the judicial consensus at the time. It had support from virtually all the serving and retired judges in the House of Lords except Lord Donaldson, who thought it required judges to become involved in matters best left to parliament.

The Conservative view

As Lord Chancellor, Lord Mackay was firmly opposed to incorporation of the European Convention into the laws of the United Kingdom. His government believed that 'Incorporation would do nothing in practice to improve the enjoyment of the rights and freedoms protected under the European Convention.'[81] Lord Mackay went further: he thought it would change the nature of the judiciary.

At present, judges may only decide a case on the facts that come before them. According to Lord Mackay, this means that a court cannot examine the effects of a range of options or decide what effect a change of course in the case before it might cause in other areas. Because the judges are limited to individual cases involving specific litigants, they are generally able to steer clear of the political arena in which policy issues are discussed. That way, he said, their independence is assured.[82]

Nevertheless Lord Mackay argued, 'incorporation of the European Convention or a Bill of Rights as the yardstick by which acts of parliament are to be measured would inevitably draw judges into making decisions of a far more political nature, measuring policy against abstract principles with possible implications for the development of broad social and economic policy' – for example, the conditions under which abortions should be allowed. In Lord Mackay's view, such decisions should be made by parliament.

If the judges were drawn into politics, people would ask whether there should be a change in the criteria for the appointment of judges, making the political stance of each candidate a matter of importance. Lord Mackay did not want to see anything like the United States Senate confirmation hearings at which nominees for the Supreme Court are questioned about their views. If that happened, the next question would be how the public's confidence in judicial independence and impartiality could be maintained.

Those would not be the only questions. As we have seen, much of the European Convention allows exceptions: article 10, for example, says the exercise of free speech is subject to such conditions as are necessary in a democratic society. 'If the Convention were incorporated into domestic law,' Lord Mackay wondered, 'which body should decide what is so necessary; the courts which are charged with the function of applying the law, or parliament which is democratically elected?'[83]

Lord Mackay's preferred answer to this rhetorical question was obvious enough. Yet why shouldn't the courts decide what restrictions are necessary? How can parliament possibly adjudicate on individual cases? How, indeed, do the judges manage in virtually all the other countries which have signed up to the Human Rights convention? As Professor Zander says, the Canadian system demonstrates 'that it is possible to have a Bill of Rights without needing to inquire into the socio-political opinions of judges . . . The introduction there of the Charter did not lead to a change in the traditional methods for the appointment of judges.'[84]

Labour's view

We have seen that Labour is committed to incorporating the European Convention. As Lord Irvine put it:

> Our country is bound by the convention. Our citizens are entitled to its protections. But to win them, they have to go to a foreign court in Strasbourg, and that can take five years and often more. Why do we not trust our own judges to secure our convention rights for us, but confine our citizens to the court in Strasbourg?
>
> We have a judiciary of high quality. Our most senior judges are as fine

167

as any in the world. What a loss it is to the development of European jurisprudence in human rights that our judges are disabled from making a British contribution. Incorporation, under the next government, will repatriate from Strasbourg to Britain the day-to-day rights to which our citizens are entitled under the convention.[85]

Even though Lord Irvine expressed his trust in the judges to uphold human rights in the United Kingdom, he thought public confidence in their decisions would be enhanced if they did not have the last word entirely to themselves:

At the final appellate level, where points of fundamental or wide-ranging importance about human rights may have to be decided, there is a strong case for adding to the judges of the final court three non-lawyer members, drawn from a panel of persons with knowledge and understanding of society and of human rights in the broad sense. That would ensure that principles are not laid down from any narrowly legal perspective. The non-lawyer members would be full members of the court, whose vote would rank equally with the judges. They would best be appointed from a list to be drawn up, after wide consultation, by an independent Judicial Appointments Commission.[86]

Lord Irvine subsequently made it explicit that he was not suggesting the lay members would be able to outvote the professional judges. The law lords normally sit in panels of five: Lord Irvine was proposing that five law lords should sit with three lay people, making up a court of eight members.[87]

This proposal is open to an obvious objection: with an even number of judges there is clearly a risk of deadlock. From time to time the judges would split four–four; in those circumstances, the final court of appeal would not be able to reach a decision. It would be possible to provide that the side with the largest number of professional judges should carry the day, but that would not be consistent with Lord Irvine's wish that the lay members should rank equally with the professional judges.

The Constitution Unit has put forward several more objections:

The definition of who would be chosen is extremely vague; nor is there any reference to who would make the appointments and how. One option would be for appointments to be subject to parliamentary hearings, as in the USA in relation to the Supreme Court. However, this could cause significant political disputes. In addition, if the final appeal court – which means the most senior and experienced judges – cannot be relied on to offer a view without lay input, it would be difficult to justify lower courts exercising judicial discretion without it. Moreover, if final responsibility for ruling on questions of compliance were given to an alternative court then the position could arise in which an European Convention on Human Rights issue came up in the House of Lords in the course of other proceedings, and the House of Lords would then need to decide whether to reconvene with the additional lay members.[88]

The idea of having three lay members sitting with the law lords does not even have the support of Lord Irvine's parliamentary colleagues. In December 1996 the shadow Home Secretary, Jack Straw MP, and the shadow Minister for the Lord Chancellor's Department, Paul Boateng MP, published a consultation paper on incorporating the convention. After summarising the case for the appointment of three lay members, the two MPs said: 'We have yet to be convinced about the merits of this proposal and welcome views on this. We are unsympathetic to any idea of creating a special constitutional court.'[89]

Labour's paper also dealt with some practical issues. The defendant at the European Court of Human Rights is always the country responsible for the alleged breach of rights. If the convention is incorporated, against whom should it be invoked? Labour argued that individuals should not be liable in the courts: action would only be possible against public authorities, including government departments, executive agencies, quangos, local authorities and other public services.

The Institute for Public Policy Research – a left-of-centre think tank – argued that Labour's plan to incorporate the convention would be of little value unless a Human Rights commission was set up in the United Kingdom. Depending on the extent of its mandate, it could 'monitor, advise, educate, investigate, mediate, adjudicate complaints and initiate legislation'.[90] Labour was lukewarm about that idea. Instead it proposed a parliamentary committee to monitor the operation of the new human rights laws.[91]

As we saw earlier, there are at least four ways of incorporating the convention. It seemed at one stage that Labour favoured the second of these, the Canadian system. There would have been a Human Rights Act which would have overridden all existing legislation, although parliament would still have been able to pass legislation inconsistent with the Human Rights Act (and presumably any court rulings made under it) provided it did so in clear terms.[92] However,

Labour's preference was clearly moving towards the much weaker New Zealand model favoured by Lord Lester.

Speaking in the House of Lords in July 1996, Lord Irvine said:

> I do not begin to accept that parliamentary sovereignty would be infringed by incorporation. Incorporation would be an exercise in sovereignty. Parliament would retain the right to repeal or amend the incorporating statute. Parliamentary sovereignty could be maintained by requiring that any statute intended to be inconsistent with the convention should say so expressly.
>
> Another mechanism, which applies in New Zealand, obliges the courts, so far as possible, to interpret statutes and apply the common law so as to conform to the convention. It is not beyond our wit both to preserve parliamentary sovereignty and to allow our citizens access to their own courts to secure their rights under the convention.[93]

Later in 1996, Lord Irvine made it plain that he was coming closer to supporting the New Zealand approach, although he would wait until the matter was debated in parliament before making up his mind.[94] Responding to an article in the *New Statesman*,[95] Lord Irvine said:

> I agree that an important issue is whether, after incorporation, the judges may strike down acts of parliament as inconsistent with the convention. This, however, need not be so. One possibility, though not the only one, is the New Zealand model. Under it the courts are required *so far as possible* to interpret statutes and apply the common law so as to conform, but may not strike down a statute which parliament plainly intended should not conform.[96]

Interviewed a month later by the same magazine, Lord Irvine said the New Zealand model repaid close attention:

> That creates the obligation for judges, so far as is possible, to construe statutes in conformity with the convention. In the overwhelming majority of cases, judges will be able to do that, but if in any case that's really impossible then I would say that parliament has to prevail. But then parliament could be faced with a situation where a court, probably the highest in the land, has decided that it can't interpret a statute consistent with the convention, that the statute in question does derogate from the European Convention on Human Rights. I would hope that at this point the matter would be a candidate for legislative action. That would be a very British compromise.[97]

Judging by the reaction of Lord Browne-Wilkinson and others, this is the option that the judges would be most comfortable with.

Anything more would risk bringing the judiciary into conflict with parliament.

In the consultation paper it published at the end of 1996, the Labour party did not explain precisely how it proposed the convention should be incorporated. Although Labour believed that in practice the convention was 'likely to enjoy a high degree of permanence in UK law', the party accepted that entrenching it would be impossible. In Labour's view, the new legislation would not affect parliamentary sovereignty: parliament would retain the right to pass 'exceptional legislation in times of national crisis'.[98]

The human rights group Liberty said that under Labour's proposals domestic law was likely to prevail in the event of any conflict: claimants who lost in the United Kingdom courts would still have to go to Strasbourg.[99]

Lord Bingham, speaking a few months before he became Lord Chief Justice, considered what would happen if legislation gave effect to the convention 'save in so far as any later act [of parliament] might expressly require otherwise' – as he understood Labour were proposing. On that basis 'There would be no question of striking down statutes as incompatible with the convention: if parliament wished to depart from the convention, it would so provide: if it did not, the courts would strive to interpret later statutes consistently with the convention, as in cases of doubt they already do.' In his view such a move would not have fundamental constitutional implications, it would not involve an important change in the judiciary's relations with the executive and it would not undermine the sovereignty of parliament.[100] He did not say whether he thought it would give the judges more power.

If Lord Irvine's plans were implemented the courts would not be able to strike down a statute as incompatible with human rights. It is obviously wise for a Labour Lord Chancellor to avoid foisting on to the judges a power they do not want and might actively resent. It is equally prudent not to ask a democratically elected parliament to surrender powers to the judges.

What then would incorporating the convention in this way actually achieve? The judges would certainly be able to overrule any previous decisions of the courts that they thought inconsistent with the convention. If there were no legislation governing a particular issue they would also be able to apply the convention in reaching a decision. However, their most important role would be to set the limits of powers granted to the executive by parliament: the judges would decide whether the actions of government ministers, officials and public bodies were compatible with human rights.

The consequences of incorporation
Lord Lester believed that if parliament were to pass his bill, and incorporate the Human Rights convention on New Zealand lines, it would reverse the effect of *Brind*,[101] a case which established that the European Convention cannot be directly invoked in the English courts to decide whether administrative discretion, exercised under broad statutory powers, has unnecessarily interfered with the rights and freedoms guaranteed by the convention.[102]

Don Brind was (and is) a BBC journalist: in 1988 he was a prominent member of the National Union of Journalists. In October of that year Mrs Thatcher's government decided to ban broadcasts by supporters of the IRA and other Irish terrorist or para-military organisations. For that purpose, the Home Secretary issued directives to the broadcasting authorities preventing them from broadcasting 'any words spoken' by supporters of banned organisations.[103] Mr Brind and five other journalists sought judicial review of the Home Secretary's decision. Their applications were dismissed all the way up to the House of Lords.

Lord Lester (not then a peer) and David Pannick (not then a QC) appeared for the journalists. They argued that the Home Secretary should have taken into account article 10 of the Human Rights convention, which says any interference with freedom of expression must be no more than is 'necessary in a democratic society'. The convention was not, of course, part of English law. Nevertheless, Lord Lester argued that parliament had intended the Home Secretary to exercise his discretion within the limits laid down by the convention.

That view was rejected by the law lords. Lord Bridge thought it would be 'a judicial usurpation of the legislative function'. Lord Ackner feared it would mean 'incorporating the convention into English domestic law by the back door'. For the first time, there would have been a presumption that parliament intended statutory powers to be exercised in accordance with the convention. Of course, that might not have helped Don Brind very much. Even if the courts had been able to rely on article 10, they may well have reached the same conclusion. Lord Templeman said: 'the interference

172

with freedom of expression is minimal and the reasons given by the Home Secretary are compelling'. Lord Ackner said: 'the extent of the interference with the right of free speech is a very modest one'. Lord Bridge said the restrictions were an 'irritant' of 'limited scope'.

Even so, Lord Lester believed his limited bill – and, no doubt, Labour's version of it – would make the European Convention on Human Rights a full part of our system of public law. It would also ensure that the Scottish courts took account of the convention.

At a dinner in his honour in 1996, the eighty-five-year-old Lord Scarman said he now thought the European Convention on Human Rights was on the point of becoming law in Britain: he only hoped he would live long enough to see this come to pass.[104] Lord Lester may well be right when he says, 'We will not have to wait much longer to have our fundamental rights secured and protected by the law of the land.'[105]

6

From *Spycatcher* to the Scott Inquiry

Q. I put it to you that [your] letter [asking the publishers for a copy of Chapman Pincher's forthcoming book *Their Trade is Treachery*] contains an untruth. That is the question.
A. It does not say that we have already got a copy of the book, that is quite true.
Q. So it contains an untruth?
A. Well, it does not contain that truth.
. . .
Q. So it contains a lie?
A. It was a misleading impression. It does not contain a lie, I don't think.
Q. What is the difference between a misleading impression and a lie?
A. A lie is a straight untruth.
Q. What is a misleading impression – a sort of bent untruth?
A. As one person said, it is perhaps being economical with the truth.

Sir Robert Armstrong, Cabinet Secretary, cross examined by
Malcolm Turnbull (1986)[1]

Q. Here the writer . . . is attributing to you a statement . . . which cannot be correct to your knowledge.
A. Well, it's our old friend being economical, isn't it?
Q. With the truth?
A. With the *actualité*.

Alan Clark, former Trade Minister, cross examined by
Geoffrey Robertson QC (1992)[2]

Mutual respect

There are many ways of judging how well a government has performed. Is the economy buoyant? Are living standards higher than they were? How are the schools doing, the hospitals, the arts? A less common assessment is to judge a government on the way it deals with the judiciary. Do judges have respect for ministers? Is there respect for the judiciary in government circles? Has one side or the other – perhaps frustrated by an apparent breakdown in normal relations – tried to overreach itself?

Readers may have drawn their own conclusions from the examples already offered. Yet there are two cases, referred to in the title to this chapter, from which we may learn valuable lessons about the relationship between the executive and the judiciary during the four Conservative administrations that governed Britain between 1979 and 1997. They also happen to be fascinating stories.

Spycatcher

In June 1986, a relatively modest news item appeared on an inside page of the *Observer*. An Australian court was about to hear an application by the British government for a permanent injunction against the publishing company Heinemann. It turned out that the British government was trying to prevent a retired MI5 officer called Peter Wright from publishing his memoirs in Australia. The government was invoking the law of confidence, created by the judges to protect people from having advantage taken of them by those they had trusted with confidential information.[3]

According to the *Observer*, Mr Wright was claiming that:

The Security Service MI5 had bugged diplomatic conferences in London.
It had also bugged foreign diplomats in London.
It had bugged the suite at Claridges used by the Soviet leader Nikita Khrushchev during his visit to London in the 1950s.
The Soviet spy Guy Burgess had attempted unsuccessfully to seduce Churchill's daughter on Soviet instructions.

The first three of these claims would have come as no surprise: they must be the stock-in-trade of any security service.[4] The fourth seemed intrinsically implausible.[5] There was more to come. The newspaper added that Peter Wright had revealed in his book details of what were described as 'two of the biggest potential unresolved post-war MI5 scandals':

The unsuccessful plot to assassinate President Nasser of Egypt at the time of Suez.
What Mr Wright's lawyers reportedly described as the 'MI5 plot' against Harold Wilson when he became Prime Minister in 1974.[6]

These allegations were more interesting. They were repeated and amplified in an inside-page story that appeared in the next day's *Guardian*.[7]

It was not the first time that anyone had known of Peter Wright and his memoirs: more than a year earlier, the *Observer* had briefly reported that he was seeking to have his book published in Australia in order to thwart any blocking moves by the security service.[8] Nor was it the first time anyone had learned of Mr Wright's allegations. Significantly, they had surfaced in a popular book written five years earlier by the security specialist, Chapman Pincher.[9] No objection had been taken by the government at the time.

Temporary injunctions

For some months after the two articles appeared in the *Observer* and the *Guardian*, the British people heard nothing more of Peter Wright's allegations.[10] Within a week, the government had obtained temporary injunctions against the two newspapers preventing them from publishing any information Mr Wright had obtained while working for the Security Service. They were 'temporary' in the sense that they were to last until a full hearing of the government's case. The Attorney General Sir Michael Havers, acting on behalf of the government rather than in any independent quasi-judicial sense, was seeking permanent injunctions against Mr Wright. The government's case was that the former MI5 officer had broken the duty of confidence he owed his employers under the ordinary principles of the common law.

The newspapers briefed Anthony Lester QC and David Pannick to challenge the temporary injunctions. Mr Lester said that if the government's arguments were accepted it would mean 'the mere assertion, or ritual incantation, of the interests of national security by the executive is sufficient to justify the prior restraint of publication of confidential information by the press'.[11] In response, John Laws for the Attorney General said that publication of material obtained by Mr Wright 'would be likely to give rise to unquantifiable injury to the security of the nation'.[12] After a three-day hearing, Mr Justice Millett upheld the original injunctions, while restricting their scope to allow the newspapers to report what was said in open court in Australia.[13] A few days later, the temporary injunctions were upheld (with further variations) by the Court of Appeal.

There the story rested until the following year, 1987. In the

176

spring, the government's application for a permanent ban on the book came to court in Australia. It was rejected in March,[14] although further appeals delayed publication there until the autumn.[15] Meanwhile, in April, the *Independent* chose to devote its entire front page to a summary of Peter Wright's allegations.[16] It was an audacious move for a paper that had been launched only six months earlier. Asked to explain itself, the newspaper said, plausibly enough, that the government had only obtained injunctions against the *Observer* and the *Guardian*, not against the media as a whole. Other papers[17] took advantage of the *Independent* move by repeating Mr Wright's claims. Later in the summer the *Sunday Times* acquired serial rights and published a long extract from the book.[18]

Following the *Independent* story, the *Guardian* and the *Observer* went back to court to ask for their injunctions to be lifted. The government, meanwhile, argued that the *Independent* was guilty of contempt of court, even though the injunction preventing publication of Mr Wright's allegations had been directed at an entirely different newspaper.

There was much to-ing and fro-ing. A senior High Court judge (the Vice Chancellor Sir Nicolas Browne-Wilkinson) found for the newspapers on both issues.[19] The Court of Appeal rapidly overturned his rulings, reinstating the injunctions[20] and deciding that one injunction would bind all newspapers.[21]

Within a few days the law lords were asked to decide whether the temporary injunctions should remain in force, even though Mr Wright's main allegations were now widely known. The question appeared even more academic because Mr Wright's book – by now entitled *Spycatcher* – had just been published in the United States.[22] The government made no attempt to stop copies being brought into the United Kingdom.[23]

Even so, at the end of July 1987[24] the law lords decided by a majority of three to two that the injunctions should remain in force until the full hearing of the government's application for a permanent ban. Lord Brandon, Lord Templeman and Lord Ackner upheld the temporary injunctions; Lord Bridge and Lord Oliver profoundly disagreed. The law lords' speeches make instructive reading.

For the majority, Lord Brandon summarised his reasons for maintaining the temporary injunctions in nine propositions:

The action brought by the Attorney General against the *Guardian* and the *Observer* has as its object the protection of an important public interest: the maintenance so far as possible of the secrecy of the British security service.

The injunctions are temporary: they remain in effect until the hearing of the Attorney General's claim.

Before the publication of *Spycatcher* in America, the Attorney General had a strong arguable case for obtaining permanent injunctions at the full hearing.

While the publication of *Spycatcher* in America has much weakened that case, it remains an arguable one.

The only way of deciding whether the Attorney General's case should succeed or fail is to have it heard.

If the injunctions are lifted now he will lose all opportunity of winning permanent injunctions at the full hearing.

If the injunctions are not lifted now and he loses at the final hearing the newspapers will then be able to publish Mr Wright's allegations.

It follows that lifting the injunctions now could cause more injustice to the Attorney General than continuing them could cause to the newspapers.

Continuing the injunctions is therefore preferable.[25]

Though logically impeccable, Lord Brandon's judgment was based on the premise that there was still something secret in Peter Wright's allegations. This, as even Lord Brandon seemed to acknowledge, was a tenuous argument. Another of the law lords, Lord Templeman, anticipated the inevitable criticism: 'I reject the argument that the law will appear ridiculous if it imposes a restriction on mass circulation when any individual member of the public may obtain a copy of *Spycatcher* from abroad. The court cannot exceed its territorial jurisdiction but the court can prevent the harm which will result from mass circulation within its own jurisdiction . . .'

As far as the media were concerned, it was not the law that appeared ridiculous – it was the judges. The *Daily Mirror* published photographs of Lord Brandon, Lord Templeman and Lord Ackner on its front page. The pictures were printed upside down. Taking up half the page was a pithy comment: YOU FOOLS.[26]

Lord Ackner was incandescent. In his written judgment, delivered a fortnight after the law lords had announced their decision, Lord Ackner said English justice would 'have come to a pretty pass if our inability to control what happens beyond our shores is to result in total incapacity to control what happens within our very own jurisdiction'. He accused the press of 'one-sided reporting': it was 'an abuse of power and a depressing reflection of falling standards and values'. There were 'elements in the press as a whole which not only lack responsibility, but integrity'.

The remaining two judges saw the case very differently. For Lord Bridge, the important question was whether 'there is any remaining interest of national security which [the original temporary] injunctions are capable of protecting and, if so, whether it is of sufficient weight to justify the massive encroachment on freedom of speech which the continuance of the . . . injunctions in present circumstances necessarily involves.' In his view, there was not. In a resounding judgment, Lord Bridge said:

> Freedom of speech is always the first casualty under a totalitarian regime . . . The present attempt to insulate the public in this country from information which is freely available elsewhere is a significant step down that very dangerous road. The maintenance of that ban, as more and more copies of *Spycatcher* enter this country and circulate here, will seem more and more ridiculous. If the government are determined to fight to maintain the ban to the end, they will face inevitable condemnation and humiliation by the European Court of Human Rights in Strasbourg. Long before that, they will have been condemned at the bar of public opinion in the free world.

He was ably supported in these prescient remarks by another judge, Lord Oliver:

> I do not for a moment dispute that there are occasions when the strength of the public interest in the preservation of confidentiality outweighs even the importance of the free exercise of the essential privileges which lie at the roots of our society. But if those privileges are to be overborne, then they must be overborne to some purpose. The argument is not perhaps assisted by homely metaphors about empty stables or escaping cats, but I cannot help but feel your Lordships are being asked in the light of what has now occurred to beat the air and to interfere with an essential freedom for the preservation of a confidentiality that has already been lost beyond recall.

It is easy to assess these speeches from a position of hindsight. Ten years on, Peter Wright is dead, his book published and all but forgotten. The Security Service may now bug and burgle without breaking the law.[27] Its offices are photographed in a glossy brochure, it advertises openly for recruits and its Director General has appeared on television.[28] Although it still relies on secrecy, there is no suggestion that its effectiveness has been seriously compromised – either by the allegations of an embittered former employee or by its own decision to emerge from the shadows. In the era of the Internet, we no longer suppose that we can stop books from crossing frontiers.

Even in 1987, it was surely not just journalists who thought the majority decision of the House of Lords was wrong. The speeches of Lord Brandon, Lord Templeman and Lord Ackner betrayed a narrow, legalistic approach. The three judges seemed to ignore what was happening in the world around them as, Canute-like, they tried to stop the in-coming tide of information. Nobody was saying that MI5 officers should be free to say what they liked, still less that they should be allowed to make money from selling the nation's secrets. As Lord Oliver's elegant nod in the direction of empty stables and escaping cats indicated, it was simply too late to stop Peter Wright.

Soon after its publication in the United States, people were bringing back copies of *Spycatcher* for their friends. By the autumn of 1987, it had become a book no fashionable home could afford to be without. The government had its temporary injunction, but the newspapers were bound to argue that it should not be made permanent. What should the government have done next?

Permanent injunctions?
Lord Bridge, who presided over the 1987 law lords' hearing but found himself in the minority, had his own advice for Margaret Thatcher and her cabinet. In a section of his judgment that read more like political comment than legal reasoning, he advised the government to 'reappraise the whole *Spycatcher* situation'. Lord Bridge bravely dared to hope that ministers would bring to this reappraisal 'qualities of vision and statesmanship sufficient to recognise that their wafer-thin victory in this litigation has been gained at a price which no government committed to upholding the values of a free society can afford to pay'.

Some hope. As Mrs Thatcher's biographer, Hugo Young, subsequently wrote, the Prime Minister 'stood firm on her conviction that, however many courts might find against her, she had a duty to fight the case until the last drop of taxpayer's money had been expended to defend the principle that spies should not talk. What some called stubbornness, even vanity, she referred to as her bounden duty.'[29]

Find against her the courts certainly did. The first judge to reject

Mrs Thatcher's plea for a permanent injunction was Mr Justice Scott[30] (of whom we shall hear more later in this chapter). Now that *Spycatcher* was an international bestseller, he considered the arguments in favour of allowing the media to report Peter Wright's allegations were of 'overwhelming weight'. Third parties no longer owed the government any duty of confidence. Mr Justice Scott said the ability of the press freely to report allegations of government scandals was 'one of the bulwarks of our democratic society'. The judge also had some strong words for ministers and their chief witness, the Cabinet Secretary Sir Robert Armstrong. He said: 'I find myself unable to escape the reflection that the absolute protection of the security service that Sir Robert was contending for could not be achieved this side of the Iron Curtain.' Not only did Mr Justice Scott lift the injunctions, he also gave a detailed account of Mr Wright's allegations which the media could safely reproduce.

The government went to the Court of Appeal. By majority rulings the appeal judges held[31] that Mr Justice Scott had been right to say that the *Observer* and *Guardian* were not in breach of their duty of confidentiality when they published their original reports (although in their view the *Sunday Times* had been in breach of that duty when it published an extract from the book). The judges agreed that the injunctions should be lifted.

The government had one last chance: the law lords. One problem was that five of the law lords had already shown their hands a year earlier. Since two of the judges who might have heard the latest appeal had already said in 1987 that they would not support temporary injunctions, it was hardly likely these judges would grant permanent injunctions a year later. It was therefore decided that the government's appeal should be heard by those law lords who had not sat before. Unfortunately, the full complement of law lords at that time was nine,[32] which was not quite enough for the normal panel of five; for this reason a retired judge, Lord Brightman, was brought in. He joined Lords Keith, Griffiths, Goff and Jauncey to hear the appeal.

In the autumn of 1988,[33] all five judges dismissed it. They decided that because of the worldwide publication of *Spycatcher*, all confidentiality had gone and permanent injunctions should be refused. As Lord Griffiths put it, 'the balance in this case comes down firmly in favour of the public interest in freedom of speech and a free press'. The government was ordered to pay the newspapers' legal costs. To celebrate, the *Guardian* published a page of 'highlights' from the book.[34]

What had the government achieved? Its perseverance was no doubt meant to deter future whistleblowers. Ministers insisted that they had to act to protect MI5 and its foreign counterpart MI6. 'Our resolution remains firm,' said the Home Secretary Douglas Hurd, 'to ensure that the vital work of the security and intelligence services, which defend the freedom of this country, is not imperilled by unauthorised disclosures by members or former members of the services.' The government said it noted with satisfaction 'that the law lords have unanimously upheld the government's contention that (to quote Lord Keith of Kinkel) "members and former members of the Security Service do have a lifelong obligation of confidence owed to the Crown. Those who breach it, such as Mr Wright, are guilty of treachery".'[35]

This was hardly a surprise. Mr Justice Millett, the first judge to give a reasoned judgment in the case, had said two years earlier that 'The Security Service must be seen to be leak-proof.' He added: 'The appearance of confidentiality is essential for its effective functioning. Its members simply cannot be allowed to write their memoirs.'[36]

In reality, the government had achieved nothing by its 'stubbornness'.[37] The £3 million it had spent trying to stop *Spycatcher* being published[38] had turned the book into a bestseller. Although it had won a temporary injunction by a 'wafer-thin' margin, it had lost at every level in its attempt to get a permanent ban on the book. That defeat was entirely predictable: indeed, it had been predicted by Lord Bridge.

He was also right in his prediction that the government would lose a challenge at the European Court of Human Rights.[39] In November 1991, the Strasbourg judges decided that once *Spycatcher* had been published in the United States all confidentiality in it had been destroyed and there was no justification for maintaining the temporary injunctions.[40] The court held unanimously that the government had broken article 10 of the Human Rights convention, which guarantees the right to freedom of expression: the newspapers had been prevented from publishing information, already available, on a matter of public concern. The case had been brought by the *Sunday Times*, the *Observer* and the *Guardian*: the government was ordered to pay £200,000 towards the newspapers' legal costs. In response, the Attorney General, Sir Patrick Mayhew, said he was 'absolutely clear that the government was right to bring these proceedings in our own courts against Mr Wright to try to prevent the publication of what he said were his memoirs'.[41]

With the exception of Lords Brandon, Templeman and Ackner – the three law lords who voted to continue the temporary orders – the English judges came out of the whole affair well. As one writer said, they recognised the importance of the freedom of the press by acknowledging that, under certain circumstances, people who were not party to the initial breach of confidence would be free to publish information obtained in that way where the public interest in its disclosure outweighed the government interest in secrecy.[42]

Although the government was broadly successful in getting and then keeping the initial injunctions, there is no suggestion that the judges were intimidated by the government of the day. Nor were they trying to curry favour with it. The judiciary may have had a naïve view of the security service: it took Lord Griffiths, who was then chairman of the Security Commission, to point out that morale among the 'close knit and dedicated' officers of MI5 would not be affected by further publication of *Spycatcher*, despite what the government had claimed. Even so, the courts' natural inclinations were to support the needs of the security service as the judges considered them to be, not what ministers claimed they were.

In the end, the government seemed to have had difficulty in remembering its own status in the litigation. This was not the Crown bringing a criminal prosecution for any alleged breach of the Official Secrets Acts. This was the government bringing a civil action under the law of confidence. For these purposes, the government was just another litigant, just another employer trying to protect its secrets. The only difference was that, because the government was using taxpayers' money, it did not show the normal inhibitions of a claimant who is told he is bound to lose his claim. Either the Prime Minister was not prepared to listen to legal advice or that legal advice had been wrong.

The Scott Inquiry

For a time, it looked as if one of the judges in the *Spycatcher* case might bring down John Major's government. Sir Richard Scott spent more than three years on his 'arms to Iraq' inquiry.[43] His report[44] was published early in 1996.[45] Ministers, he decided, had misled

183

parliament. The government's legal advisers, he believed, had got the law wrong. Within a fortnight, though, the government had won a Commons debate by one vote[46] and Whitehall returned to business as usual.[47] What had gone wrong?

The Matrix Churchill prosecution[48]
First, some background. Iraq invaded Iran in 1980; the two countries were officially at war until Iraq called a ceasefire in 1988. Two years later, Iraq invaded Kuwait, precipitating the Gulf War.

Throughout the 1980s, the British government had legal powers to restrict exports of arms and related goods to Iraq: exporters had to apply for licences.[49] Even so, ministers allowed manufacturers to send the Iraqis considerable quantities of machine tools, which they could then use to make weapons. One such machine tool manufacturer was Matrix Churchill Ltd of Coventry.

In October 1990, three senior executives of Matrix Churchill, including the managing director Paul Henderson, were arrested by Customs and Excise officers.[50] The following February, the three were charged with serious export-control offences. It was alleged they had lied about the intended use of machine tools when applying for export licences.

It was known before their trial started that the Matrix Churchill defendants would be putting forward two main lines of defence. First, they would say that the government had encouraged exporters to be less than frank when applying for licences: they claimed manufacturers had been told they should suppress the intended military use of the machine tools. Indeed, an apparently well-informed newspaper had reported that the former Trade minister, Alan Clark, and officials at the Department of Trade and Industry had surreptitiously encouraged companies such as Matrix Churchill to export machine tools to Iraq for the production of weapons.[51]

Second, the Matrix Churchill defendants would say that the government had known all along that their machine tools would probably be used to manufacture munitions; despite this, ministers had deliberately turned a blind eye. Mr Henderson knew the government had this information because he had given it to them: while working as an exporter he had also been an agent for MI6, the British Secret Intelligence Service.

The Customs and Excise prosecutors realised that to support their arguments the defendants' lawyers would be asking to see a number of government documents dealing with arms exports. They decided to resist these requests. For this purpose, they asked ministers to sign what are called public interest immunity certificates, opposing disclosure of certain classes of documents on the ground that serious damage would be caused to the public interest if they were released. Four ministers agreed to sign.[52]

The Matrix Churchill trial had been due to start before Judge Smedley and a jury at the Old Bailey in the middle of October 1992. Earlier in the month, defence lawyers persuaded the judge to disclose the documents they had wanted to see. These documents were used to cross-examine Alan Clark and two officials from the Department of Trade and Industry. In the light of Mr Clark's evidence, which was inconsistent with his previous written statement, Alan Moses QC for the prosecution concluded that the case should be dropped.[53] The result was all three defendants acquitted and champagne glasses outside the Old Bailey.[54]

Scott to the rescue
The Matrix Churchill acquittals led to two charges against the government. First, ministers were accused of helping arms exporters in a way that was inconsistent with the government's publicly expressed policy on exports to Iraq. Second, it was claimed that ministers had used public interest immunity certificates to cover up their own wrongdoing, knowing that there was a risk that the defendants might be wrongly convicted and imprisoned if they were denied access to the papers they needed.[55]

When serious allegations like these begin to circulate, the natural reaction in Whitehall is to set up some sort of inquiry, ideally headed by a judge. Public inquiries into disasters, natural or otherwise, have a number of advantages. They give ministers a valuable breathing space ('all these are questions for the inquiry' becomes their normal response) and – like the reports on football safety and prison reform from Lord Justice Taylor and Lord Justice Woolf, as they were at the time – they may provide the public with valuable information and advice.

It used to be common for judges to head public inquiries. As Professor Robert Stevens noted, between 1945 and 1979 the English judges 'chaired over a third of the Royal Commissions and Departmental Committees which in those days played such a significant role in British public life. It was not just inquiries

185

about spying or errant ministers, or Indian boundaries or colonial insurrections: it covered the range of pay awards, from dockers to doctors – and all aspects of public life, from the unions and company law to compensation and income tax'.[56]

It was therefore no surprise that the Prime Minister announced a 'full and independent inquiry'[57] into the events surrounding the Matrix Churchill case. In particular, the inquiry was to investigate whether ministers and officials had operated in accordance with government policies on arms exports; it was also to examine the decisions taken in the Matrix Churchill case. The terms of reference were widely drawn.

Rather harder to understand was John Major's decision to appoint Lord Justice Scott[58] to carry out the inquiry. The Prime Minister must have taken advice from the Lord Chancellor on a suitable judge. Lord Mackay would certainly have known that Sir Richard Scott was no pushover. As we saw earlier in this chapter, in December 1987 the then Mr Justice Scott had rejected the government's claim for a permanent ban on *Spycatcher* because the arguments in favour of press freedom were of 'overwhelming weight'.

Why then pick a judge who had already demonstrated a healthy scepticism towards the government's policies? Was it because the Prime Minister wanted the toughest judge he could find?[59] Was it because the Lord Chancellor wanted to make sure that any wrongdoing on the part of his cabinet colleagues would not escape attention? Was it purely a mistake? Unfortunately, this is one question on which Sir Richard Scott is unable to help us. Those who know are not saying either. Normally the cock-up theory of history is to be preferred, although on this occasion it may have been a 'conspiracy' by Lord Mackay to ensure that the inquiry was as effective as possible.

An informal inquiry
With the agreement of its chairman, the Scott Inquiry was conducted on an informal, non-statutory basis. This meant that the inquiry team had no powers to compel witnesses to attend, no power to punish anyone for lying and no power to prevent prejudicial public comment. Such powers would have been available if the inquiry had been set up under the Tribunals of Inquiry (Evidence) Act 1921.

Even so, ministers chose to behave as if they were unable to speak about the issues being investigated by the Scott Inquiry while it was under way. No doubt this suited the government well. Yet as Sir Richard Scott made clear, there was no need for such restraint: it had neither been required by law nor requested by him.[60]

Although his inquiry was non-statutory, Sir Richard Scott could still have allowed witnesses to be legally represented at the formal hearings he held. That was not how he chose to operate. He had begun with what he called a 'paperchase' through Whitehall, a search through 200,000 pages of official documents.[61] These files gave Sir Richard Scott and his team 'an unrivalled insight into the whole picture': one which even those directly involved did not have at the time.[62]

Having reached their provisional views on the facts and likely inferences, the Scott team then asked more than 250 witnesses to respond to his initial assessments. About a third of them were then invited to give oral evidence. They were allowed lawyers, paid out of public funds, to assist them at both written and oral stages.

It was at this stage that Sir Richard Scott could have allowed witnesses' lawyers to question other witnesses at the inquiry. However, he believed this would have 'turned the oral proceedings into a procedural morass to the serious detriment of the conduct of the inquiry and with no gain to those affected save that of serious delay'.[63] Instead he decided that the people whom he might criticise should be shown his comments before his report was published: they would then be invited to comment. Those comments turned out to be voluminous, and in turn they meant further inquiries were necessary. The process lasted for more than a year, and had a 'pivotal' position in the process.[64] In some cases, Sir Richard was persuaded to tone down or even remove his original criticisms.[65] In other cases, they remained.[66]

Procedural attacks
The procedure adopted by the Scott Inquiry was heavily criticised by Lord Howe, who had been Foreign Secretary at the time the government changed its guidelines on exports to Iraq and Iran.[67] His most scathing criticism appeared in the *Spectator* just before the Scott Report was published.[68] As a former government law officer who had appeared before and presided over previous public inquiries, he was well able to look after himself at such events. Nevertheless, he made it clear in his article that he objected strongly to the fact that witnesses were being denied legal representation.

When he gave his evidence at the inquiry, Lord Howe had startled Sir Richard Scott by accusing him of acting as 'detective, inquisitor, advocate and judge'.[69] Apparently stung by this attack, Sir Richard issued an immediate statement saying, 'It would be ludicrous to permit legal representation to each person or department who might have an interest in particular issues.'[70]

Lord Howe considered that Sir Richard Scott should have followed the six principles defined thirty years earlier by the Royal Commission on Tribunals of Inquiry,[71] chaired by Lord Justice Salmon.[72] The so-called Salmon principles provide that:

1. Before any person becomes involved in an inquiry, the tribunal must be satisfied that there are circumstances which affect him and which the tribunal proposes to investigate.
2. Before any person who is involved in the inquiry is called as a witness he should be informed of any allegations which are made against him and the substance of the evidence in support of them.[73]
3. (a) He should be given an adequate opportunity of preparing his case and of being assisted by legal advisers.
(b) His legal expenses should normally be met out of public funds.
4. He should have the opportunity of being examined by his own solicitor or counsel and of stating his case in public at the inquiry.
5. Any material witness he wishes called at the inquiry should, if reasonably practicable, be heard.
6. He should have the opportunity of testing by cross-examination conducted by his own solicitor or counsel any evidence which may affect him.

These principles were recommendations for the procedures to be adapted by statutory inquiries established under the 1921 legislation. Sir Richard Scott considered that these principles, with their emphasis on the 'case' which a witness was to prepare or state, did not apply to an inquisitorial procedure based largely on written documents. In his view, they were not required to ensure fairness.[74]

Lord Howe also objected to the role of counsel to the inquiry as it was taken by Presiley Baxendale QC.[75] Normally during a public hearing, counsel to the inquiry sits or stands facing the chairman, addressing him or her as an advocate addresses a judge. Indeed, although Lord Howe may not have known it, this was how Miss Baxendale carried out the role when she was counsel to two child abuse inquiries chaired by Sir Louis Blom-Cooper QC in the mid-1980s.[76] However, during the Scott Inquiry she and the judge sat alongside each other. Ministerial critics said they were 'like partners in a double-barrelled inquisition';[77] she was accused of behaving more like a prosecuting advocate than an independent seeker after truth.[78] If that was so, it was because of the way Sir Richard Scott had chosen to conduct the inquiry.

Lord Howe's comments are not just interesting reflections on the procedures to be adopted at public inquiries. They may be seen as yet another round in the battle between the executive and the judiciary. The more involved the judges get in 'political' inquiries, the more risk there is that the judiciary will be damaged by attacks from politicians of this kind. Commenting on Lord Howe's accusation that Sir Richard Scott was 'detective, inquisitor, advocate and judge', the Labour leader, John Smith said he was 'gravely concerned' by what he called a 'deliberate and clearly premeditated attempt to undermine the findings of the inquiry'.[79]

Sir Richard Scott was often accused of not understanding how Whitehall operated. In particular, his opponents claimed he did not realise that governments could not function properly if every decision they took was open to public scrutiny. In June 1995, the *Daily Telegraph* political editor reported that 'for months' there had been 'a whispering campaign in government and the higher levels of the Tory Party to discredit the Scott inquiry'. The newspaper said Sir Richard had 'been described as a "Boy Scout" blundering around the corridors of Whitehall, with no appreciation of the real world of politics. One senior cabinet minister was quoted as saying that Sir Richard was "astonishingly ignorant" of the workings of government: he did not even know the meaning of the initials PPS, Parliamentary Private Secretary.'[80]

If that were so, it was probably the fault of those who appointed him to conduct a one-man inquiry. The Labour MP, Tony Benn, thought it was 'entirely wrong that such political matters should be handed to a judge who knew nothing about administration'.[81] Lord Howe thought he should have had experts sitting with him.[82] However, Sir Richard's view[83] was that experts were not necessary and would have damaged the perceived impartiality of his inquiry. It was, after all, his independence from government that qualified him for appointment in the first place.

Faced with government criticism, the judges traditionally keep their own counsel. Nevertheless, the Lord Chief Justice often sums up the judicial mood in his speech at the annual dinner given for the judges by the Lord Mayor of London.

Speaking at the Mansion House in July 1995, Lord Taylor of Gosforth turned his attention to criticism of Sir Richard Scott. 'If a judge appointed by the government to investigate a matter of public concern reports – or is thought to be going to report – adversely about individuals or groups within his terms of reference, cries are raised that he has got above himself.' Lord Taylor said phrases like 'power-hungry' and 'frustrated politicians' were entering the commentators' lexicon. The suggestion seemed to be that 'the senior judiciary had decided to mount a bloodless coup and seize the commanding heights of the constitution. But,' said the Lord Chief Justice, 'nothing could be further from the truth.'

As far as judicial inquiries were concerned, the Lord Chief Justice said people had confidence in the system. They accepted that our criminal justice system ensured thoroughness and excluded cover-ups. A judge, Lord Taylor suggested, had no political axe to grind. 'Providing, therefore, the judge acts within his terms of reference, it is inappropriate to seek to undermine his position by suggesting he has no business to do that which he was appointed to do.' Lord Taylor concluded by expressing his confidence that 'the separation and the balance of powers is and will be properly maintained'.

Lord Taylor was right to act as Sir Richard Scott's defence counsel on this occasion. The more difficult question – which he did not confront – was whether the Lord Chief Justice should have allowed a judge to head such an obviously 'political' inquiry in the first place.

The Howe guidelines
The first question Sir Richard Scott's inquiry was asked to investigate was whether the government had followed its publicly declared policy on defence exports to Iraq.

The policy on arms sales to Iraq and Iran was expressed in four principles, known as the 'Howe Guidelines'.[84] These guidelines were adopted in December 1984, at the height of the Iran-Iraq war, but parliament was not told about them until October 1985. The first guideline reaffirmed a total ban on sales of 'lethal equipment' to the two countries. The third, which was crucial, dealt with non-lethal 'defence' exports. It read: 'We should not, in future, approve orders for defence equipment which, in our view, would significantly enhance the capability of either side to prolong or exacerbate the conflict?'

In 1989, following the Iran-Iraq ceasefire, three junior ministers – William Waldegrave of the Foreign Office, Alan Clark of the Department of Trade and Industry and Lord Trefgarne of the Ministry of Defence – decided to implement a less restrictive policy towards exports of non-lethal equipment.[85] Under this policy, export licences would be refused only if the equipment would be 'of direct and significant assistance to either side in the conduct of offensive operations in breach of the ceasefire'.[86] However, 'a conscious decision was taken by the junior ministers that there should be no public announcement' of the new policy.[87] The government took the view that there had been no change in the Howe guidelines: they were designed to be operated flexibly and it was only their application or implementation which was being adjusted.

Sir Richard Scott disagreed. To say the new policy was merely an interpretation of the old did not seem 'to correspond with reality'. He thought that claim was 'incapable of being sustained by serious argument'.[88] Although ministers including William Waldegrave 'did not . . . have any duplicitous intention',[89] there had been a 'deliberate' failure to inform parliament of the government's policy on non-lethal arms sales to Iraq. He said it was an inevitable result of the agreement between three junior ministers – William Waldegrave, Alan Clark and Lord Trefgarne – 'that no publicity would be given to the decision to adopt a more liberal, or relaxed, policy, or interpretation of the guidelines'.[90] Parliament and the public had repeatedly been given information 'that was by design incomplete and in certain respects misleading'.[91]

William Waldegrave was the only one of the three junior ministers still in the government. Yet despite these damning criticisms of a serving minister, Mr Waldegrave felt he had no reason to resign.

Public interest immunity

The second question for Sir Richard Scott to decide was whether ministers had used public interest immunity certificates to cover up their own wrongdoing, knowing that there was a risk that the defendants might be wrongly convicted and imprisoned if they were denied access to the papers they needed.

Normally each party in a civil case, or the prosecution in a criminal case, has a duty to supply the other side with relevant documents.

191

Public interest immunity is a ground for refusing to disclose a relevant and material document. A claim to public interest immunity can be justified only if the public interest in preserving the confidentiality of the document outweighs the public interest in securing justice.[92]

Public interest immunity is a rule of law which has been built up by the judges.[93] It sank to its lowest depths in 1939 along with the submarine *Thetis*, which failed to resurface after a test dive in Liverpool bay. Relatives of the ninety-nine men who lost their lives in the disaster sued the shipbuilders, Cammell Laird. To establish negligence they needed to see plans of the submarine. As it was wartime the government said national security would be damaged if the plans were released. That was an established ground for claiming public interest immunity (or 'Crown privilege', as it was then called). The law lords ruled in 1942 that if a minister claimed public interest immunity for documents falling into a protected class then the courts had to take his word for it. Judges could not look at the contents of the documents to see if they did indeed deal with matters of national security.[94]

The relatives of those who died in the submarine were therefore unable to sue. Though it was little consolation to them, their rights had been properly sacrificed in the greater national interest: it emerged after the war that the *Thetis* was fitted with a new type of torpedo tube which had to be keep secret. Nevertheless, as Lord Justice Simon Brown commented in 1994;

> it was regrettable that, by a unanimous decision, the House of Lords laid down a sweeping rule that a court could never question a claim of Crown privilege made in proper form, regardless of the nature of the documents sought to be withheld. History teaches that the executive behaves more scrupulously (or do I mean even more scrupulously?) when subjected to a measure of judicial control.[95]

This 'sweeping rule' laid down in the case of *Duncan v. Cammell Laird* remained in force for twenty-five years. Fortunately, we did not need to wait until the appointment of judges like Lord Justice Simon Brown before the courts started modifying it.

Taking advantage of newly assumed powers to overturn their own decisions, the law lords changed the law in 1967. In a case called *Conway v. Rimmer*,[96] they ruled that it must be for the courts to decide whether a document should be disclosed. A judge would inspect the document and do his best to decide its significance. The effect was that the minister's word was no longer decisive: a judge would strike a balance between the damage to national security if the document were released and the damage to a claimant's case if the document were withheld.

At that time, public interest immunity could be claimed if either the *contents* of the particular document required it to be withheld; or it belonged to a *class* of documents which ought not to be disclosed. 'Class' claims were much more common than 'contents' claims. In a class claim, some of the documents that came within the class might have been relatively or even totally innocuous; however, the class itself was considered worthy of protection. The classes of documents covered by public interest immunity included advice to ministers, national security matters, documents dealing with international relations, details of informers, papers dealing with the integrity of the criminal investigation process and judicial communications.

It was not surprising to find at a time when the courts were beginning to act as a check on the executive in the field of judicial review that they were also no longer prepared to accept the minister's word as conclusive when he or she claimed public interest immunity. Lord Woolf and Professor Jeffrey Jowell said the case of *Conway v. Rimmer* 'was of the highest importance'. Even so, the judges were taking on a difficult job for themselves: Professor Stanley de Smith had thought English judges were 'poorly equipped' to balance competing public interests.[97]

Conway v. Rimmer still represented the law in January 1992 when the Attorney General Sir Nicholas Lyell took advice on public interest immunity from three leading barristers. John Laws,[98] Michael Kalisher QC[99] and Nicholas Ainley[100] were asked what the government should do about documents that fell into a class to which the courts had said the immunity applied.

> First, they advised, the minister must tell the defendant the document exists.
> Next, the minister *must* claim public interest immunity (whether he wants to or not).
> Then the court will carry out a balancing exercise and decide whether the document should be handed over.
> The minister can hand over the document himself only in a 'very exceptional case' where counsel advises that a court is bound to order disclosure anyway.

This advice relied heavily on a judgment given by Lord Justice

Bingham in an appeal called *Makanjuola*. That case had been decided in March 1989 but for three years it lay unnoticed by all but the government's lawyers, who prized it greatly and relied on it frequently. Giving judgment in that case, Lord Justice Bingham said:

> Where a litigant asserts that documents are immune from production or disclosure on public interest grounds he is not (if the claim is well founded) claiming a right but observing a duty. Public interest immunity is not a trump card vouchsafed to certain privileged players to play when and as they wish. It is an exclusionary rule, imposed on parties in certain circumstances, even where it is to their disadvantage in the litigation.

Lord Justice Bingham said this did not mean someone had to claim public interest immunity even when there was a clear balance in favour of disclosure. Nevertheless, it did mean

> that public interest immunity cannot in any ordinary sense be waived, since, although one can waive rights, one cannot waive duties;
> that, where a litigant holds documents in a class prima facie immune, he should (save perhaps in a very exceptional case) assert that the documents are immune and decline to disclose them, since the ultimate judge of where the balance of public interest lies is not him but the court; and
> that, where a document is, or is held to be, in an immune class, it may not be used for any purpose whatever in the proceedings to which the immunity applies, and certainly cannot (for instance) be used for the purposes of cross-examination.[101]

Four ministers were advised that these remarks were an accurate and binding summary of the law. Defence lawyers in the Matrix Churchill case were seeking documents which they hoped would show their clients were innocent. Nevertheless, ministers were told they could not disclose these vital papers: only a judge could decide whether they ought to be handed over. As a result, they signed public interest immunity certificates covering classes of documents. Ministers were assured that these certificates were not 'gagging orders': they simply alerted the judge to the 'balancing exercise' he was required to perform.

It is well established that public interest immunity applies in criminal trials as well as civil cases. Yet until the Matrix Churchill prosecution there had been virtually no criminal cases in which *class* claims had been made: in previous criminal cases virtually all claims had been made on a contents basis.[102] All the leading judgments were in civil cases.

John Laws, Michael Kalisher and Nicholas Ainley were experienced counsel. The Attorney General must have thought he was taking the best advice that money could buy. Their advice was supported by James Hunt QC, who appeared for one of the Matrix Churchill defendants[103] and by several other leading criminal and public law counsel.[104] As we shall see, it was also supported by Lord Bingham. Even so, it may have been wrong.

One wonders what advice the Attorney General would have received in 1992 if he had gone to different counsel. Writing in March 1994 – after the Matrix Churchill acquittals but before the law lords changed the law yet again – David Pannick QC criticised the advice given by Sir Nicholas Lyell to the four ministers as 'impossible to reconcile with principle, practice or precedent':

> As a matter of principle, ministers bear the primary responsibility for deciding whether the national interest requires the suppression of evidence. If a minister believes that no damage would be done by supplying the documents . . . it would be surprising were the law to require that a claim of public interest immunity must be made.
>
> As a matter of practice, the Crown has frequently supplied to courts information for which it *might* be able to claim public interest immunity . . . Indeed, out of court, ministers regularly provide to parliament, and to the press, material for which public interest immunity could be claimed in court proceedings. It would be extraordinary if the law were to forbid ministers from supplying in a criminal case what ministers have the legal power to publish out of court.
>
> As a matter of precedent . . . the Divisional Court . . . held that in criminal cases the prosecution may voluntarily disclose, without a court order, documents which might otherwise be covered by public interest immunity, so long as the prosecution itself has weighed the competing public interests and keeps a record of voluntary disclosures.[105]

It appeared that David Pannick was placing far less reliance on the *Makanjuola* case than everyone else: he was apparently suggesting that the decision did not require the Attorney General to advise Ministers in the way he did. If David Pannick had been asked to advise the Attorney instead of the Laws-Kalisher-Ainley team, the whole history of the Matrix Churchill affair might have been very different.

The four ministers
The Home Secretary, Kenneth Clarke, approved a certificate covering the work of the Security Service MI5 and the Secret Intelligence
Service MI6. Uniquely, this certificate authorised an individual
intelligence service officer to give evidence at the forthcoming trial:
his witness statement had already been disclosed to the defence. This
officer was Mr Henderson's contact at MI6: prosecution lawyers were
seeking to establish that Mr Henderson had not told the government's
intelligence service about the military use of machine tools. However,
as Sir Richard Scott observed in his report, on the government's view
of the law 'it was not open to ministers to waive protection and
permit disclosure' of a statement from an intelligence service officer:
it fell 'fairly and squarely' within a class of document to which public
interest immunity applied.[106] Despite this, they had done so. Nobody
seemed to think it odd that ministers could allow an MI6 officer to
give evidence when they could not allow an MI6 document to be
handed over.

The next certificate was signed by the Foreign Office minister,
Tristan Garel-Jones. He had been asked to consider the matter
overnight in the absence abroad of the Foreign Secretary, Douglas
Hurd. The minister's certificate dealt mainly with internal government documents. There were also papers dealing with an informant
and documents relating to the security and intelligence services.
In his certificate, Mr Garel-Jones asserted that 'disclosure of any
sources or alleged sources of intelligence information . . . would
cause unquantifiable damage to the functions of the security and
intelligence services'.[107] In his evidence to the Scott Inquiry, Mr
Garel-Jones explained that 'unquantifiable damage' could mean
either 'unquantifiably large' or 'unquantifiably small'. Sir Richard
Scott dismissed as 'risible' Mr Garel-Jones's suggestion that a judge
might understand 'unquantifiable' to mean 'minuscule'.[108]

The Defence Secretary, Malcolm Rifkind, was next to sign. His
certificate was similar to that approved by Tristan Garel-Jones. Mr
Rifkind, a QC, said he was familiar with the rule that a minister
was obliged to claim public interest immunity if he was satisfied the
papers in question came within the categories of advice to ministers
or intelligence papers.[109]

Finally, the President of the Board of Trade, Michael Heseltine,
was asked to sign a certificate. He was not a lawyer, but on one

reading of the law he was the only person in the government to get it right: certainly Mr Heseltine's approach was in line with the view of public interest immunity taken by Sir Richard Scott and also subsequently by the law lords.[110]

Mr Heseltine told his officials that although he was satisfied that the documents fell within the categories of advice to ministers and intelligence matters he was not willing to sign the public interest immunity certificate. He did not feel the documents should be withheld from the defence; on the contrary, he thought disclosure would be in the public interest.

Faced with this rebellion, the Attorney General, Sir Nicholas Lyell, advised Mr Heseltine it was his duty to claim public interest immunity. However, a special certificate was drafted for him, making it clear that he was not asserting that the documents in question should in fact be withheld. On that basis, and after taking the trouble to read *Makanjuola* in the law reports, Mr Heseltine agreed to sign.[111] He had been led to believe his anxieties would be put to Judge Smedley. Yet Alan Moses QC,[112] who was prosecuting on behalf of Customs and Excise, was not briefed about Mr Heseltine's concerns and therefore did not pass them on to the court.

Officials in the Treasury Solicitor's department were criticised for ignoring Mr Heseltine's views in preparing the brief for Mr Moses.[113] However, Sir Richard Scott said that, in his opinion, major responsibility for the inadequacy of counsel's instructions should be borne by the Attorney General. Alan Moses had even been to see the Attorney General three days after Sir Nicholas had promised Mr Heseltine that his concerns would made known to the court, but the Attorney General had failed to tell Mr Moses about the minister's reluctance to sign. It was plain from the Scott Report that Alan Moses behaved entirely properly: he was later appointed to the High Court bench.

In his report, Sir Richard Scott accepted that Sir Nicholas Lyell genuinely believed he was personally blameless. 'But,' said Sir Richard in a damning sentence, 'I do not accept that he was not personally at fault.'[114] There was 'an absence of the personal involvement by the Attorney General that Mr Heseltine's stance and its implications had made necessary'.[115] Like Mr Waldegrave, Sir Nicholas Lyell remained a member of the government.

Judge Smedley to the rescue
As we have seen, Judge Smedley was called upon to perform a balancing exercise at the Old Bailey: he had to decide whether the public interest in disclosing the documents outweighed the public interest in maintaining confidentiality. Ministers had claimed public interest immunity in three classes of document:

A: Information from a confidential informant.
B: Ministerial and departmental documents.
C: Security and intelligence papers.

There were only a couple of pieces of paper covered by category A. The judge inspected the documents, decided they would not help the defendants and therefore did not order their disclosure.

Category B involved a much larger number of papers. The judge inspected them, decided that they were relevant to the proposed cross-examination of prosecution witnesses, and decided they should be shown to the defence.

His initial reaction had been to refuse disclosure of documents in category C. As Judge Smedley himself said later, he was 'not really in a position to weigh the effect of disclosure of information concerning the security and intelligence services on the public interest. That is a matter on which the Home and Foreign Secretaries can be the only judges.'[116] Notwithstanding, Geoffrey Robertson QC representing Paul Henderson argued that what MI6 had been told by the defendants was fundamental to their defence.

As a result, Judge Smedley ordered the intelligence documents to be disclosed. They were heavily edited (or, to use the preferred official term, 'redacted') with black marker pen. Armed with these documents, defence lawyers were able to obtain the crucial admission from the former minister Alan Clark, that he had advised exporters they need not tell the truth when applying for export licences.[117]

Must ministers claim immunity?
The most controversial legal question arising from the Scott Report is whether the four ministers who signed public interest immunity certificates were obliged to do so. Sir Richard Scott thought not: 'In my opinion, the view of the law on which the making of the public interest immunity class claims in the Matrix Churchill case was based was unsound. There was no clear prior judicial authority approving

the making of public interest immunity class claims in *criminal* trials
in order to keep from disclosure material documents which might
be of assistance to the defence.'[118]

Sir Richard had common sense on his side. As David Pannick
pointed out, ministers frequently disclose (or even leak) documents
covered by public interest immunity. If they decide papers ought to
be released, especially if they are doing so to make sure that a criminal
prosecution is fair, why should a judge want to stop them? Indeed,
if all the government has to do is to decide whether documents fall
into a particular class, and if there is no discretion to be exercised,
why does the job need to be done by a senior minister? Is he not
just acting as a 'postman', or a rubber stamp? Judges expect rather
more of them: indeed, they rely on ministers to let them know how
important it is that a particular document should be withheld.

Sir Richard's conclusions were also based on his reading of the legal
authorities.[119] Taking the *Makanjuola* case on which the government
had relied so heavily, he said that 'Nothing in the judgment of Lord
Justice Bingham suggests there is any duty to assert public interest
immunity in circumstances where the disclosure to the defendant
would not in the view of the . . . minister . . . be damaging to the
public interest.'[120]

The Attorney General firmly disagreed. 'This is in direct conflict
with the accepted view,' his office said.[121] 'The government is
satisfied that the Attorney General's advice was correct,' insisted a
press statement.[122]

A few days later, Sir Nicholas Lyell received unexpected support
from Sir Thomas Bingham himself. The then Master of the Rolls
said pointedly that Sir Richard Scott's view on the question of public
interest immunity was 'not one that all judges and practitioners would
have shared'. Sir Thomas Bingham stressed that he was not judging
the Scott Report or the Attorney General; still less was he seeking to
take part in any political debate. Nevertheless, he said he had been
somewhat concerned because he himself had given one of the leading
judgments on public interest immunity.[123] 'So far as I can see,' said
Sir Thomas, 'the Attorney General was really doing his best in good
faith to give effect to that judgment according to what it said'.[124]

Yet again in this episode, we see how uneasy was the relationship between the ministers and the courts. Neither of them
really understood what the other was trying to do. Ministers
thought the courts wanted them to claim public interest immunity.

The courts thought ministers wanted them to keep documents confidential.

It is remarkable that on such a sensitive issue as this that the law should be so uncertain. One can sympathise with the government's legal advisers in their efforts to understand the law. One senior judge thought they had it wrong. Another judge, equally senior at the time, thought they had it right. If the judges cannot agree among themselves, there is little hope for the rest of us.

Yet our sympathy with the government's lawyers is not unlimited. There must be a suspicion that they treasured *Makanjuola* because it suited their purposes. They did not stop to think whether, as Sir Richard Scott said, it creat^d 'any duty to assert public interest immunity in circumstances where the disclosure to the defendant would not in the view of the . . . minister . . . be damaging to the public interest'.[125] Indeed, the only person who gave any serious thought to the government's position was Michael Heseltine.

Interesting though it is to follow this debate on what the law was – or perhaps ought to have been – at the time of the Matrix Churchill trial, it was simply not the law any more by the time Sir Richard Scott published his report.

The law moves on
In July 1994, the law lords had reconsidered the law on public interest immunity in a case called *Wiley*.[126] Broadly speaking, they decided that ministers could now weigh the public interest for themselves, and disclose documents if they thought it would be in the public interest to do so.

This was a major change. In the course of his judgment Lord Templeman, the most senior of the law lords who heard the case, said:

> If a document is relevant and material then it must be disclosed unless it is confidential and unless a breach of confidentiality will cause harm to the public interest which outweighs the harm to the interests of justice caused by non-disclosure. It has been said[127] that the holder of a confidential document for which public interest immunity may be claimed is under a duty to assert the claim, leaving the court to decide whether the claim is well founded. For my part I consider that when a document is known to be relevant and material the holder of the document should voluntarily

200

disclose it unless he is satisfied that disclosure will cause substantial harm.

Lord Templeman said that if the holder were in doubt he could refer the matter to the court. The judge stressed that 'a rubber stamp approach to public interest immunity by the holder of a document is neither necessary nor appropriate'.[128]

Lord Woolf, who was broadly supported by the other law lords, managed to distance himself from Lord Justice Bingham's remarks in *Makanjuola*. Referring to the paragraphs quoted above, he politely suggested that they might have been applied in a manner which went beyond what Lord Justice Bingham had intended. Lord Woolf said he was sure Lord Justice Bingham had not been intending to extend the principles of public interest immunity or to make their application any more rigid than before.

The law lord pointed out that *Makanjuola* had not involved a government department: instead, it was the police who were seeking to withhold documents. He then suggested that if a government minister – as opposed to anyone else taking legal action – concluded that any public interest in documents being withheld from production was outweighed by the public interest in the documents being available for purposes of litigation, then the court would probably agree. Lord Woolf added:

> the principle which was established in *Conway v. Rimmer* is that it is the courts which should have the final responsibility for deciding when both a contents and a class claim to immunity should be upheld. The principle was not that it was for the courts to impose immunity where, after due consideration, no immunity was claimed by the appropriate authority . . . As far as contents of documents are concerned I cannot conceive that their lordships in *Conway v. Rimmer* would have anticipated that their decision could be used, except in the most exceptional circumstances, so that a department of state was prevented by the courts from disclosing documents which it considered it was appropriate to disclose.

If the case of *Wiley* had been decided two years earlier, Mr Heseltine would have been allowed to disclose his documents when he wanted to. The Matrix Churchill trial might still have gone ahead: it was Alan Clark's evidence, rather than disclosure of government papers, which caused its collapse. Nevertheless, critics would not have been able to accuse the government of using 'gagging orders'[129] and the Scott Inquiry might never have been needed.

Public interest immunity revisited
In his report, Sir Richard Scott recommended that in criminal cases there should no longer be *class* claims for public interest immunity. Contents claims – covering specified documents – could still be made where, in the view of the person making the claim, disclosing the contents of a specific document would cause 'substantial harm'. Even then, he thought the minister or other person claiming public interest immunity should consider the use of 'redactions' – editing out sensitive parts of the documents.[130]

Shortly before Christmas 1996, the government broadly accepted these recommendations. The Attorney General told parliament there would be a 'new approach' to public interest immunity:

> Under the new approach, ministers will focus directly on the damage that disclosure would cause. The former division into class and contents claims will no longer be applied. Ministers will claim public interest immunity only when it is believed that disclosure of a document would cause real damage or harm to the public interest. That new approach constitutes a change in the practice to be adopted by ministers, but fully respects existing legal principles, as developed by the courts, and is subject to the supervision of the courts. It also accords with the view expressed by the present Lord Chief Justice that 'public interest immunity should only be claimed for the bare minimum of documents for which the claim of serious harm can be seen to be clearly justified'.

The Attorney General said it was impossible to give a complete list of the circumstances in which 'serious harm' might follow. 'It may relate to the safety of an individual, such as an informant, or to a regulatory process; or it may be damage to international relations caused by the disclosure of confidential diplomatic communications.' Sir Nicholas said that normally it would be direct or immediate harm that was being avoided; in some cases it might be indirect or longer-term damage. Either way, public interest immunity certificates would set out in greater detail than before both what the document was and what damage its disclosure would be likely to do (unless to do so would itself cause the damage which the certificate aimed to protect).[131]

This was a remarkable change. Responding to the government's statement in the House of Lords, Lord Irvine of Lairg said that if there had been this spirit of openness ten years earlier, the events leading to the Scott Report would never have occurred.[132] The government's view, of course, was that it had no choice in the matter before the decision in *Wiley* two years earlier.

Public interest immunity has now risen from the icy depths to which it was dragged by the *Thetis* disaster. Ministers will no longer claim immunity in files of innocuous papers merely because they happen to fall into a class that has traditionally been protected. Judges will no longer have to assess wordy certificates in the hope of discovering whether a minister really wants a document to be released or withheld. The law has moved much closer to common sense. All this – and not a finger lifted by parliament.

At first sight, this may seem like a shift in the balance of power. Before Matrix Churchill ministers could – and, they believed, should – claim public interest immunity in documents merely because they happened to be of a particular type. There was a reasonable chance that judges would accept these certificates at face value, giving public authorities an advantage in litigation or a stronger chance of getting a conviction. Now, because the judges have spoken, ministers can no longer be sure their private papers will be protected from disclosure. Better, then, to make a virtue of it and disclose most of them anyway.

Plus ça change, plus c'est la même chose. Although ministers claimed public interest immunity, judges decided what documents should be released. There may be fewer claims for public interest immunity in future but judges will still have the last word.

How not to publish a report

The way in which Sir Richard Scott handled the publication of his report beggars belief.

First, he allowed the government more than a week in which to read the report and prepare its response.[133] This would not have mattered so much if the opposition front bench had been given a comparable period: in fact, Robin Cook, the shadow Trade and Industry spokesman, had just three hours to master some 1,800 pages.[134]

Then Sir Richard allowed the government to dictate when his report would be published. Not surprisingly, it was 3.30 p.m. on a Thursday. Thursdays are good from the government's point of view: most MPs leave London for their constituencies that evening, and it is difficult to get a head of steam going in parliament until the following week. The time of 3.30 p.m. has two advantages for the government. It is the time at which the Prime Minister stops answering MPs' questions on a Tuesday and Thursday: if a report has not been published by that time, he can refuse to answer questions about it in parliament. Publication of a report in the late afternoon, especially if copies are not released in advance under embargo, also means that reporters do not have enough time to read the document before summarising it for the early evening news bulletins and inside pages of the newspapers.

All that would have mattered less if Sir Richard Scott had provided a summary of his conclusions, or even a guide to where they might be found. He offered two lame excuses: 'a summary would risk distortion,' he said, and he 'had reached a point of writing fatigue at which I was not prepared to write any more'.[135] Though his press officer did what he could to help, Sir Richard's decision meant that reporters were floundering as they attempted to plough through five heavy volumes, plus an appendix.

Sir Richard might still have redeemed the situation if he had been prepared to brief the media properly at the news conference he held at 4.30 p.m. Instead, he pointedly refused to summarise his report for the benefit of journalists who had not had time for more than a cursory glance at it. As reporters grew increasingly desperate, Sir Richard seemed reluctantly to accept that the government's phrase 'no conspiracy and no cover-up' amounted to 'a fair summary' of his report. He then went on holiday, refusing all further interviews. The misleading phrase soon found its way into the headlines.

Sir Richard's unhelpful approach left the way open for the government. It had responded by issuing a 'press pack', a plastic folder containing twelve separate press releases running to more than sixty pages. Some of these were background notes ('What is the Export Control Organisation?', 'The Role of the Attorney General') which a cynic might think were intended to distract rather than assist. Others, understandably, painted the government in as positive a light as possible.

An article in the respected academic journal *Public Law* accepted that this should not have come as a surprise. However, the author of the *Public Law* article concluded that the press pack 'went further than selective quoting and flattering portraiture: it contained a number of lies and deliberate misrepresentations about the contents and conclusions of the Scott report'.[136]

Many of these involved the former Foreign Office minister, William Waldegrave. The Scott Report pointed out that between February and July 1989 Mr Waldegrave had signed nearly forty letters to MPs whose constituents had asked about government policy on arms sales to Iraq. The letters said: 'British arms supplies to both Iran and Iraq continue to be governed by the strict application of guidelines which prevent the supply of lethal equipment or equipment which would significantly enhance the capability of either side to resume hostilities. These guidelines are applied on a case by case basis.' In the last twenty-seven of these letters he added: 'The government have not changed their policy on defence sales to Iraq or Iran.'

The Scott Report concluded:

D4.4 The reference in each of these letters to the criterion that governed the supply of non-lethal defence equipment to Iraq was not accurate. Since the end of February 1989 the criterion for Iraq had been the new formulation, namely, that there would be no supply of equipment which would be of direct and significant assistance to Iraq in the conduct of offensive operations in breach of the cease-fire. The inaccuracy should have been noticed by Mr Waldegrave, who had been one of the midwives at the birth of this new formulation . . .

D4.5 The statement in the letters that 'the government have not changed their policy on defence sales to Iraq or Iran' was untrue. After the cease-fire Lord Howe had advocated, and the Prime Minister, with the concurrence of senior ministers, had accepted, that a more liberal policy, designed to enable British exporters to take advantage of the glittering opportunities for defence-related sales to Iraq that it was believed would be available, should gradually be adopted . . . Agreement by the junior ministers had led, by February 1989, to a new, more liberal, policy in the form of revised guideline (iii) being implemented on a trial basis . . .

D4.6 Mr Waldegrave knew, first hand, the facts that, in my opinion, rendered the 'no change in policy' statement untrue. I accept that, when he signed these letters, he did not regard the agreement he had reached with his fellow ministers as having constituted a change in policy towards Iraq. In his evidence to the Inquiry, he strenuously and consistently asserted his belief, in the face of a volume of, to my mind, overwhelming evidence to the contrary, that the policy on defence sales to Iraq had, indeed, remained unchanged. I did not receive the impression of any insincerity on his part in giving me the evidence he did. But it is clear, in my opinion, that policy on defence sales to Iraq did not remain unchanged.

One of the government press releases issued to coincide with publication of the Scott Report gave a different impression. It was issued from the Treasury, where Mr Waldegrave was then Chief Secretary. Here is an extract:

Does Scott say Waldegrave misled Parliament?

No. He says that William Waldegrave and others did not believe there had been a change of the guidelines (they still do not).

D 3.113 sets out the facts.

D 3.122 This argument (that the relaxation of the guidelines agreed upon by the junior ministers did not constitute a change in the guidelines) is not one that was produced by its proponents for the purposes of meeting questions put by the Inquiry. It was a viewpoint widely expressed at the time.

Scott does not accept the argument, but . . .

D 3.124 I accept that Mr Waldegrave and the other adherents of the 'interpretation' thesis did not, in putting forward the thesis, have any duplicitous intention and, at the time, regarded the relaxed interpretation, or implementation, of guideline (iii) as being a justifiable use of the flexibility believed to be inherent in the guidelines.

Scott says 'I accept also that in deciding that the agreed approaches to defence exports to Iraq and Iran respectively could be described as being interpretations of the 1985 Guidelines, the junior ministers believed they were avoiding a formal change of the 1985 Guidelines.' (D 3.125)

The government was simply not telling the truth when it answered the question at the beginning of this press release in the negative. The Scott Report said Mr Waldegrave told MPs something that was not true. In that sense, he misled parliament. He may not have intended to do so. He does not think he ever did so. However, Sir Richard Scott said he did. Furthermore, the fact that he misled parliament is implicit in remarks Mr Waldegrave himself made in his press release. He said: 'Sir Richard Scott clears me of lying to parliament or *intending to* mislead anyone in the letters I signed.[137]

There would have been no need for Mr Waldegrave to add the words in italics if the Scott Report had cleared him of misleading parliament.

The only reference in the Treasury press release to the three paragraphs quoted above (D 4.4 to D4.6) is a selective quotation from paragraph D4.6: 'I did not receive the impression of any insincerity on his part in giving me the evidence he did'. The rest of the paragraph is ignored.

There are other selective quotations from this section of the Scott Report. Thus, the press release says:

Scott clears Waldegrave of lying to parliament or in letters.

I accept that he [Waldegrave] did not intend his letters to be misleading and did not so regard them. (D 4.12)

Reading the sentence in context gives a very different impression:

D4.12 . . . Taken overall, the terms of Mr Waldegrave's letter to Mr [Tom] Sackville [MP] and his other letters in like terms were, in my opinion, apt to mislead the readers as to the nature of the policy on export sales to Iraq that was currently being pursued by the government. Mr Waldegrave was in a position to know that although I accept that he did not intend his letters to be misleading and did not so regard them.

One may speculate on whether Sir Richard's first draft ended on the words 'Mr Waldegrave was in a position to know that' and whether the qualification was added at the Minister's request. If so, Sir Richard will have seen how useful the qualification was to Mr Waldegrave when officials were preparing his press release.

Other extracts from Mr Waldegrave's press notice were equally misleading. 'I accept also that . . . the junior ministers believed they were avoiding a formal change to the 1985 guidelines' the press release quoted Sir Richard Scott as saying. Yet in his report Sir Richard said the ministers 'were, in any ordinary use of language, agreeing on a change of policy. I regard the explanation that this could not be so because the approval of senior minister and the Prime Minister had not been obtained as sophistry.'[138]

All this may be treated as part of the rough and tumble of everyday politics. However, its importance is far greater. It is yet another example of ministers and their officials doing their best to belittle a senior judge, to make light of his concerns and criticisms. In court, the judge is supreme. Nevertheless, as soon as he steps into the political arena he is no match for the government. Judges always come off second best when they are playing away from home.

That might be tolerable if it were temporary. The problem is that once a judge's reputation has been tarnished in an encounter with the government it takes a lot of polishing before the judge can restore it. The next time Sir Richard Scott rules against a minister in court his political friends will no doubt remind journalists that this was the judge who 'didn't understand Whitehall', this was the judge whose severe criticisms were easily brushed aside by the government. It is the judiciary as a whole which suffers when ministers shoot poisoned arrows against an individual judge.

The Commons debate

In parliament, the government's approach was to pretend that the Scott Inquiry had been set up to decide two questions: whether ministers had been guilty of a secret plot to arm the Iraqi ruler, Saddam Hussein, and whether the government had suppressed documents that could have led to a miscarriage of justice. Opening a Commons debate ten days after the Scott Report had been published, the President of the Board of Trade, Ian Lang, said that on those 'serious and defamatory charges . . . the government now stand acquitted'.[139] As the editor of *Public Law* pointed out, those were not the charges Sir Richard Scott was asked to investigate.[140] Despite criticism from its own back benches, the government survived the division by 320 votes to 319 after arm-twisting by the Whips and behind-the-scenes deals with the Ulster Unionists. The government, and all its ministers, survived.

In what was perhaps the final irony, Labour's spokesman, Robin Cook, told MPs that the Iraqis had not even paid for the machine tools they had imported: the government had extended Iraq's export credits despite mounting evidence that it did not have the money and the British taxpayer was left with a bill for £700 million.

An unsatisfactory outcome

Sir Richard Scott fully recognised that 'one of the main purposes behind the setting up of the inquiry' was 'the allaying of public disquiet'.[141] This is one reason why most of the important witnesses gave evidence in public.[142] Nonetheless, it is hard to believe that the Scott Report achieved that aim.

Lord Howe, while conceding that he was a partisan witness, said it was 'difficult to recall an inquiry which has provoked a more deeply felt sense of injustice and disbelief on the part of those

208

investigated'.[143] He added: 'The risk is that [the Scott Inquiry] may, in Denis Healey's phrase, have done for public or judicial inquiries what the Boston Strangler did for doorstep selling.'[144] As it turned out, all those investigated by the Scott Inquiry kept their jobs (or were promoted). From the government's point of view, it was as successful as ministers and officials had dared hope.

That was not because they escaped criticism: as we have seen, they were found to have misled parliament, which should be a serious matter in a parliamentary democracy. The government's saving grace was that these criticisms were all but drowned in a sea of words.

Why did Sir Richard Scott pull his punches when it came to publication? Why did he allow ministers the advantages we have seen? There can be two possible explanations: either ministers persuaded him that it would be fair and right to behave in this way or after three years he was still innocent about the ways of Whitehall.

He may have felt that once he had submitted his report the government was entitled to decide how and when it would be published. Like so much in our constitution this is no more than a convention: if Sir Richard had insisted on his own arrangements there would have been nothing that Whitehall could have done to stop him. Furthermore it was entirely his choice to avoid providing a summary of his report or a briefing for the media: if that was because he wanted reporters to reflect the subtleties of his conclusions when covering his report he was certainly being unrealistic. Of course, he may have thought that the presentation and immediate impact of his report mattered less than its long-term effect. If that was his approach, it was certainly naïve.

In his report, Sir Richard Scott gave some thought to the way inquiries of the sort he had conducted should operate.[145] The government invited comments on his recommendations. Those comments in turn were considered by the Council on Tribunals, an independent advisory body set up in 1958. In July 1996, the council submitted its advice to the Lord Chancellor; Lord Mackay published it four months later.[146] The council's advice tended to be woolly: on the whole, it left difficult questions to be decided in the light of circumstances. However, there were two implicit criticisms of Sir Richard Scott's procedures. 'Where there is a need for forceful questioning of witnesses,' the report said, 'it is often better if this is undertaken by counsel to the inquiry, rather than by the tribunal itself. Otherwise, the tribunal may be seen as having already formed a certain view.'[147] Also, the Council on Tribunals said it agreed with a number of commentators who urged 'that inquiry reports of any length should provide for an executive summary of the findings and recommendations.'[148]

How then do we remember Sir Richard Scott and his hugely expensive public inquiry? Sir Richard proved not to be the crusty old judge of popular myth: the fellow even wore a cloth cap and actually turned up on a bicycle. Yet it is hard to see what the public gained in the end, except perhaps a new ministerial approach to public interest immunity. Even that followed more from the decision in *Wiley* than from Sir Richard's recommendations. It was also agreed that the Attorney General would keep a closer eye on some customs prosecutions. In the light of Matrix Churchill, he would probably have done so anyway.

The government, on the other hand, gained a valuable breathing space: much longer, thanks to Sir Richard, than they could ever have hoped for. Cynics would say that was all they wanted.

Judges and inquiries

Professor Robert Stevens noted that judges had not been asked to head public inquiries until the present century; it was inevitable that they would be subject to public criticism now that they were taking on these broader responsibilities.[149] Whether the value to society of judicial inquiries outweighs the risks to public respect for the judiciary is another of the delicate balancing exercises which judges may have to conduct in the future.

Judges should be very careful before they take on public inquiries. Few people can associate any particular decision with a specific judge, but Sir Richard Scott is remembered for his 'arms to Iraq' inquiry as Lord Justice Taylor[150] is for his investigation of the Hillsborough tragedy and indeed Lord Denning still is for the Profumo report of 1963. The more the judges get involved in investigations of this kind the more risk there is that they will be dragged into matters of political controversy. The more that happens, the less able they will be to do the job of judging. It is no doubt difficult for a judge to refuse an invitation to chair a public inquiry, but before they do so they should think carefully about every stage of the process – and take advice from those who understand the risks.

Professor John Griffith has well-known misgivings about the neutrality of the judiciary: for that reason he considered it 'false' for judges to be presented as 'neutral arbiters capable of providing unpolitical solutions to political problems or of expressing unpolitical opinions on political issues'.[151] Professor Gavin Drewry agreed that there was a strong case for holding that judicial inquiries should be used 'sparingly and selectively'. However, he thought there was an equally strong case for saying that 'Some such inquiries are from time to time essential mechanisms of accountability and reassurance in a system where the investigative will and capability of an executive-dominated House of Commons is so very weak.' He added:

> The Scott Inquiry may have had its shortcomings, and in the end the report's bulk and the technicality both of the subject and of the remedies proposed have made it inaccessible to the public that it was meant to reassure. But, paradoxically, that very same bulk and technicality, underpinned by the authority of a senior judge who was seen to make William Waldegrave squirm and Lord Howe scowl, provided to some degree its own reassurance.[152]

In the United Kingdom, we are used to the idea of judges chairing public inquiries. But as the Lord Chief Justice pointed out in November 1996, 'in many countries, the participation of judges in commissions, inquiries and committees not devoted to law reform or the administration of justice is regarded as inconsistent with the independence of the judiciary'. Lord Bingham accepted that there might not be any threat to judicial independence if the judge's final report was accepted by the government, at any rate where the report also commanded broad public acceptance. The Lord Chief Justice then sounded a word of warning:

> The situation plainly becomes more difficult when a report is rejected by the government, as the Macmillan Government rejected Mr Justice Devlin's report on Central Africa; or when a report is the subject of acute political controversy and hostile publicity before publication, as was the case with Sir Richard Scott's recent report on arms to Iraq; or when a major recommendation is instantly rejected, like Lord Cullen's recommendation on hand-guns; or when a report is regarded as unpersuasive by significant sections of opinion, as proved to be the case with Lord Widgery's report on 'Bloody Sunday'.[153]

Two comments immediately spring to mind. The first is that, as we

211

have seen, parts of Sir Richard Scott's report were rejected by the government on publication as well as being criticised in advance. The second, and more important point, is that no judge who agrees to take on a public inquiry can exclude the possibility that his or her report will fall foul of one or more of Lord Bingham's four elephant traps.

The Lord Chief Justice thought that the judges had generally survived with their reputations intact:

> To date, I think that the standing of the judges involved and the quality of the reports produced have almost always won for such reports a degree of acceptance denied to those who reject or criticise them. But I think that this is an area in which great caution is needed. The reputation which judges generally enjoy for impartiality and skill in arriving at the truth is a priceless asset, not to be lightly squandered.[154]

Though understated, this was a serious warning from the head of the English judiciary. In support, Lord Bingham cited a comment made by Lord Devlin in 1979: 'In our own country the reputation of the judiciary for independence and impartiality is a national asset of such richness that one government after another tries to plunder it.'[155]

It will be interesting to see whether serving judges become mysteriously unavailable the next time a government which finds itself suffering from a political mishap is looking for someone to preside over a long-running public inquiry. Of course, the Lord Chief Justice has no power to prevent a judge taking on a task of this kind. Nevertheless, he does have influence and if the misgivings he expressed in 1996 become stronger as the months go by it will be a brave judge who chooses to defy his wishes.

The judiciary should waste no time in thinking what to do. Judicial inquiries are often announced at short notice: before the next telephone call from Downing Street, the judges should decide what their response will be.

One compromise would be for judges to refuse to sit alone. Lord Denning's report on the Profumo affair and Sir Richard Scott's 'arms to Iraq' inquiry demonstrated the exposed position of a judge who is obliged to write his report in the first person singular. Another possibility is to make use of retired judges. However, the retirement age for newly appointed judges is seventy, which means they still retire later than most other people. It is not generally a good idea to give someone in his seventies a demanding job of this kind. The best way of getting a job done quickly is to give it to someone who is busy.

Concluding thoughts

The story of *Spycatcher* was one of grudging respect for the judiciary. The government may have behaved stubbornly, even petulantly, but it played the game by the legal rules. Ironically, it failed in its political judgments: it seemed unable to accept that the judges would reject its attempts to preserve the secrecy of information that was no longer secret.

The judges' attitude to the government is harder to categorise. It was natural enough for the courts to impose temporary injunctions at an early stage: the courts would have done so whoever was before them. By the summer of 1987, when *Spycatcher* was available in Britain, it was absurd for the Court of Appeal and a majority of the law lords to uphold the temporary ban. The appeal judges were closer to the government's way of thinking than seemed healthy.

Then the tide turned. The courts took their lead from the minority of the law lords and demonstrated a robust independence. Sir Richard Scott, then merely a High Court judge, upheld the right of the media to report alleged government misdeeds. This judicial independence was to flourish during the following decade. It was a decade when Lord Mackay was on the woolsack, when the old order was breaking down, and when the government could no longer rely on the unquestioning support of the judges it had appointed.

Predictably enough, Sir Richard Scott supported the principle of openness in his report on the Matrix Churchill affair. Underlying his report was the assumption that in a parliamentary democracy the public should be told what ministers are up to. Ministers, on the other hand, regarded it as axiomatic that 'the processes of government cannot be conducted in a goldfish bowl', watched by the world.[156] Neither of them is entirely right. The Scott Report and the government's reaction show that the executive and the judiciary are no nearer to understanding one another.

How then should we answer the questions posed at the start of this chapter? Do judges have respect for ministers? On the whole, no. Is there any respect for the judiciary in government circles? Not as much as there should be. Has one side or the other tried to overreach itself? Yes, both have. Can anything be done to make amends? Yes, given goodwill on both sides and a willingness to change established practices.

Failing that, the trial of strength will continue. However, as Lord Steyn said in the quotation at the beginning of Chapter 1, 'It is when there is a state of perfect harmony between the judges and the executive that citizens need to worry.'

Notes

Titles such as 'Home Secretary' will be used in references throughout this book, even though the Law Reports normally list cases under a more formal title, such 'Secretary of State for the Home Department'. Square brackets around a date indicate that it is an essential part of the reference; round brackets indicate that the date is given purely for information. Unexplained initials generally refer to the various law reports: Appeal Cases, Queen's Bench Reports and so on. A further subtlety is explained in Chapter 3, note 3.

Introduction

1 *Hansard*, House of Lords, 27 January 1997, cols. 1002–3.
2 (1765) 19 State Trials 1030.
3 *Hansard*, House of Lords, 20 January 1997, col. 406.
4 *Ibid.* col. 416.
5 Contents, 161; Not-Contents, 161. *Hansard, House of Lords*, 28 January 1997, col. 1097.

Chapter 1   Battle Lines

1 Lord Steyn, 'The Weakest and Least Dangerous Department of Government', Administrative Bar Association Annual Lecture, 27 November 1996.
2 Lord Nolan, 'The Judiciary', third Radcliffe Lecture, Warwick University, 5 December 1996.
3 *R. v. Home Secretary ex p. Norney*, [1996] Crown Office Digest 81.
4 In the judicial review sense: see Chapter 3.
5 BBC Radio 4, 29 September 1995.
6 Interview with the author, 5 September 1996. The judge asked not to be named.
7 Interview with the author, 30 September 1996. Lord Mackay was not told which particular example the author had in mind.
8 *Erskine May*, 21st edn., p. 380, n. 1.
9 Interview with Marcel Berlins, *Law in Action*, BBC Radio 4, 19 October 1996.
10 He had been suffering from heart disease which led to his early death, but it was not at his choice that he retired so soon after taking up his appointment.

11 Information provided by the Home Secretary, 14 January 1997.
12 Interview with the author, 14 January 1997.
13 *R. v. Home Secretary ex p. Moon*, (1996) 8 Administrative Law Reports 477.
14 *The Times*, 3 November 1995. The MP was David Faber (Westbury).
15 Interview with the author, 14 January 1997.
16 *The Times*, 3 November 1995.
17 Interview with the author, 14 November 1996.
18 Some people doubted whether the public was ready for the two most senior judicial posts in England to be held by Jews at the same time. Others said that those who took that view were being paranoid.
19 Judicial assistants, as they were called, were comparable to American law clerks; Lord Mackay was against the idea of providing judicial assistants for the law lords (interview with the author, 18 June 1993).
20 Michael Howard, questioned by the author at a Home Office briefing, 25 October 1996.
21 Interview with the author, 14 January 1997. Incorporation of the European Convention is discussed in Chapter 5.
22 This argument had been put forward on the brothers' behalf by Michael Beloff QC. It was used successfully against him by David Pannick QC in the *Moon* case (mentioned above) when Mr Beloff was appearing for the Home Secretary.

23 *R. v. Home Secretary ex p. Fayed*, 13 November 1996.
24 For example, at the end of 1992 Lord Justice Glidewell issued a four-page summary of his ruling in *R. v. British Coal ex p. Vardy* [1993] IRLR 104.
25 Private conversations.
26 Interview with the author, 14 November 1996.
27 Leader, *Daily Telegraph*, 16 November 1996. The naïveté of this criticism will be exposed in Chapter 4.
28 On 15 November 1996 the High Court decided the Home Secretary had been wrongly calculating release dates for prisoners serving concurrent sentences (see Chapter 3) and the European Court of Human Rights said the Home Secretary's plans to deport a Sikh activist to India would be a breach of his human rights.
29 Michael Gove, *The Times*, 16 November 1996, p. 2.
30 Will Hutton, *The State We're In*, p. 36.
31 No date is given for this reference.
32 Will Hutton, *The State We're In*, pp. 35–6.
33 Sir Thomas Bingham, 'The Courts and the Constitution', lecture at King's College London, 14 February 1996, *Kings College Law Journal*, vol. 7, p. 19.
34 *Liversidge v. Anderson* [1942] AC 206.
35 In *Nakkuda Ali v. Jayaratne* [1951] AC 66 Lord Radcliffe said it would be a very unfortunate thing if *Liversidge*'s case were regarded as laying down any general rule.
36 Lord Diplock in *R. v. Inland Revenue Commissioners ex p. Rossminster* [1980] AC 952.
37 See Chapter 6.
38 The Lord Chancellor's woolsack is a large square bag of wool (and a little horsehair) inside a wooden frame, covered with red cloth and placed in front of the throne. It has no formal back or sides although a small, supposedly temporary, backrest provides some comfort during long debates.
39 Although, ironically, at that time he was probably too young.
40 All fourteen said their second choice would have been Lord Justice Kennedy. The Lord Chancellor subsequently appointed Lord Justice Kennedy to be vice-president of the Queen's Bench Division of the High Court and Lord Justice Rose to be vice-president of the criminal division of the Court of Appeal. These unpaid honours were seen as consolation prizes.
41 On 21 May 1996.
42 Author's sources.
43 See Chapter 2.
44 See Chapter 6, 'Must ministers claim immunity?'
45 News conference, 4 October 1996. There is a full discussion of judicial review in Chapter 3.
46 See Anthony Bevins, 'Senior Judges round on the Tories', *Independent*, 9 October 1996.
47 In *The Search for Justice*, pp. 9–10.
48 On 12 July 1995.
49 Home Affairs Committee, *Judicial Appointments Procedures*, 5 June 1996, vol. II, Q. 459.
50 Home Affairs Committee, *Judicial Appointments Procedures*, above, para. 126.
51 *Ibid.*, para. 128.
52 *Guardian*, 29 June 1996.
53 Scotland's senior law officer, the Scottish counterpart of the English Attorney General.
54 Short for Alexander.
55 See Chapter 4.
56 See Chapter 2.
57 Interview with Ian Hargreaves, *New Statesman*, 6 December 1996, p. 18.
58 Which is kept personally by the Lord Chancellor.
59 Although, of course, higher courts may overrule lower ones.
60 The full story is told in Chapter 6.
61 Lord Nolan, 'The Judiciary', third Radcliffe Lecture, Warwick University, 5 December 1996. Some journalists who were acquainted with Mr Justice Sedley no doubt assumed that Mr Justice Smedley was merely a misprint.
62 There are comparable overlaps in Scotland and Northern Ireland.
63 Italics added. In the absence of good faith, those appointed to positions which involve both political and legal decisions would act more as politicians than as lawyers.
64 *Hansard*, House of Lords, 3 July 1996, col. 1450.
65 The 'law lords'.
66 He is also president of the High Court and the Court of Appeal, but in practice he sits in these courts only on ceremonial occasions.
67 In his lecture to the Administrative Bar Association, 'The Weakest and Least Dangerous Department of Government', 27 November 1996.
68 Figuratively speaking: he only has one.

See Joshua Rozenberg, *The Search for Justice*, p. 14.

69 As above.

70 Lord Mackay of Clashfern, 'Parliament and the Judges – a Constitutional Challenge?', speech to the Citizenship Foundation, 8 July 1996.

71 *Hansard*, House of Lords, 18 January 1994, col. 506.

72 Although Strasbourg-based British officials were clearly irritated by the intrusion of British reporters on to their territory. They had rather more to worry about when the Home Secretary became involved: see Chapter 5, 'The convention's origins'.

73 Geoffrey Bindman, *Gazette*, 27 November 1996, p. 5.

74 He eventually found a seat.

75 In January 1997, the law lords, in order of precedence, were: Lord Goff of Chieveley, Lord Browne-Wilkinson, Lord Mustill, Lord Slynn of Hadley, Lord Lloyd of Berwick, Lord Nolan, Lord Nicholls of Birkenhead, Lord Steyn, Lord Hoffmann, Lord Hope of Craighead, Lord Clyde and Lord Hutton. Lord Mustill had announced his intention to retire in the spring of 1997.

76 Such as Derek Wheatley QC, writing in *Consumer Policy Review*, published by the Consumers' Association, September/October 1996.

77 Fifty-nine in 1995, of which twenty-eight were allowed.

78 Unless the Master of the Rolls is already a member of the House of Lords on appointment (as Lord Denning and Lord Woolf were) he or she may have to wait some years for a peerage; the Lord Chief Justice receives one immediately.

79 John Patten, 'Let's reform the Lord Chancellor', *Daily Telegraph*, 10 July 1996.

80 The cross benches, being in the middle of the chamber, are occupied by peers who identify with neither the government nor the opposition. When the law lords have the chamber to themselves for judicial proceedings, they spread themselves around the two front benches (with the senior law lord sitting on the woolsack). During Lord Taylor's last speech as Lord Chief Justice (23 May 1996) there were so many law lords in the chamber that some had to sit on the opposition benches.

81 Lord Mackay of Clashfern, 'Parliament and the Judges – a Constitutional Challenge?', speech to the Citizenship Foundation, 8 July 1996.

82 Or 1688: both dates are used. Article 9 provided 'that the freedom of speech and debates or proceedings in parliament ought not to be impeached or questioned in any court or place out of parliament'.

83 7 May 1996. The amendment became s. 13 of the act.

84 In a huge front-page headline, 1 October 1996. In response, he said he could not afford to sue the paper for libel.

85 Clare Dyer, *Guardian*, 2 October 1996. The amendment was passed by 157 votes to 57. It seems unlikely that more than 200 peers would have turned up to vote without an unofficial whip. One account said that Conservative peers were phoned directly from Downing Street to preserve the fiction of a free vote. It quoted a Conservative peer saying 'it was made absolutely clear to me that the Prime Minister was relying on my support'. (David Leigh and Ed Vulliamy, *Sleaze*, 1997, p. 198.)

86 Hugo Young, *Guardian*, 8 October 1996, citing a remark by the Prime Minister: 'If the government were so concerned about perverting the natural course of justice, why did I help steer a bill through the House of Commons so that Neil Hamilton could take his case to court?'.

87 Letter to the author, 28 November 1996.

88 They normally take knighthoods. Juries must be bemused to hear them addressed in court as 'Mr Attorney' and 'Mr Solicitor'. Usually, they are neither attorneys, nor solicitors, nor misters.

89 The Crown Prosecution Service, the Serious Fraud Office and some of the prosecutions brought by H. M. Customs and Excise.

90 'The Weakest and Least Dangerous Department of Government', lecture to the Administrative Bar Association, 27 November 1996.

91 In his Hamlyn Lectures, *Protection of the Public – A New Challenge*, 1990, pp. 103–13.

92 Lord Jenkins of Hillhead, *Hansard*, House of Lords, 26 February 1996, cols. 1242–3. The Scott Report is discussed in Chapter 6. Silks are QCs.

93 30 January 1997.

94 The others were Sir Ivan Lawrence QC (Conservative) and Alex Carlile QC (Liberal Democrat). Mr Carlile announced he would be leaving the Commons in 1997.

95 *Hansard*, House of Lords, 20 October

1992, WA 84 (which gives the latest available figures).

96 Joshua Rozenberg, *The Case for the Crown*, 1987, p. 44.

97 The European Court of Human Rights in Strasbourg and the European Court of Justice in Luxembourg.

98 *EastEnders*. Who says judges are out of touch?

99 *AG v. MGN and others*, Divisional Court, 31 July 1996 (Lord Justice Schiemann and Mr Justice Smedley).

100 *Independent*, *Guardian*, 5 October 1995 (Judge Sanders).

101 Government lawyers knew they had fourteen days in which to appeal but had not realised that the date of the original judgment was reckoned as the first day of the period. They missed the deadline by one day: there is no provision for late appeals. This incident gives further support to those who are convinced that the conspiracy theory of history is always less plausible than the cock-up theory.

102 17 January 1997.

103 What a coincidence, the jury must have thought: a lawyer whose surname is Solicitor.

104 The case was *Pepper v. Hart* [1993] AC 593. Pepper was the Inspector of Taxes. Although all seven law lords found against the Inland Revenue, Lord Mackay did not want to change a well-established rule that could have a substantial effect in increasing the costs of litigation. His department funds the cost of legal aid, among other matters. Lord Mackay said afterwards that there were precedents for a Lord Chancellor sitting in tax cases.

105 The same may apply to governments that take advice from in-house lawyers: see *The prisons fiasco*, p.109.

106 Scott Report G13.125: see Chapter 6.

Chapter 2 The Sentence of the Judge

1 Speech at the Conference of Chief Justices and Attorneys General of the European Union, Lisbon, 18–21 May 1994. Lord Taylor repeated these remarks in a speech to the Commonwealth Judges' and Magistrates' Association Hertfordshire Symposium, 15 April 1996.

2 *Observer*, 9 June 1996.

3 *Electronic Telegraph*, 11 October 1995.

4 *Hansard*, House of Lords, 1 November 1995, cols. 1425–7.

5 Chairman of the Prison Reform Trust.

6 Speech at the Lord Mayor's Dinner, 15 July 1992.

7 As note 1 above.

8 Speech at the Conference of Chief Justices, above.

9 The source of this anecdote is Lord Windlesham. See *Responses to Crime*, vol. 2, p. 250 and, more fully, vol. 3, p. 6.

10 Interview with Patricia Wynn Davies, *Independent*, 9 February 1990.

11 The story is told in Joshua Rozenberg, *The Search for Justice*, chapter 6, and more fully in Lord Windlesham, *Responses to Crime*, vol. 3, chapter 1.

12 *Today* programme, BBC Radio 4, 4 May 1993.

13 Letter from David Maclean to the author's source, 18 August 1993.

14 Criminal Justice Act 1993. The government depicted this U-turn as a triumph.

15 Lord Taylor, speech to the Law Society of Scotland, Gleneagles, 21 March 1993.

16 See Joshua Rozenberg, *The Search for Justice*, p. 289.

17 To allow time to train judges and magistrates. It took effect in October 1992.

18 *Responses to Crime*, vol. 2, p. 181.

19 *Sunday Times*, 22 November 1981.

20 See Joshua Rozenberg, *The Search for Justice*, p. 39.

21 Interview with the author, 14 January 1997.

22 14 October 1995.

23 'Continuity and Change in the Criminal Law', speech delivered at King's College London, 6 March 1996, printed in *King's College Law Journal*, vol. 7, p. 8.

24 Royal Commission on Criminal Justice Report, Cm 2263, July 1993, chapter 4, para. 22.

25 As drafted, the legislation would have required the magistrates or judge to call the defendant into the witness box and order him to give evidence in his own defence.

26 That defendants facing charges which could be tried either by magistrates or by a jury should lose the right to insist on a jury trial.

27 See paragraph 70 of the Final Government Response, published by the Lord Chancellor's Department, the Home Office and the Law Officer's [sic] Department in June 1996. However, in February 1997 Michael Howard put the issue back on the political agenda with a Home Office report which was criticised by Lord Bingham.

28 Criminal Justice and Public Order Act 1994, s. 35.
29 *R. v. Cowan and others* [1995] 4 All ER 939.
30 *R. v. Secretary of State for Defence ex p. Smith and others*, [1996] QB 517.
31 The grounds for judicial review will be explained more fully in Chapter 3.
32 *Hansard*, House of Commons, 3 May 1950, col. 1762.
33 *Judicial Independence*, Inaugural address to the Judicial Studies Board, 5 November 1996.
34 PA News, 7 November 1996.
35 *Hansard*, House of Lords, 7 April 1989, col. 1331.
36 The Lord Chief Justice, the Master of the Rolls and the President of the Probate, Divorce and Admiralty Division.
37 Addressed 'Dear Jacob' to show he was writing to an equal.
38 The letter is dated 12 December 1955. It is printed in [1986] *Public Law* 384.
39 The Harry Street Lecture, University of Manchester, 13 February 1986. It is printed in [1986] *Public Law* 220. There is a full discussion of judicial review in Chapter 3.
40 A brief extract was broadcast on *Law in Action*, Radio 4, 14 February 1986.
41 *R. v. Commissioner for the Special Purposes of the Income Tax Acts, ex p. Stipplechoice Ltd, The Times*, 23 January 1985.
42 Lord Hailsham, *A Sparrow's Flight*, p. 432. Lord Hailsham did not identify the judges concerned.
43 *Hansard*, House of Lords, 5 February 1985, col. 945.
44 Lord Hailsham, *A Sparrow's Flight*, p. 432.
45 Lord Mackay of Clashfern, 'Parliament and the Judges – a Constitutional Challenge?', speech to the Citizenship Foundation, 8 July 1996.
46 News conference, 3 November 1987 (*Daily Telegraph*, 4 November 1987).
47 See below.
48 Lord Mackay of Clashfern, letter to Lord Lane, 16 October 1989, unpublished (extracts quoted by Lord Irvine of Lairg, *Hansard*, House of Lords, 5 June 1996, col. 1257).
49 Letter to Lord Justice Watkins VC dated 11 June 1991.
50 England and Wales are divided into six circuits. Each circuit has at least two *presiding* judges, who are responsible for the running of judicial business within

the circuit. At each Crown Court centre there is a *resident* judge responsible for the listing of cases and their allocation to individual judges.
51 By the author.
52 Letter to the author, 13 January 1997.
53 Prisoners serving twelve months or less were released automatically and unconditionally after serving half their sentences. Prisoners serving over twelve months but less than four years were also released automatically after they had served half their time, but they were subject to supervision until the three-quarters point of their original sentence. Prisoners serving four years or more became eligible for release on licence after serving half their sentence, but they could be kept in prison until they had served two-thirds of their sentence. Again they were subject to supervision until the three-quarters point. They were also at risk of recall until the end of their sentence.
54 Criminal Justice Act 1991, Part II.
55 Michael Howard, speech to Conservative party conference, Blackpool, 12 October 1995.
56 Held near Northampton, 3 February 1996.
57 Lord Taylor, statement to the Press Association, 12 October 1995. As the statement was being issued Lord Taylor was saying *kaddish*, the Jewish prayer for the dead, at his wife's memorial service in the Temple Church.
58 Private letter to the author, 8 September 1996.
59 Interview with the author, 14 January 1997.
60 *Independent*, 14 October 1995.
61 On *The World at One*, 6 December 1993.
62 Interview in *The Times*, 21 November 1995.
63 Interview with the author, 30 September 1996.
64 *The Times*, 5 November 1996.
65 3 February 1996.
66 It did nothing for Lord Justice Rose's chances of becoming Lord Chief Justice when a vacancy arose a few months later.
67 *The Times*, 1 February 1996.
68 'Continuity and Change in the Criminal Law', speech delivered at King's College London, 6 March 1996, printed in *King's College Law Journal*, vol. 7.
69 *Independent*, 14 October 1985.
70 Section 48 of the Criminal Justice and Public Order Act 1994.

71 *Protecting the Public*, Cm 3190, May 1996, para. 9.2.
72 *Ibid.*, para. 10.1.
73 *Ibid.*, para. 10.11.
74 *Ibid.*, para. 11.4.
75 *Ibid.*, para. 12.9.
76 Interview with the author, 14 January 1997.
77 *Hansard*, House of Lords, 23 May 1996, col. 1025.
78 *Ibid.*, col. 1025–6.
79 Home Office, *Crime, Justice and Protecting the Public*, Cm 965, February 1990, para. 2.16
80 Lord Taylor was supported by a former Home Secretary (Lord Carr) and four former Home Office ministers (Lords Belstead, Carlisle, Windlesham and Elton). All were Conservatives.
81 *Hansard*, House of Lords, 23 May 1996, col. 1074. Surely the government could have done so three years earlier?
82 The White Paper fully reflected Douglas Hurd's views, even though he had left the Home Office four months before it was published.
83 24 May 1996.
84 *Hansard*, House of Lords, 23 May 1996, cols. 1071–2. The Lord Chancellor's Department has confirmed the accuracy of the *Hansard* report.
85 Letter to the author from the Lord Chancellor's Head of Information, 13 January 1997.
86 Since Lord Lane's attack on Lord Mackay's plans to reform the legal profession (quoted later in this chapter).
87 'The government fights back.'
88 Lord Donaldson, BBC interviews, 25 October 1996.
89 See Joshua Rozenberg, *The Search for Justice*, p. 41. Without referring to Lord Donaldson by name, Lord Bingham said that if it was true 'that a judge, otherwise obviously fitted for preferment, was denied such preferment because his judicial decisions and pronouncements had excited the hostility of an incoming government . . . the incident must represent a serious blot on the record of those responsible.' ('Judicial Independence', Inaugural Address to the Judicial Studies Board, 5 November 1996).
90 PA News, 25 October 1996.
91 Home Office Background Notes, 25 October 1996.
92 Interview with the author, 14 January 1997.
93 *The Times*, 5 November 1996.
94 *Hansard*, House of Commons, 4 November 1996, col. 914.
95 Powers of Criminal Courts Act 1973, s. 22(2)(b) as amended by Criminal Justice Act 1991.
96 Lord Bingham, BBC *Breakfast with Frost*, 10 November 1996.
97 Interview with the author, 16 November 1996.
98 *Hansard*, House of Lords, 27 January 1996, col. 971.
99 It followed that the three-year minimum for burglars would be the equivalent of a four-and-a-half-year sentence under the old arrangements; the seven years for drug dealers would be equal to a sentence of ten and a half years.
100 *Hansard, op.cit.*, Col. 985. Lord Bingham also pointed out that the maximum discount of twenty per cent allowed under the bill from the mandatory minimum penalty was below current rate and well below the discount allowed where a defendant was willing to give valuable information to the police or to spare a victim the trauma of giving evidence.
101 *Ibid.*, Col. 986.
102 *Ibid.*, Col. 988.
103 *Ibid.*, Col. 990.
104 *Ibid.*, Col. 997.
105 He modestly omitted the fact that he had also been Lord President, the Scottish equivalent of the Master of the Rolls. He had been appointed to these positions from his post of Dean of the Faculty of Advocates, the Scottish equivalent of Chairman of the Bar, overtaking all the serving judges in Scotland.
106 Lewd conduct covers a very wide range of sexually deviant behaviour ranging from indecent exposure to the serious sexual abuse of young children. Clandestine injury to women is committed when a man has intercourse with a woman who is unconscious or asleep. Both offences are unique to Scotland.
107 *Hansard*, House of Lords, 27 January 1996, col. 971.
108 *Hansard*, House of Lords, 18 March 1997
109 *Hansard*, House of Lords, 3 February 1993, col. 1040.
110 By the author, press conference, 28 May 1993.
111 Interview with the author, 4 June 1996.
112 House of Lords Internet pages: http: //www.parliament.the-stationery-office. co.uk/pa/ld199697/ldinfo/ld08judg/

ld08judg.htm#history

113 Professor Robert Stevens, interview with the author, 30 May 1996.

114 Interview with Marcel Berlins, *Law in Action*, BBC Radio 4, 18 October 1996.

115 See p.84.

116 Professor Rodney Brazier, *Constitutional Practice*, 2nd edn., 1994, p. 281.

117 House of Commons Disqualification Act 1975, s. 1(1) and Schedule 1, Part I.

118 See Home Affairs Committee, *Judicial Appointments Procedures*, June 1996, para. 202. The committee endorsed this policy, although it concluded that the aim of a balanced bench had not yet been achieved.

119 Peter Brooke MP, *Hansard*, House of Commons, 4 November 1996, col. 951.

120 See *Independent*, 24 and 27 September 1996. The newspaper, which carries no libel insurance, agreed to make a payment to charity after the judge had sent a solicitor's letter.

121 Professor Rodney Brazier, as above.

122 See Joshua Rozenberg, *The Search for Justice*, p. 63.

123 Lord Mackay, 'Parliament and the Judges – a Constitutional Challenge', speech to the Citizenship Foundation, 8 July 1996.

124 *Hansard*, House of Lords, 5 June 1996, cols. 1258/9.

125 *Ibid.*, col. 1259.

126 Interview with Marcel Berlins, *Law in Action*, BBC Radio 4, 18 October 1996.

127 They had in fact decided this thirty years earlier: see *Practice Statement (Judicial Precedent)* [1966] 1 WLR 1234 (26 July 1966).

128 *Hansard*, House of Lords, 5 June 1996, cols. 1272–3.

129 *Ibid.*, cols. 1310–1.

130 See Joshua Rozenberg, *The Search for Justice*, p. 65.

131 Fortunately, it did not prevent him becoming Master of the Rolls three years later.

132 The Lord Chief Justice, the Master of the Rolls, the Vice-Chancellor of the Chancery Division and the President of the Family Division.

133 However, both these topics have resource implications.

134 Interview with Marcel Berlins, *Law in Action*, BBC Radio 4, 19 October 1996.

135 Lord Jowitt, Lord Chancellor 1945–51. Jowitt wrote to Denning shortly after his book was published in 1949. See Robert Stevens, *The Independence of the Judiciary*, p. 93.

136 11 May.

137 Lord Bingham of Cornhill, 'Judicial Independence', Inaugural Address to the Judicial Studies Board, 5 November 1996.

138 He considered that a front-page headline in the *Independent* on 5 October 1996 – 'Top judge lambasts Howard' – did not accurately reflect his views.

139 Those who have forgotten Judge Pickles are referred to Joshua Rozenberg, *The Search for Justice*, pp. 112–5.

140 *Hansard*, House of Lords, 27 January 1997, col. 992

141 As above, col. 991.

142 To the Conference of Chief Justices and Attorneys General of the European Union, Lisbon, 18–21 May 1994.

143 For their early attempts, see Joshua Rozenberg, *The Search for Justice*, pp. 101–3.

144 Nick Chibnell took on the job in September 1996.

145 Tom Kennedy.

Chapter 3   Judicial Review

1 Speaking to PA News.

2 Speaking at the Newspaper Press Fund lunch.

3 *M. v. Home Office* [1992] QB 270, 314. (Note for non-lawyers: this reference means the report begins on page 270 of the 1992 Queen's Bench law reports although the quotation is from page 314). The formulation had been advanced by *M*'s counsel, Stephen Sedley QC (later Mr Justice Sedley).

4 2 February 1997.

5 Suicide Act 1961, s. 2.

6 de Smith, Woolf and Jowell, *Judicial Review of Administrative Action*, 5th edn., 1995.

7 *Rooke's Case* (1598) 5 Coke's Reports 99b. The report continues: 'For discretion is a science or understanding to discern between falsity and truth, between wrong and right, between shadows and substance, between equity and colourable glosses and pretences, and not to do according to their wills and private affections.'

8 *Padfield v. MAFF* [1968] AC 997.

9 Wade and Forsyth, *Administrative Law*, 7th edn., p. 390.

10 *Associated Provincial Picture Houses v. Wednesbury Corporation* [1948] 1 KB 223. The cinema needed a licence from the council, which could impose 'such conditions as the authority think fit'. The council decided no children under fifteen should be admitted on a Sunday. The Court of Appeal held that this condition was not unreasonable.

11 Sir Stephen Sedley, 'Governments, Constitutions, and Judges' in *Administrative Law and Government Action*, edited by Genevra Richardson and Hazel Genn, p. 38.

12 Sir Stephen Sedley, 'The Common Law and the Constitution', Radcliffe Lecture, University of Warwick, 14 November 1996.

13 In *Short v. Poole Corporation* [1926] Chapter 66.

14 *Associated Provincial Picture Houses v. Wednesbury Corporation* (above).

15 *Council of Civil Service Unions v. Minister for the Civil Service* [1985] AC 374.

16 At p. 410.

17 Wade and Forsyth, p. 401.

18 See de Smith, Woolf and Jowell, para. 13–005 onwards.

19 As Lord Donaldson says, 'irrational' casts doubt on the mental capacity of the decision-maker, 'a matter which, in practice, is seldom if ever in issue': *R. v. Devon CC ex p. G* [1988] 3 WLR 49, 51.

20 de Smith, Woolf and Jowell, p. 375.

21 *Ibid.*, p. 417.

22 *Nemo judex in causa sua* (or . . . *in re sua*).

23 *Audi alterem partem*.

24 de Smith, Woolf and Jowell, p. 295.

25 *R. v. Social Security Secretary, ex p. JCWI and B.* [1996] 4 All ER 385.

26 Lord Justice Neill made his remarks during the course of a dissenting judgment.

27 Sir John Laws, 'Law and Democracy' [1995] *Public Law* 72, 77.

28 Lord Irvine of Lairg QC, 'Judges and Decision-Makers: The Theory and Practice of *Wednesbury* Review' [1996] *Public Law* 59, 74.

29 S. A. de Smith, *Judicial Review of Administrative Action*, 1959, p. 24.

30 Wade and Forsyth, *Administrative Law*, p. 19.

31 de Smith, Woolf and Jowell, pp. 6, 8.

32 *Ibid.*, p. 9.

33 Although Professor Stanley de Smith had recently published his own *Judicial Review of Administrative Action*, a book which was much more detailed but had less breadth of vision.

34 Wade, *Administrative Law*, 1961, pp. 11–12.

35 Lord Irvine of Lairg QC, 'Judges and Decision-Makers: The Theory and Practice of *Wednesbury* Review' [1996] Public Law 59.

36 Sir Stephen Sedley, 'Human Rights: a Twenty-First Century Agenda' [1995] *Public Law* 386, 388.

37 Lord Woolf, '*Droit Public* – English Style' [1995] *Public Law* 57, 58–9.

38 *R. v. Home Secretary ex p. Fire Brigades Union*, [1995] 2 AC 513, 567. The case is discussed later in this chapter. (Note: the figure preceding the comma indicates the page on which the law report begins; the subsequent figure is the page on which the specific quotation will be found.)

39 Interviewed by the author, 5 September 1996.

40 See p.39.

41 Wade and Forsyth, p. 19.

42 *Ibid.*, p. 22–3.

43 Interview with the author, 14 November 1996.

44 Sir Harry Woolf, Harry Street Lecture, University of Manchester, 13 February 1986, [1986] *Public Law* 220, 221–2.

45 Author's sources.

46 Boris Johnson, 'The Long Arm of the Law', *Spectator*, 17 June 1995.

47 Both quoted above.

48 Interview with the author, 26 July 1993.

49 Robert Stevens, 'Judges, politics, politicians and the confusing role of the judiciary', Hardwicke Building Lecture, 21 May 1996.

50 Sir Thomas Bingham, interview with David Rose, *Observer*, 9 May 1993.

51 *Hansard*, House of Lords, 5 June 1996, col. 1255.

52 Interview with Ngaire Woods, *Analysis*, BBC Radio 4, 1 February 1996.

53 *Ibid.*

54 *Ibid.*

55 Home Affairs Committee, *Judicial Appointments Procedures*, vol. II, June 1996, col. 39, evidence of Lord Taylor given 14 June 1995.

56 *Certiorari, mandamus*.

57 Speech at the Lord Mayor's Dinner, 17 July 1996.

58 Interview with the author, 14 November 1996.

59 Sir Thomas Bingham, 'The Courts and the Constitution', lecture at King's College London, 14 February 1996, *King's College Law Journal*, vol. 7, p. 19.

60 Wade and Forsyth, p. 38–9.

61 *Ibid.*, p. 40.

62 *Ibid.*, p.40–1.

63 *R. v. Social Security Secretary, ex p. JCWI and B.* [1996] 4 All ER 385.

64 Lord Mackay of Clashfern, 'Parliament and the Judges – a Constitutional Challenge?', speech to the Citizenship Foundation, 8 July 1996. Lord Mackay made

no reference to this particular case and it seemed he was speaking generally.

65 *R. v. Kensington and Chelsea RB and others ex p. Kihara and others.* The point was academic: as a result of the judgment mentioned in the previous note these asylum-seekers were entitled to social security and were therefore no longer entitled to priority housing.

66 *Hansard*, House of Commons, 25 June 1996, col. 152.

67 15 July 1996.

68 22 July 1996.

69 2 February 1997.

70 Sections 9, 10, 11 and Schedule I.

71 Lord Keith in *R. v. Home Secretary ex p. Fire Brigades Union*, [1995] 2 AC 513, 546, referring to the view of the majority (see below).

72 Home Office, *Compensating Victims of Violent Crime*, December 1993, Cm 2434, para. 38.

73 *R. v. Home Secretary ex p. Fire Brigades Union*, [1995] 2 AC 513.

74 Put by Patrick Elias QC and Dinah Rose, their highly regarded junior counsel.

75 Lord Mustill wrote 1688; it was changed in the law reports to 1689.

76 [1995] 2 AC 513, 568.

77 The Criminal Injuries Compensation Act 1995 came into force in April 1996.

78 Such as dependency claims in fatal cases and provision for some loss of earnings and care costs. There are more generous time limits and a larger list of specified injuries than there were under the unlawful 1994 tariff. On the other hand, payments were held down to 1994 levels and victims are still not treated as individuals.

79 By, for example, Richard Mullender in [1996] LQR 182, 185, who cited the judge's refusal to accept the health authority's view that the treatment sought was experimental. See also Sir Thomas Bingham's remarks later in this section.

80 *R. v. Cambridge HA ex p. B* [1995] 1 WLR 898, 905. The girl's father raised money for her treatment but Jaymee Bowen died little more than a year later, in May 1996.

81 *R. v. Foreign Secretary ex p. World Development Movement* [1995] 1 All ER 611, 620.

82 Sir Stephen Sedley, 'The Common Law and the Constitution', Radcliffe Lectures, University of Warwick, 14 November 1996.

83 *Ibid.*

84 *R. v. Home Secretary ex p. Venables and*

Thompson, The Times, 7 May 1996 (Div. Court), 7 August 1996 (CA).

85 *R. v. Home Secretary ex p. Venables and Thompson, The Times*, 7 August 1996.

86 Strictly speaking, the Divisional Court of the Queen's Bench Division of the High Court.

87 *R. v. Home Secretary ex p. Venables and Thompson, The Times*, 7 May 1996.

88 PA News, 2 May 1996.

89 *R. v. Home Secretary ex p. Venables and Thompson, The Times*, 7 August 1996.

90 *The Times*, 31 July 1996.

91 *Ibid.*

92 Although Lord Woolf did criticise the decision to put off a review of the case for twelve years.

93 *The Times*, letters, 5 August 1996.

94 See s. 67(1) Criminal Justice Act 1967 as amended.

95 Before remission.

96 Again, the example ignores remission. The two examples are freely adapted from hypothetical cases given by Lord Justice Simon Brown during his judgment: see *R. v. Home Secretary ex p. Naughton, The Times*, 17 September 1996.

97 In *R. v. Governor of Brockhill Prison ex p. Evans*, 15 November 1996.

98 In his Crime (Sentences) Bill.

99 Interview with the author, 14 November 1996.

100 Lord Bingham, *Breakfast with Frost*, BBC1, 10 November 1996.

101 Lord Nolan, 'The Judiciary', third Radcliffe Lecture, Warwick University, 5 December 1996.

102 Lord Bingham of Cornhill, 'Judicial Independence', speech to the Judicial Studies Board, 5 November 1996.

103 See Robert Stevens, *The Independence of the Judiciary*, p. 173.

104 Lord Nolan, 'The Judiciary', third Radcliffe Lecture, Warwick University, 5 December 1996. Lord Nolan also referred (though not by name) to the last Labour government's refusal to promote Mr Justice Donaldson (later Lord Donaldson) to the Court of Appeal; however, that was 'unique'.

Chapter 4   Laying Down the Law

1 Writing to the Lord Chancellor, the first Lord Hailsham, and quoted by Professor Robert Stevens, 'Judges, Politics, Politicians and the Confusing Role of the Judiciary', Hardwicke Building Lecture, 21 May 1996.

2 Writing in 'Governments, Constitutions, and Judges' in *Administrative Law and Government Action*, edited by Genevra Richardson and Hazel Genn, p. 38.

3 Sir Thomas Bingham, 'Should there be a law to protect rights of personal privacy?', Lecture to the Association of Liberal Democrat Lawyers, 21 May 1996.

4 The café owner René in *'Allo, 'Allo*: see *Kaye v. Robertson* [1991] FSR 62.

5 *A. G. v. Guardian Newspapers* (No. 2) [1990] 1 AC at pp. 255D–256C.

6 [1993] *Public Law* 269, 284–5, which gives a full citation of the authorities relied on.

7 *Hallewell v. Chief Constable of Derbyshire* [1995] 1 WLR 804, 807. Lawyers for Diana, Princess of Wales had apparently intended to put forward similar arguments after a newspaper published photographs of her exercising in a gym; the case was settled before it came to court.

8 Lord Hoffmann, 'Mind Your Own Business', Goodman Lecture, 22 May 1996.

9 *Hansard*, House of Lords, 5 June 1996, col. 1259.

10 The lecture is discussed later in this chapter.

11 *Hansard*, House of Lords, 5 June 1996, col. 1313.

12 *Ibid.*, col. 1311.

13 *The Times*, 2 July 1996.

14 News conference, 4 October 1996.

15 By the author, news conference, 4 October 1996.

16 Article 17. See D. J. Harris and Sarah Joseph, *The International Covenant on Civil and Political Rights and United Kingdom Law*, Chapter 12.

17 Article 8. See Chapter 5.

18 Lord Mackay, 'Parliament and the Judges – a Constitutional Challenge?', speech to the Citizenship Foundation, 8 July 1996.

19 Sir Stephen Sedley, 'Human Rights: a Twenty-First Century Agenda', [1995] *Public Law* 386, 387.

20 *Plessey v. Ferguson* 163 US 537 (1896).

21 *Brown v. Board of Education of Topeka* 347 US 483 (1954).

22 *Morgentaler v. The Queen* [1988] 1 SCR 30.

23 B Verf G 928.5.1993, B Verf GE 88, 203.

24 *Short v. Poole Corporation* [1926] Ch 66.

25 *Associated Provincial Picture Houses v. Wednesbury Corporation* [1948] 1 KB 223. The case was discussed in Chapter 3.

26 Lord Reid, The Judge as Law Maker, (1972) *Journal of the Society of Public Teachers of Law*, vol. 12 p. 22.

27 On 9 July 1990 the law lords granted the applicants interim relief; written reasons were delivered on 11 October 1990. The European Court decision and the law lords' ruling are reported as *R. v. Transport Secretary ex p. Factortame (No. 2)* [1990] 1 AC 603.

28 As it is still called.

29 *Hansard*, House of Lords, 3 July 1996, col. 1450–1.

30 Interview with Ngaire Woods, *Analysis*, BBC Radio 4, 1 February 1996.

31 *Seaford Court Estates Ltd. v. Asher* [1949] 2 KB 481. I am indebted to Lord Lester of Herne Hill QC for this example and much else in this chapter; see Anthony Lester, 'English Judges as Law Makers', [1993] *Public Law* 269.

32 Sir Stephen Sedley, 'The Common Law and the Constitution', Radcliffe Lecture, University of Warwick, 14 November 1996.

33 *Magor and St. Mellons RDC v. Newport Corporation* [1950] 2 All ER 1226, 1236. (CA). Denning was at that time a Lord Justice of Appeal. As was so often the case, he was in a minority of one.

34 *Magor and St. Mellons RDC v. Newport Corporation* [1952] AC 189, 191. Another of the law lords, Lord Morton of Henryton, agreed with Lord Simonds in almost identical words.

35 Anthony Lester, 'English Judges as Law Makers', [1993] *Public Law* 269, 273.

36 [1993] AC 593

37 And, arguably, the 'notes on clauses' prepared by government departments for the parliamentary draftsman if these are available: Lord Lester referred to them in arguing the Diane Blood case (*R. v. HFEA ex p. Blood*) before the Court of Appeal in January 1997.

38 Although it does not hear criminal appeals from Scotland.

39 Some of the cases to be discussed in this section are mentioned by Dr Gary Slapper in *The Times*, 2 July 1996, p. 35.

40 See, for example, the case of Tony Bland, the young man whose injuries at the Hillsborough football disaster in 1989 had left him in a 'persistent vegetative state': *Airedale NHS Trust v. Bland* [1993] 1 All ER 821, and see Joshua Rozenberg, *The Search for Justice*, pp. 29–30.

41 Although Hale had died sixty years earlier, in 1676. This seems a little slow, even by publishers' standards.

42 Who cannot be named to avoid identifying his wife.

43 *Reg. v. R.* [1992] 1 AC 599.

44 *Ibid.*

45 *CR v. UK* [1996] 21 EHRR 363.

46 By s. 142 of the Criminal Justice and Public Order Act 1994, which (among other things) removed the word 'unlawful' from the previous statutory definition of rape. However, if the courts were right in saying the word was 'mere surplusage' (in other words, meaningless) its removal will have made no difference. The amendment was moved by Lord Lester of Herne Hill QC.

47 *Woolwich Equitable Building Society v. Commissioners of Inland Revenue* [1993] AC 70.

48 [1932] AC 562. This was the famous 'snail in the bottle' case from which the entire modern law of negligence is derived: a woman who claimed she had become ill through drinking contaminated ginger beer sued the manufacturer for damages.

49 See Chapter 3.

50 An injunction which enables the court to freeze the assets of a defendant. This prevents him from thwarting legal action by taking the assets abroad. Anyone seeking this powerful remedy must satisfy the court he has an arguable claim against the defendant. The *Mareva* case was decided in 1975.

51 *Woolwich Equitable Building Society v. Commissioners of Inland Revenue* [1993] AC 70, 173–4.

52 [1993] AC 70, 176.

53 [1994] AC 180.

54 The term comes from Australia. The author is assured it is genuine.

55 [1994] AC 180, 195.

56 Unfortunately, Lord Browne-Wilkinson used the word 'cohabitee'. This word is commonly used, but is quite wrong: it must mean someone who receives cohabitation. A person who cohabits is a cohabiter, or better still, a cohabitant.

57 In *Shaw v. DPP* [1962] AC 220, 275.

58 Private Aindow was later sentenced to two years imprisonment for perverting the course of justice.

59 *R. v. Clegg* [1995] 1AC 482, 492.

60 [1995] 1 AC 482, 500.

61 Press Statement, Northern Ireland Office, 16 January 1997.

62 *Forensic* means 'of, or used in, courts of law'. A forensic scientist is a scientist who examines evidence for the purposes of a

court. Sir Patrick presumably meant to say 'scientific evidence'.

63 *C. v. DPP* [1996] 1 AC 1, 9.

64 There were also a couple of adverse precedents from the Court of Appeal, but Mr Justice Laws felt he could ignore them because the desirability of keeping the presumption was not specifically addressed. A year later five law lords decided Mr Justice Laws was wrong on all three points: see *C. v. DPP* [1996] 1 AC 1, 36–7.

65 Lord Justice Mann: highly experienced but soon to retire.

66 *Crime, Justice and Protecting the Public*, Cm 965 (1990), para. 8.4.

67 *C. v. DPP* [1996] 1 AC 1, 26.

68 *Ibid.*, 40.

69 Lord Woolf, '*Droit Public* – English Style', F. A. Mann Lecture, 15 November 1994, printed in [1995] *Public Law* 57, 66.

70 *R. v. Home Secretary ex p. Doody* [1994] 1 AC 531.

71 *Anisminic Ltd v. Foreign Compensation Commission* [1969] 2 AC 147.

72 In fact, as Professor Wade pointed out, such provisions do appear in recent legislation. Both the Security Service Act 1989 and the Intelligence Services Act 1994 provide that 'the decisions of the Tribunal and the Commissioner under [Schedule 1 to this Act] (including decisions as to their jurisdictions) shall not be subject to appeal or liable to be questioned in any court.' A similar provision appears in the Interception of Communications Act 1985.

73 Emphasis added.

74 See Chapter 6.

75 *Public Law* Project Lecture, 12 May 1994. A version of it appears as 'Law and Democracy' in [1995] *Public Law* 72.

76 See *Ridge v. Baldwin* [1964] AC 40.

77 See *Padfield v. Minister of Agriculture* [1968] AC 997.

78 [1995] *Public Law* 72, 84–5.

79 As indeed it did from 1935 to 1945.

80 Sir Stephen Sedley, 'Human Rights: a Twenty-First Century Agenda' [1995] *Public Law* 386, 389.

81 Sir Stephen Sedley, 'The Common Law and the Constitution', Radcliffe Lecture, University of Warwick, 14 November 1996, citing Lord Bridge of Harwich in *X. v. Morgan-Grampian* [1991] AC 1, 48, where he said 'in our society the rule of law rests on twin foundations: the sovereignty of the Queen in parliament

in making the law and the sovereignty of the Queen's courts in interpreting and applying the law'.

82 *Daily Telegraph*, 7 December 1995.

83 *Daily Telegraph*, 8 December 1995.

84 Lord Mackay of Clashfern, 'Parliament and the Judges – a Constitutional Challenge?', speech to the Citizenship Foundation, 8 July 1996.

85 'Judges and Decision-Makers: The Theory and Practice of *Wednesbury* Review' [1996] *Public Law* 59, 75. See Chapter 3.

86 See Chapter 5.

87 *Hansard*, House of Lords, 5 June 1996, col. 1255.

88 Marcel Berlins, *New Statesman*, 1 November 1996, p. 16.

89 Letter, *New Statesman*, 8 November 1996, p. 36.

90 In lectures or articles rather than in court.

91 Interview with Ian Hargreaves, *New Statesman*, 6 December 1996, p. 18.

92 Sir Thomas Bingham, 'The Courts and the Constitution', lecture at King's College London, 14 February 1996, *King's College Law Journal*, vol. 7, p. 26.

93 Speech at the Lord Mayor's Dinner, 17 July 1996.

94 *Ibid.*

95 Interviewed by the author, 5 September 1996.

96 Interview with the author, 14 November 1996.

97 *Barclays Bank v. O'Brien*.

98 Interview with Marcel Berlins, *Law in Action*, BBC Radio 4, 18 October 1996.

99 Although it may be harder to prove than non-marital rape.

100 It is a sign of age when law lords seem to be getting younger. It is even more alarming to discover that a retired law lord has children younger than one's own.

101 [1993] *Public Law* 269, 280.

102 *Ibid.* 281.

103 *Ibid.*, 278–9.

104 Professor Conor Gearty, 'The Judicialisation of Democracy', paper delivered to the Administrative Bar Association conference, 7 July 1996.

Chapter 5   A Bill of Rights

1 Quoted by Lord Lester of Herne Hill QC, 'European Human Rights and the British Constitution', in Jeffrey Jowell and Dawn Oliver, *The Changing Constitution*, 3rd edn., 1994, p. 35.

2 'European Human Rights and the British Constitution', above, p. 36.

3 Incorporation is also supported by the Liberal Democrats.

4 Tony Blair, 'Democracy's second age', *The Economist*, 14 September 1996.

5 John Smith QC MP, 'A Citizen's Democracy', Charter 88 Lecture, 1 March 1993.

6 The Labour Party, *A New Agenda for Democracy: Labour's Proposals for Constitutional Reform*, September 1993.

7 Interview with Ian Hargreaves, *New Statesman*, 6 December 1996, p. 18.

8 May to August. As Lord Kilmuir, he was Lord Chancellor from 1954 to 1962.

9 See Anthony Lester QC, 'Fundamental Rights: the United Kingdom Isolated?', [1984] *Public Law* 46, 49. His research forms the basis of the historical account in this introductory section.

10 Lord Jowitt, cabinet papers, quoted by Lord Lester QC, 'European Human Rights and the British Constitution', above, p. 36.

11 On 3 September.

12 See Anthony Lester, 'Fundamental Rights: the United Kingdom Isolated?', above, at pp. 60–1.

13 *Hansard*, House of Commons, col. 235, 7 December 1965.

14 See Joshua Rozenberg, *The Search for Justice*, pp. 211–3.

15 For five years. Sir Nicholas Bonsor, parliamentary written answer, 13 December 1995.

16 Clare Dyer, *Guardian*, 17 January 1997, and author's sources. Lord Mackay's visit to Strasbourg in November 1996 is discussed in Chapter 1.

17 The convention does not ban discrimination as such: it merely guarantees that the specific rights available should be enjoyed without discrimination.

18 *Brogan v. UK* (1989) 11 EHRR 117.

19 *Brannigan and McBride v. UK* (1994) 17 EHRR 539.

20 Such as John Wadham, Director of the human rights group Liberty. This section is based on his contribution to *Law Reform for All*, ed. David Bean, 1996, p. 122.

21 Doug Henderson MP, speaking at a seminar on 14 November 1996.

22 See *Bringing Rights Home*: Labour's plans to incorporate the European Convention on Human Rights into UK law, December 1996, p. 2: 'the most speedy, practical and effective remedy would be to pass legislation that would incorporate the standards of the European Convention on Human Rights in to UK law.'

23 Press release, 18 December 1996.

24 They were deliberately constructed to accommodate the smaller but much more prestigious international body. However, a new debating chamber for the European Parliament has now been built in Strasbourg.

25 The river Ill, printed in the Michelin guide as the almost unreadable *I'lll.*

26 Formerly Sir Richard Rogers.

27 That came later.

28 Lord Irvine of Lairg QC, speech to the Bar Conference, 28 September 1996.

29 Source: Council of Europe Press Office. Four cases had been struck off (following 'friendly settlements') and twelve were pending. The figures may vary because joint applications are sometimes counted as one case and sometimes as more.

30 Lord Mackay of Clashfern, *Hansard*, House of Lords, 3 July 1996, col. 1452.

31 England and Wales, Scotland and Northern Ireland.

32 Ireland has not incorporated the convention, but it does have a written constitution.

33 *Guillot France*, 24 October 1996.

34 In *Abdulaziz* (1985) 7 EHRR 471 the government responded to a decision that the Immigration Rules discriminated between men and women by treating them both equally badly.

35 As did Mr Justice Dyson in the case of *Norney*: see Chapter 1.

36 Lord Bingham of Cornhill, maiden speech, House of Lords, *Hansard*, 3 July 1996, cols. 1465–7.

37 Nicole Smith, Assistant Director, The Constitution Unit, citing research by Francesca Klug, letter to the author, 19 November 1996.

38 Although the government would not be able to appeal to the European Court if the British courts had decided that there *was* a breach of the convention: governments do not have human rights.

39 Anthony Lester QC, 'English Judges as Law Makers, [1993] *Public Law* 269, 271.

40 *Independent*, 2 August 1995.

41 Letter to the author, 15 August 1995.

42 4th edn., 1991; 5th edn. to be published 1997.

43 Letter, *Independent*, 8 August 1995.

44 J. A. G. Griffith, *The Politics of the Judiciary*, 4th edn, p. 325.

45 Melanie Phillips, *Observer*, 12 November 1995.

46 Keith Ewing and Conor Gearty, *Democracy or a Bill of Rights*, Society of Labour Lawyers, 1991.

47 Professor Conor Gearty, 'The Judicialisation of Democracy', paper delivered to the Administrative Bar Association conference, 7 July 1996.

48 In Chapter 4.

49 Lord Irvine of Lairg QC, 'Judges and Decision-Makers: The Theory and Practice of *Wednesbury* Review' [1996] *Public Law* 59, 77.

50 For example, by requiring a two-thirds majority in the legislature. Although some countries require special procedures to pass or amend constitutional legislation, it is possible to give entrenched legislation superior status without these procedures.

51 Article 9 of the Bill of Rights was amended by s.13 of the Defamation Act 1996.

52 For example, by the Specialist Adviser to the House of Lords Select Committee on a Bill of Rights, HL 176, 1978.

53 Section 2(4).

54 Wade, *Administrative Law*, 7th edn., p. 31.

55 *R. v. Transport Secretary ex p. Factortame* (*No. 2*) [1990] 1 AC 603. The decision was announced on 9 July 1990 and full reasons were given on 11 October of that year.

56 See Wade and Forsyth, *Administrative Law*, 7th edn., p. 31.

57 This section draws heavily on *Human Rights Legislation*, published in November 1996 by the Constitution Unit, paras. 55–66. The unit was a research project set up in April 1995 to inquire into constitutional reform.

58 Michael Zander, *A Bill of Rights?*, 4th edn., 1997, p. 117.

59 It might be thought governments would be reluctant to abrogate human rights, except in unforeseen circumstances. However, the Canadian precedent is not very encouraging. Although the Canadian Justice Minister had assured parliament that the 'notwithstanding' clause would be an infrequently used 'safety valve', the National Assembly in Quebec (which had opposed Canada's new constitutional arrangements in 1982) immediately passed legislation amending all existing Quebec statutes to include a 'notwithstanding' provision.

60 Although Professor Zander, writing in September 1996, disagrees: see *A Bill of Rights?*, 4th edn., p. 118.

61 Section 5 of the New Zealand measure provides that 'Wherever an enactment can be given a meaning that is consistent with the rights and freedoms contained in

this Bill of Rights, that meaning shall be preferred to any other meaning.'

62 The Constitution Unit, *Human Rights Legislation*, para 63.

63 See Anthony Lester, p. 62. His original Bill of Rights would not have been enforceable by the judges until they could be trusted to apply it in a 'progressive and liberal spirit'.

64 See Michael Zander, *op cit.*, Chapter 1, for a full history.

65 Discussed in Chapter 1.

66 Leslie Scarman, *English Law – The New Dimension*.

67 Interview with the author, 7 February 1985.

68 Formerly the Conservative MP Sir Derek Walker-Smith.

69 *Hansard*, House of Lords, col. 1285, 1 May 1995.

70 Clause 1(3) said: 'An act of parliament . . . (whether passed . . . before or after the passing of this act) shall not be enforced and may not be relied on in any legal proceedings . . . if and to the extent that to do so would deprive a person of any of the rights and freedoms defined in Schedule 1.' Schedule 1 set out articles 2 to 18 of the convention and the first protocol, as amended.

71 Lord Lester of Herne Hill QC, 'The Mouse that Roared: the Human Rights Bill 1995' [1995] *Public Law* 198, 199.

72 *Ibid.*

73 *Ibid.*, p. 201.

74 He meant, one hopes, both men and women, English and not.

75 *Hansard*, House of Lords, col. 1280–1, 1 May 1995.

76 Interview with Marcel Berlins, *Law in Action*, BBC Radio 4, 18 October 1996.

77 *Ibid.*

78 Interview with the author, 14 November 1996.

79 HL Bill 11, published 31 October 1996. It was clearly not, in his view, the best possible way of incorporating the convention: instead, it was in the form he thought most likely to win support from peers and MPs. After campaigning for thirty years, he wanted to see something, at least, on the statute book.

80 Articles 2–18 inclusive and articles 1–3 of the first protocol, subject to the two derogations which were already in force. The first of these allowed detention under the Prevention of Terrorism Act (mentioned above). The second, made in 1952,

provided that the 'right of parents to ensure . . . education and teaching in conformity with their own religious and philosophical convictions' was accepted 'only so far as it is compatible with the provision of efficient instruction and training, and the avoidance of unreasonable public expenditure'. The United Kingdom courts were to take 'judicial notice' of the decisions of the European Commission of Human Rights and the European Court of Human Rights.

81 *Hansard*, House of Lords, col. 1284, 1 May 1995 (Baroness Blatch).

82 Even so, there can be little doubt that judges do consider the implications of their decisions when giving judgment in an individual case.

83 Lord Mackay of Clashfern, 'Parliament and the Judges – a Constitutional Challenge?', speech to the Citizenship Foundation, 8 July 1996, and *Hansard*, House of Lords, 3 July 1996, col. 1452.

84 Michael Zander, *op. cit.*, p. 146.

85 Lord Irvine of Lairg QC, speech to the Bar Conference, 28 September 1996.

86 Lord Irvine of Lairg QC, in *Law Reform for All*, p. 20.

87 Letter to the author, 6 November 1996.

88 The Constitution Unit, *Human Rights Legislation*, para 106.

89 *Bringing Rights Home*: Labour's plans to incorporate the European Convention on Human Rights into UK law, December 1996, p. 13.

90 Institute for Public Policy Research, *A Human Rights Commission for the UK*, December 1996.

91 *Bringing Rights Home*: Labour's plans to incorporate the European Convention on Human Rights into UK law, December 1996, p. 11–12.

92 See *Human Rights Legislation*, above, paras. 67–92, and The Labour Party, *A New Agenda for Democracy*, 1993.

93 *Hansard*, House of Lords, 3 July 1996, col. 1460–1

94 Letter to the author, 6 November 1996.

95 By Marcel Berlins, 1 November 1996.

96 *New Statesman*, 8 November 1996, p. 36.

97 Interview with Ian Hargreaves, *New Statesman*, 6 December 1996.

98 *Bringing Rights Home*: Labour's plans to incorporate the European Convention on Human Rights into UK law, December 1996, p. 10.

99 Press release, 18 December 1996.

100 Sir Thomas Bingham, 'The Courts and the

Constitution', lecture at King's College London, 14 February 1996, *King's College Law Journal*, vol. 7, p. 25–6.

101 *R. v. Home Secretary, ex p. Brind* [1991] 1 AC 696.

102 See Lord Lester of Herne Hill QC, 'The Mouse that Roared: the Human Rights Bill 1995' [1995] *Public Law* 198, 199.

103 Their words could be reported, provided they were not heard saying them. This provided an unexpected windfall for the Belfast-based actors who spoke their words, deliberately out of sync with the pictures so the viewers would realise what was going on. Being a terrorist's mouthpiece was not without its dangers and the actors were never named.

104 Conversation with the author, 10 December 1996.

105 [1995] *Public Law* 198, 202.

Chapter 6   From *Spycatcher* to the Scott Inquiry

1   18 November 1986, during the British government's attempts to stop *Spycatcher* being published in Australia, quoted in Malcolm Turnbull, *The Spycatcher Trial*, p. 74–5.

2   5 November 1992, during the Matrix Churchill trial: Scott Report (see below) G17.29. The symmetry is enhanced by the fact that it was Geoffrey Robertson who recommended Malcolm Turnbull to the Australian publishers of *Spycatcher*: see *The Spycatcher Trial* (above) p. 1.

3   The definition is adapted from one given by Lord Griffiths: see AG v. *The Observer and others* [1990] 1AC 109, 267. 'People' on this occasion means 'the government'.

4   These activities were, however, illegal at the time.

5   The reference should have been to Winston Churchill's niece, Clarissa (later, Lady Avon). Peter Wright said that 'Burgess was appalled by the task. For one thing, he was an inveterate homosexual; for another, Clarissa was scarcely better-looking than her uncle.' (Peter Wright, *Spycatcher*, Viking, New York, 1987, p. 242).

6   *Observer*, 22 June 1986.

7   23 June 1986. The Security Service MI5 said subsequently that a vigorous internal enquiry had failed to produce any evidence to substantiate Peter Wright's claim that MI5 had plotted to undermine Harold Wilson. It added that Mr Wright himself had subsequently admitted they were false. (*The Security Service*, HMSO, 1993, pp. 27–8).

8   *Observer* Diary, 31 March 1985. Malcolm Turnbull says that Geoffrey Robertson told him 'someone at Heinemann in London was fool enough to leak this [plan to publish in Australia] to a gossip columnist at the *Observer*. The government read about it [and] commenced proceedings'. See *The Spycatcher Trial* p. 1. At the time, the government regularly began legal actions of this type on the strength of little more than a newspaper cutting.

9   Chapman Pincher, *Their Trade is Treachery*, 1981.

10 Except for a speech in the House of Commons by Dale Campbell-Savours MP (*Hansard*, 21 July 1986, col. 52). His speech was reported in the *Guardian*.

11 *Guardian*, 9 July 1986.

12 *Guardian*, 10 July 1986.

13 PA News, 11 July 1986: see also [1987] 1 WLR 1248.

14 By the doughty Mr Justice Powell: 13 March 1987.

15 13 October 1987.

16 27 April 1987: 'How MI5 Plotted Wilson's Fall'.

17 Such as the *Evening Standard*, 27 April 1987.

18 12 July 1987.

19 On 2 June 1987 that the *Independent* was not in contempt: [1988] Ch 333, 337; on 22 July 1987 that the injunctions against the *Observer* and the *Guardian* should be lifted: [1987] 1 WLR 1248, 1253.

20 24 July 1987: [1987] 1 WLR 1248, 1271. Even so, the Court of Appeal thought the injunctions were now too wide. Publication in the United States meant there was no point in trying to keep the allegations secret and the Court of Appeal said newspapers should be allowed to publish a summary of Mr Wright's allegations in general terms. That order was suspended pending the appeal to the House of Lords.

21 Decision 15 July 1987; reasons 17 July 1987: [1988] Ch 333, 357. The decision was upheld by the House of Lords on 11 April 1991: *AG v. Times Newspapers* [1992] 1 AC 191.

22 On 13 July 1987: see bibliography for details.

23 To the disappointment of an ITN reporter who apparently wanted to film Customs officers at Heathrow airport stopping him and confiscating the book.

24 30 July 1987: [1987] 1 WLR 1248, 1282.
25 *AG v. Guardian* Newspapers Ltd and others 13 August 1987 [1987] 1 WLR 1248, 1287. Author's summary. Subsequent remarks by the four other law lords are taken from the same report.
26 31 July 1987.
27 Security Service Act 1989, s. 3.
28 Stella Rimington gave the Richard Dimbleby lecture, 12 June 1994.
29 Hugo Young, *One of Us*, 1989, p. 462.
30 21 December 1987: [1990] 1 AC 109, 117.
31 10 February 1988: [1990] 1 AC 109, 175.
32 It is now twelve.
33 13 October 1988: [1990] 1 AC 109, 253.
34 14 October 1988.
35 Home Office press release, 13 October 1988.
36 11 July 1986.
37 To borrow Hugo Young's description of Mrs Thatcher.
38 According to an estimate in the *Guardian*, 14 October 1988.
39 *The Sunday Times v. UK (No. 2)*: (1992) 14 EHRR 229; *The Observer and Guardian v. UK*: (1992) 14 EHRR 153.
40 Indeed ten of the twenty-four judges thought the original injunctions had not been justified either.
41 BBC Nine O'Clock News, 26 November 1991.
42 Rodney Austin, in Jowell and Oliver (eds.), *The Changing Constitution*, 1994, p. 417.
43 It is fair to say that the government never licensed the export of 'arms' to Iraq, only equipment which could be used to make arms. This distinction may have been of little consequence to anyone on the receiving end of munitions made in Iraq in British-equipped factories.
44 *Report of the Inquiry into the Export of Defence Equipment and Dual-Use Goods to Iraq and Related Prosecutions*, HC 115, 5 vols. plus index, £45, 7.5 kg. ('Scott Report').
45 15 February.
46 26 February 1996: see *Hansard* cols. 589–694.
47 As David Pannick said: *The Times*, 27 August 1986.
48 This account is taken from the Scott Report (above).
49 And Iran.
50 The others were Trevor Abraham and Peter Allen.
51 *Sunday Times*, 2 December 1990: How

MINISTER HELPED BRITISH FIRMS TO ARM SADDAM'S SOLDIERS.
52 The President of the Board of Trade Michael Heseltine (reluctantly, as we shall see), the Home Secretary Kenneth Clarke, the Defence Secretary Malcolm Rifkind and a Foreign Office minister, Tristan Garel-Jones.
53 Scotland Yard were asked to investigate apparent inconsistencies between Alan Clark's evidence in court and his earlier statements (BBC News, 17 November 1992). However, Mr Clark chose not to make a statement to the police. The Director of Public Prosecutions subsequently decided not to take further action because the Crown Prosecution Service had been 'unable to establish with sufficient certainty which of the inconsistent statements made by Mr Clark was not true' (BBC News, 3 March 1993).
54 9 November 1992.
55 See any of the broadsheet Sunday newspapers, 15 November 1922.
56 Professor Robert Stevens, 'Judges, Politics, Politicians and the Confusing Role of the Judiciary', Hardwicke Building Lecture, 21 May 1996.
57 *Hansard*, House of Commons, 10 November 1992, col. 743.
58 As he then was. When he was subsequently promoted to the post of Vice Chancellor of the Chancery Division, he lost the title 'Lord Justice'.
59 Andrew Marr suggested that the government 'was so lacking in authority that it was protecting itself, for the time being, with the borrowed authority of Lord Justice Scott' (*Independent*, 8 June 1995).
60 Scott Report, A2.11 (references are to paragraphs).
61 See Scott Report, Appendix A, Part D2(xvi), para. 14.
62 *Ibid.* para. 17.
63 Scott Report, B2.29.
64 *Ibid.*, B2.23.
65 *Ibid.*, B2.24.
66 In his draft report he rejected as 'sophistry' Mr Waldegrave's explanation that because the favourable tilt towards arms sales to Iraq had never been approved by senior ministers and the Prime Minister, it had not become Government policy (leak to the BBC, reported in the *Daily Telegraph*, 7 June 1995). The criticism remained unchanged: see para. D3.125, quoted below.
67 See [1996] *Public Law* 445.

68 27 January 1996.

69 PA News, 12 January 1994.

70 Read out by the inquiry secretary, 12 January 1994.

71 Cmnd. 3121 (1966). It had been set up in response to criticism of Lord Denning's one-man inquiry into the 1963 Profumo scandal.

72 Later Lord Salmon. He had a home in Kent: hence Lord Salmon, of Sandwich.

73 Communications from the inquiry staff informing witnesses of the allegations and evidence against them are known as 'Salmon letters'.
See his lecture to the Chancery Bar Association, 2 May 1995, referred to by Lord Howe in [1996] Public Law 445.

75 Presiley Lamorna Baxendale became something of a star. Possessed of a mellifluous name and a disarming giggle, she proved to be a powerful and fearless interrogator.

76 See A Child in Trust, report of the inquiry into the death of Jasmine Beckford, London Borough of Brent, 1985 and A Child in Mind, report of the inquiry into the death of Kimberley Carlile, London Borough of Greenwich, 1987.

77 Lord Howe, above, p. 457.

78 Sir Richard Luce, Sunday Telegraph, 29 October 1995.

79 PA News 12 January 1994.

80 George Jones, Daily Telegraph, 7 June 1995.

81 Hansard, House of Commons, 26 February 1996, col. 620.

82 Lord Howe of Aberavon CH QC, [1996] Public Law 445, 455–6.

83 Which can presumably be inferred from a lecture given by the inquiry secretary: Scott Report, Appendix A, Part D2(xvi), para. 38.

84 Sir Geoffrey Howe, later Lord Howe of Aberavon, was Foreign Secretary at the time.

85 Scott Report, D3.65.

86 Ibid., D3.122.

87 Ibid., D3.107.

88 Ibid., D3.123.

89 Ibid., D3.124.

90 Ibid., D4.42.

91 Ibid., D4.60.

92 Slightly adapted from the definition given by Lord Templeman in R. v. Chief Constable of West Midlands ex p. Wiley [1995] AC 274 .

93 It can be traced back 200 years: R. v. Hardy (1794) 24 St. Tr. 199 (public interest in protecting informer's identity).

94 Duncan v. Cammell Laird [1942] AC 624.

95 Sir Simon Brown, 'Public Interest Immunity', [1994] Public Law 579.

96 [1968] AC 910.

97 See de Smith, Woolf and Jowell, Judicial Review of Administrative Action, para. 1–138 and 1–139 n. 65.

98 Subsequently Mr Justice Laws.

99 Who sadly died in 1996. He was Chairman of the Criminal Bar Association, 1991–3.

100 An experienced junior counsel. The three barristers revised their opinion five times before it was signed.

101 Makanjuola v. Metropolitan Police Commissioner [1992] 3 All ER 617, 623.

102 Scott Report, G10.10.

103 Letter, The Times, 13 November 1992.

104 Letter, The Times, 17 February 1996.

105 David Pannick QC, The Times, 15 March 1994. He was referring to the case of R. v. Horseferry Road Magistrates' Court, ex p. Bennett (No 2) [1994] 1 All ER 289. This case had been decided in November 1993, a year after the Matrix Churchill prosecution and nearly two years after the Attorney General had taken advice on the law. However, Mr Pannick was writing four months before the law lords supported his view of the law in the case of Wiley (discussed below). David Pannick appeared for a third party in that case.

106 Scott Report G13.9–G13.14.

107 Ibid., G13.24 (para. 8).

108 Ibid., G13.32.

109 Ibid., G 13.46.

110 In the case of Wiley: see below.

111 See above: Mr Heseltine marked the passage in which Lord Justice Bingham said 'the ultimate judge of where the balance of public interest lies is not [the minister] but the court' (Scott Report G13.69)

112 Subsequently Mr Justice Moses.

113 Scott Report G13.115.

114 Ibid., G13.125. Reporters did not accept that Sir Richard's double negatives were not designed to make his sentences any harder to follow.

115 Ibid., G13.125. Sir Richard said he would have expected Sir Nicholas Lyell to have recognised that important constitutional and legal issues were raised by Mr Heseltine's stand and to have made sure that Alan Moses was adequately briefed.

116 Quoted by Adam Tomkins, [1993] Public Law 650, 654.

117 Ibid., G17.31. The documents also established that Mr Henderson had risked being executed for spying when he visited Iraq

(as the journalist Farzad Bazoft was in 1990). Mr Henderson's MI6 handler told the jury Mr Henderson was 'a very very brave man'. The head of Customs and Excise, Sir Brian Unwin, complained to the head of MI6, Sir Colin McColl, about this testimonial. MI6 rightly (in Sir Richard's view) sent Customs a robust reply (Scott Report, G17.25).

118 *Ibid.*, G18.94. Emphasis added.

119 Authorities are binding decisions in previous cases.

120 Scott Report, G18.52. *Makanjuola* was not a criminal case.

121 Public interest immunity: the government's response, press release from Attorney General's Chambers, 15 February 1996.

122 No specific source given, but included in the government's 'press pack' issued on 15 February 1996 (see below).

123 *Makanjuola* (see above).

124 Interview with the author, 23 February 1996, BBC *Nine O'Clock News*.

125 Scott Report, G18.52 (above).

126 *R. v. Chief Constable of West Midlands ex p. Wiley* [1995] AC 274.

127 In cases like *Makanjuola* (above).

128 [1995] AC 274, 281.

129 As public interest immunity certificates were invariably though inaccurately called.

130 Scott Report, K6.18.

131 *Hansard*, House of Commons, 18 December 1996, col. 949.

132 *Ibid.*, col. 1509.

133 Ministers had already seen first drafts of the passages in which they were criticised some months earlier.

134 That was the government's decision, but it could hardly have surprised Sir Richard; had he chosen to let the opposition MPs read it earlier, it is difficult to see on what grounds the government could have objected.

135 News conference, 15 February 1996.

136 Adam Tomkins, School of Law, King's College London, 'Government Information and Parliament: Misleading by Design or by Default?' [1996] *Public Law* 472, 489.

137 Italics added.

138 Scott Report, D3.125.

139 *Hansard*, House of Commons, 26 February 1996, col. 589.

140 Professor Dawn Oliver, [1996] *Public Law* 365.

141 Sir Richard Scott, 'Procedures at Inquiries – The Duty to be Fair', [1995] *Law Quarterly Review* 596, 615.

142 Scott Report, B2.8.

143 [1996] *Public Law* 445, 459.

144 *Ibid.*, 445, 460.

145 Scott Report, K1.1 to K1.6.

146 Council on Tribunals, *Advice to the Lord Chancellor on the procedural issues arising in the conduct of public inquiries set up by ministers*, July 1996.

147 Scott Report, para. 5.21.

148 *Ibid.*, para 7.17. 'Executive summary' is a modern phrase. Its meaning may be further summarised: it means 'summary'.

149 *Law in Action*, BBC Radio 4, June 1995.

150 The title he held at the time was fixed in the public's mind as if in aspic: for the same reason, people still refer to Lord Woolf as Lord Justice Woolf.

151 J. A. G. Griffith, *The Politics of the Judiciary*, 4th edn., p. 73.

152 Gavin Drewry, [1996] *Public Law* 368, 371–2.

153 Lord Bingham, 'Judicial Independence', inaugural address to the Judicial Studies Board, 5 November 1996.

154 Lord Bingham, above.

155 Patrick Devlin, *The Judge*, 1979, p. 9.

156 Lord Howe of Aberavon, *Spectator*, 27 January 1996, p. 12.

Bibliography

Bean, David, (ed.), *Law Reform for All*, Blackstone Press, 1996

Brazier, Rodney, *Constitutional Practice*, 2nd edn., Oxford University Press, 1994

Boulton, C. J., (ed.), *Erskine May's treatise on the law, privileges, proceedings and usage of Parliament*, 21st edn., Butterworths, 1989

Devlin, Patrick, *The Judge*, Oxford University Press, 1979

Griffith, J. A. G., *The Politics of the Judiciary*, 4th edn., Fontana, 1991

Hailsham, Lord, *A Sparrow's Flight*, Collins, 1990

Harris, D. J. and Joseph, Sarah, *The International Covenant on Civil and Political Rights and United Kingdom Law*, Clarendon Press, 1995

Hutton, Will, *The State We're In*, Jonathan Cape, 1995

Jowell, Jeffrey and Oliver, Dawn, (eds.), *The Changing Constitution*, 3rd edn., Clarendon Press, 1994

Leigh, David and Vulliamy, Ed, *Sleaze: the Corruption of Parliament*, Fourth Estate, 1997

Pincher, Chapman, *Their Trade is Treachery*, Sidgwick and Jackson, 1981

Richardson, Genevra and Genn, Hazel, *Administrative Law and Government Action*, Oxford University Press, 1994

Rozenberg, Joshua, *The Case for the Crown*, Thorsons, 1987

Rozenberg, Joshua, *The Search for Justice*, Hodder and Stoughton, 1994; revised edition, Sceptre, 1995

Scarman, Leslie, *English Law – The New Dimension*, Stevens, 1974

de Smith, S. A., *Judicial Review of Administrative Action*, Stevens, 1959

de Smith, Woolf and Jowell, *Judicial Review of Administrative Action*, 5th edn. by Lord Woolf and Professor Jeffrey Jowell, Sweet and Maxwell, 1995

Turnbull, Malcolm, *The Spycatcher Trial*, Heinemann, 1988

Wade, H. W. R., *Administrative Law*, Clarendon Press, 1961

Wade, W. R. and Forsyth, C. F., *Administrative Law*, 7th edn., Oxford University Press, 1994

Wright, Peter, *Spycatcher*, Viking, New York, USA, 1987; Heinemann, Victoria, Australia, 1987

Young, Hugo, *One of Us*, Macmillan, 1989

Zander, Michael, *A Bill of Rights?*, 4th edn., Sweet and Maxwell, 1997

Index

235

Index